MOVIE PREQUEL

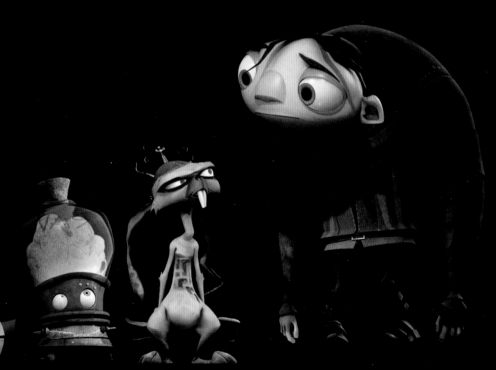

IDW Publishing • San Diego, CA

IGOR

MOVIE PREQUEL

Written by
Dara Naraghi

Art and colors by
Grant Bond

Letters by
Neil Uyetake

Series edits by
Chris Ryall and Tom Waltz

Collection edits by
Justin Eisinger

Collection design by
Neil Uyetake

Cover by
Grant Bond

ISBN: 978-1-60010-262-2
11 10 09 08   1 2 3 4

THE WEINSTEIN COMPANY   EXODUS FILM GROUP

Advertising Sales: (858) 270-1315 x 101
www.idwpublishing.com

Special thanks to Bruce Auerbach, Lisa Bluemel, Maria Flagg,
Max Howard, John McKenna, Charis Orchard for their
invaluable assistance.

IDW Publishi■

Operatio■
Moshe Berger, Chairm■
Ted Adams, Preside■
Clifford Meth, EVP of Strategi■
Matthew Ruzicka, CPA, Controll■
Alan Payne, VP of Sal■
Lorelei Bunjes, Dir. of Digital Servic■
Marci Hubbard, Executive Assista■
Alonzo Simon, Shipping Mana■

Editor■
Chris Ryall, Publisher/Editor-in-Ch■
Scott Dunbier, Editor, Special Proje■
Justin Eisinger, Edi■
Kris Oprisko, Editor/Foreign L■
Denton J. Tipton, Edi■
Tom Waltz, Edi■

Desi■
Robbie Robbins, EVP/Sr. Graphic Ar■
Ben Templesmith, Artist/Desig■
Neil Uyetake, Art Direc■
Chris Mowry, Graphic Ar■
Amauri Osorio, Graphic Ar■

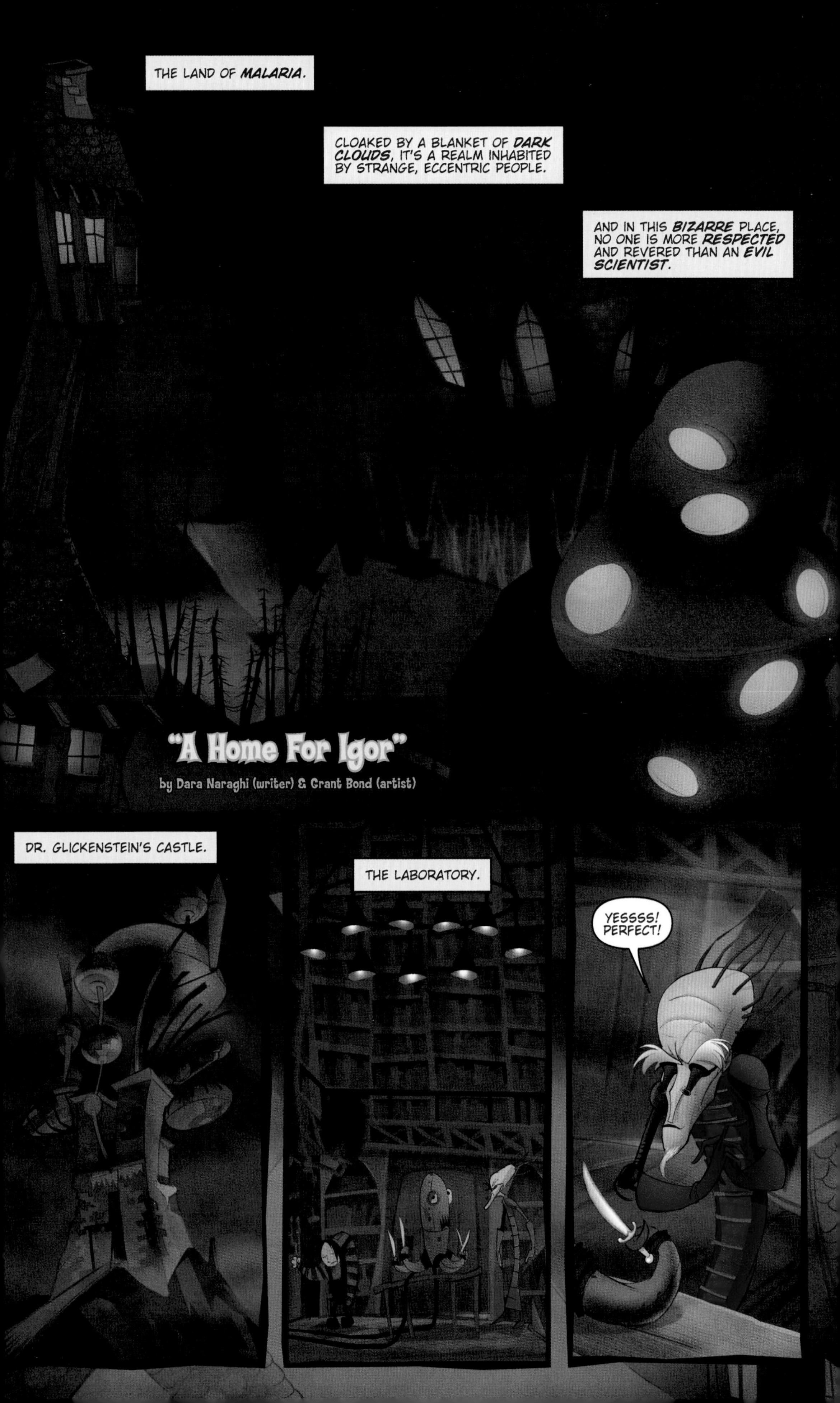
THE LAND OF MALARIA.
CLOAKED BY A BLANKET OF DARK CLOUDS, IT'S A REALM INHABITED BY STRANGE, ECCENTRIC PEOPLE.
AND IN THIS BIZARRE PLACE, NO ONE IS MORE RESPECTED AND REVERED THAN AN EVIL SCIENTIST.
"A Home For Igor"
by Dara Naraghi (writer) & Grant Bond (artist)
DR. GLICKENSTEIN'S CASTLE.
THE LABORATORY.
YESSSS! PERFECT!

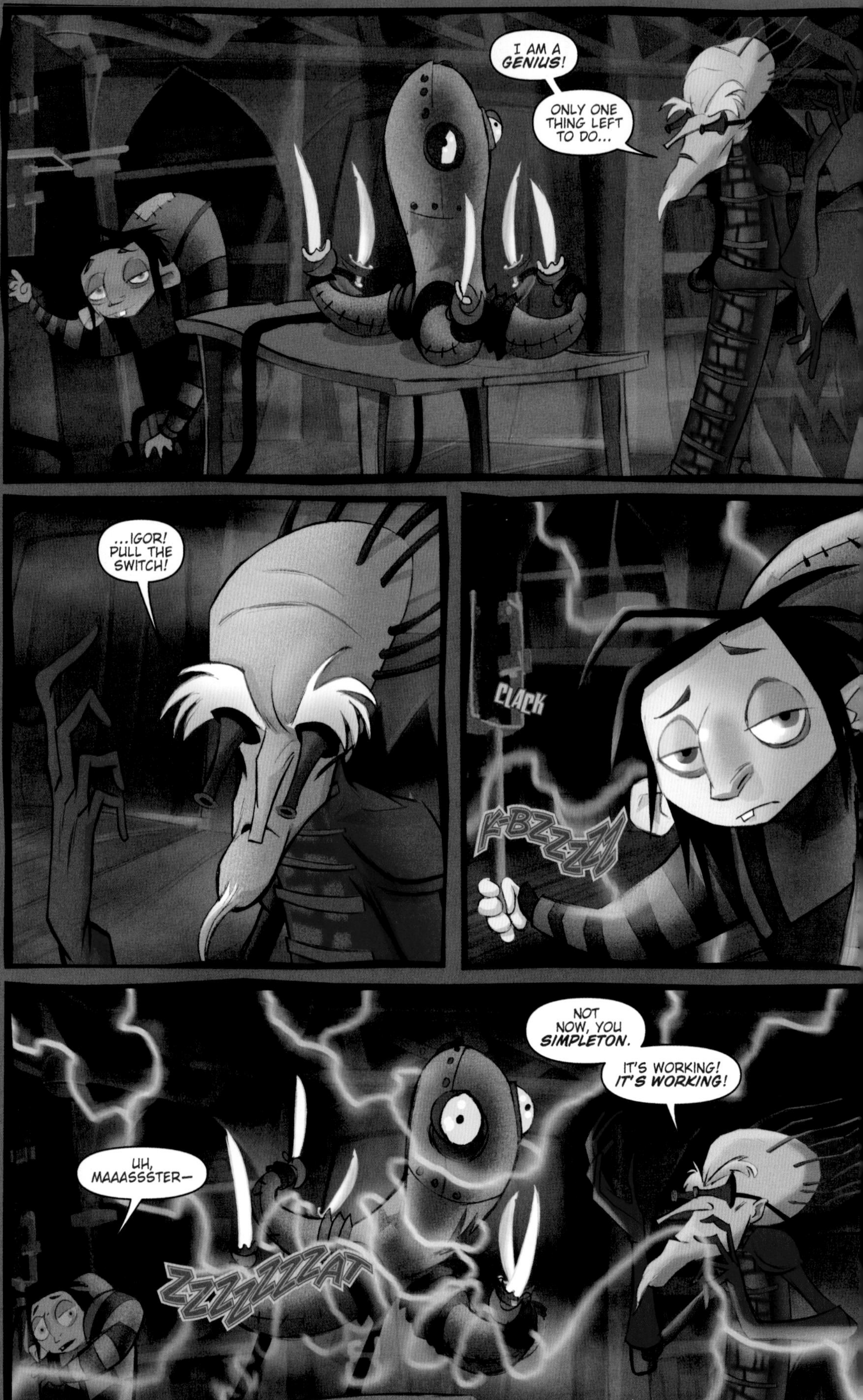
I AM A *GENIUS*!
ONLY ONE THING LEFT TO DO...
...IGOR! PULL THE SWITCH!
CLACK
K-BZZZZZM
NOT NOW, YOU *SIMPLETON*.
IT'S WORKING! *IT'S WORKING!*
UH, MAAASSSTER—
ZZZZZZZZAT

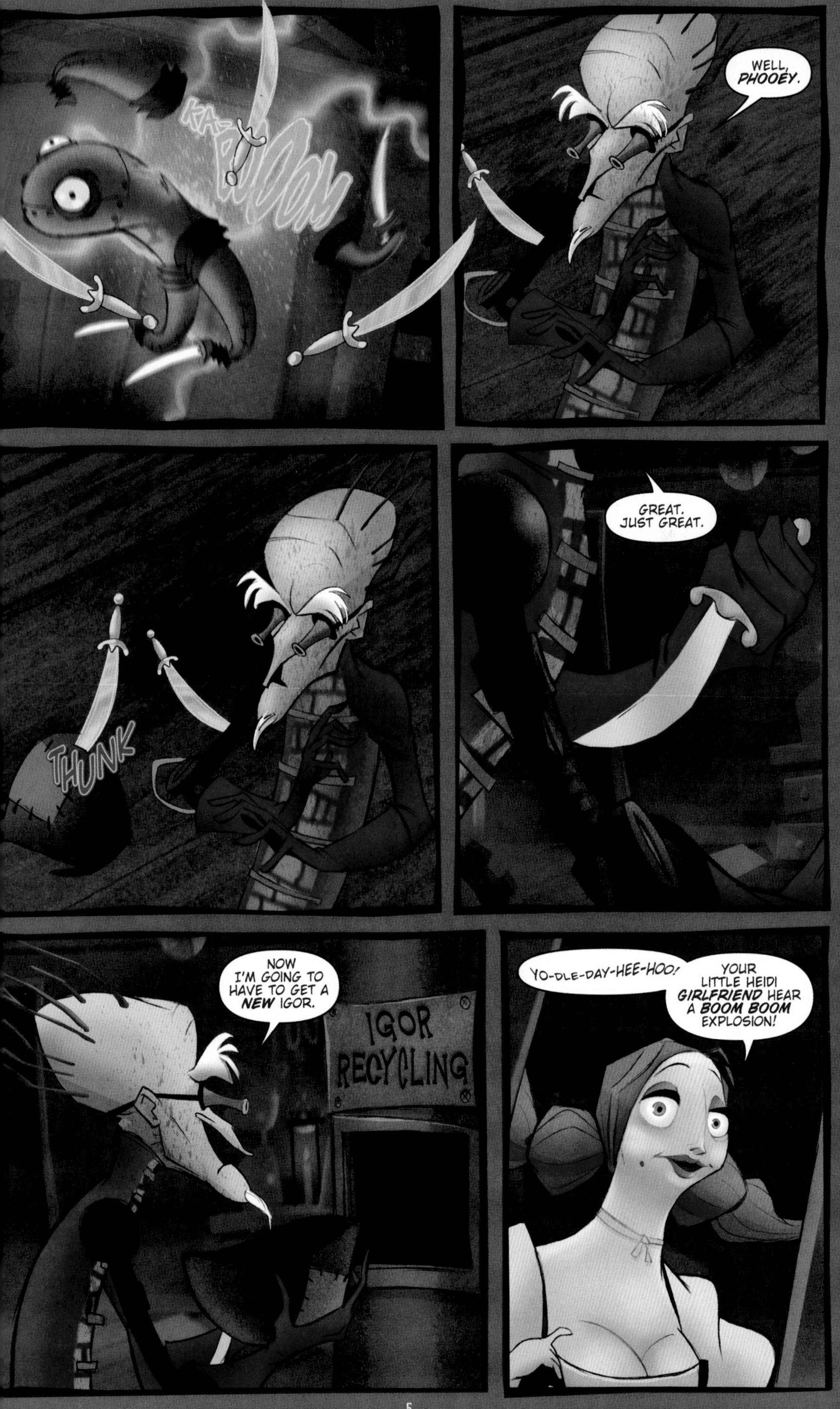
KA-BLOOM
WELL, PHOOEY.
THUNK
GREAT. JUST GREAT.
NOW I'M GOING TO HAVE TO GET A NEW IGOR.
IGOR RECYCLING
YO-DLE-DAY-HEE-HOO!
YOUR LITTLE HEIDI GIRLFRIEND HEAR A BOOM BOOM EXPLOSION!

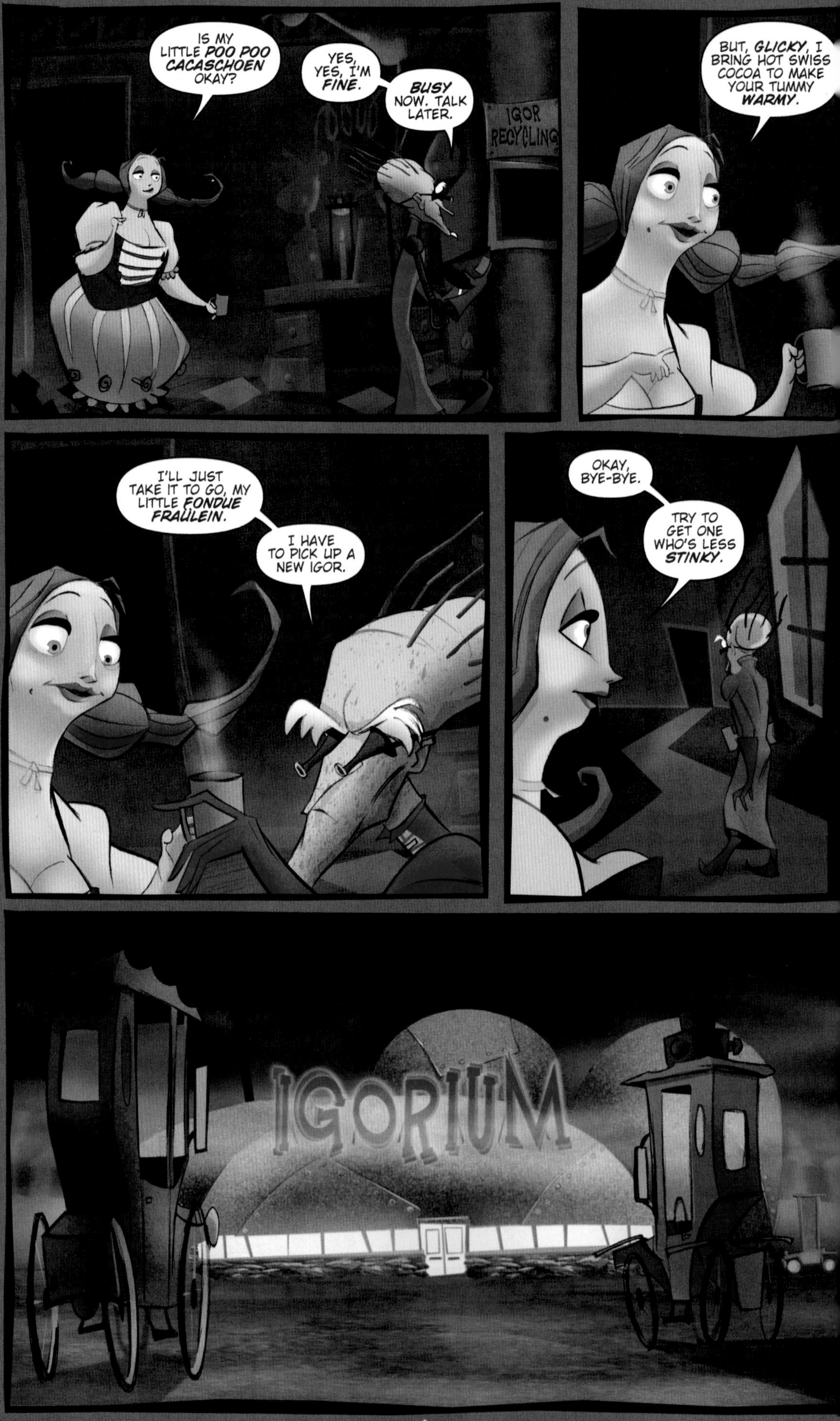
IS MY LITTLE POO POO CACASCHOEN OKAY?
YES, YES, I'M FINE.
BUSY NOW. TALK LATER.
IGOR RECYCLING
BUT, GLICKY, I BRING HOT SWISS COCOA TO MAKE YOUR TUMMY WARMY.
I'LL JUST TAKE IT TO GO, MY LITTLE FONDUE FRAÜLEIN.
I HAVE TO PICK UP A NEW IGOR.
OKAY, BYE-BYE.
TRY TO GET ONE WHO'S LESS STINKY.
IGORIUM

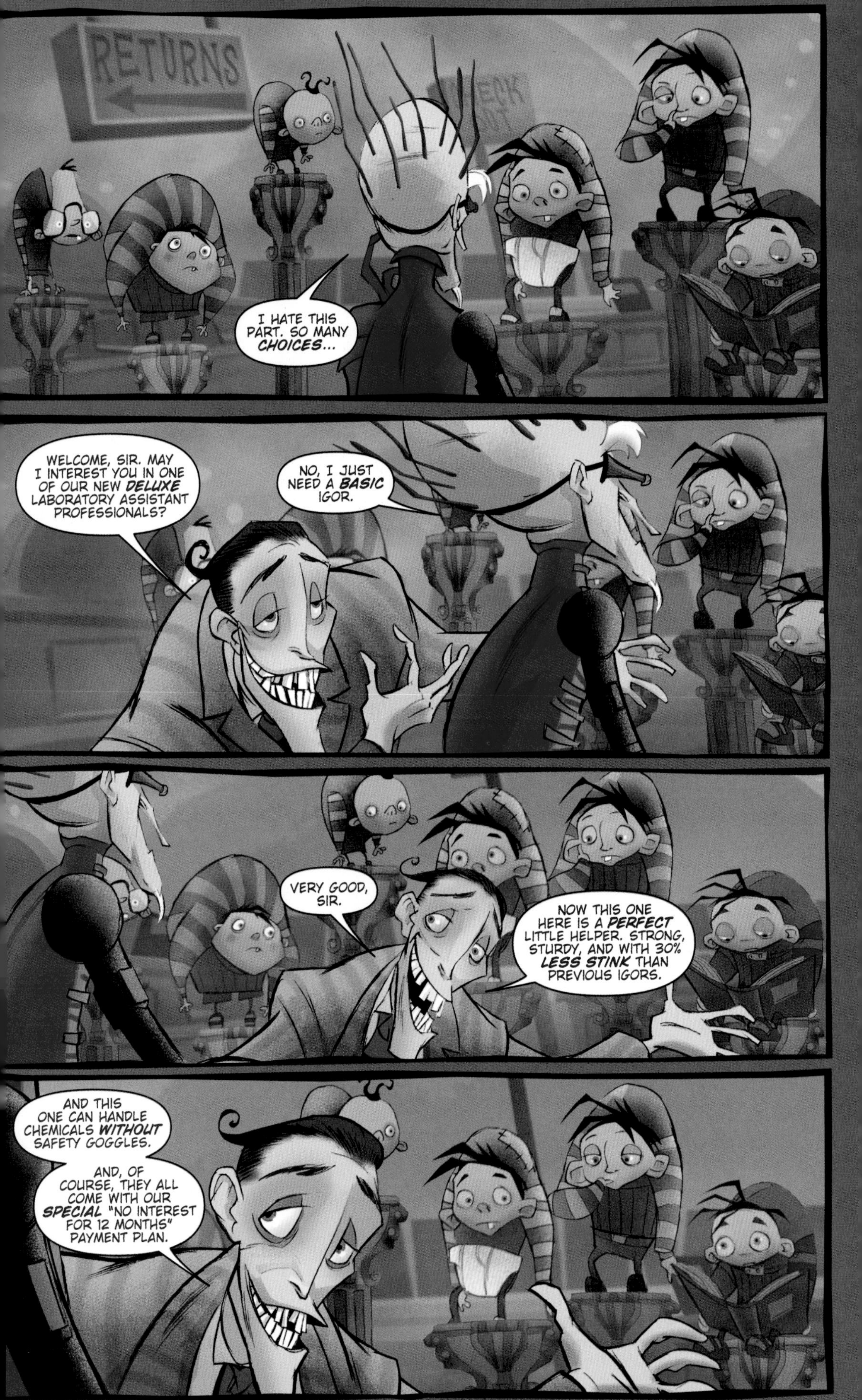
RETURNS
I HATE THIS PART. SO MANY *CHOICES*...
WELCOME, SIR. MAY I INTEREST YOU IN ONE OF OUR NEW *DELUXE* LABORATORY ASSISTANT PROFESSIONALS?
NO, I JUST NEED A *BASIC* IGOR.
VERY GOOD, SIR.
NOW THIS ONE HERE IS A *PERFECT* LITTLE HELPER. STRONG, STURDY, AND WITH 30% *LESS STINK* THAN PREVIOUS IGORS.
AND THIS ONE CAN HANDLE CHEMICALS *WITHOUT* SAFETY GOGGLES.
AND, OF COURSE, THEY ALL COME WITH OUR *SPECIAL* "NO INTEREST FOR 12 MONTHS" PAYMENT PLAN.

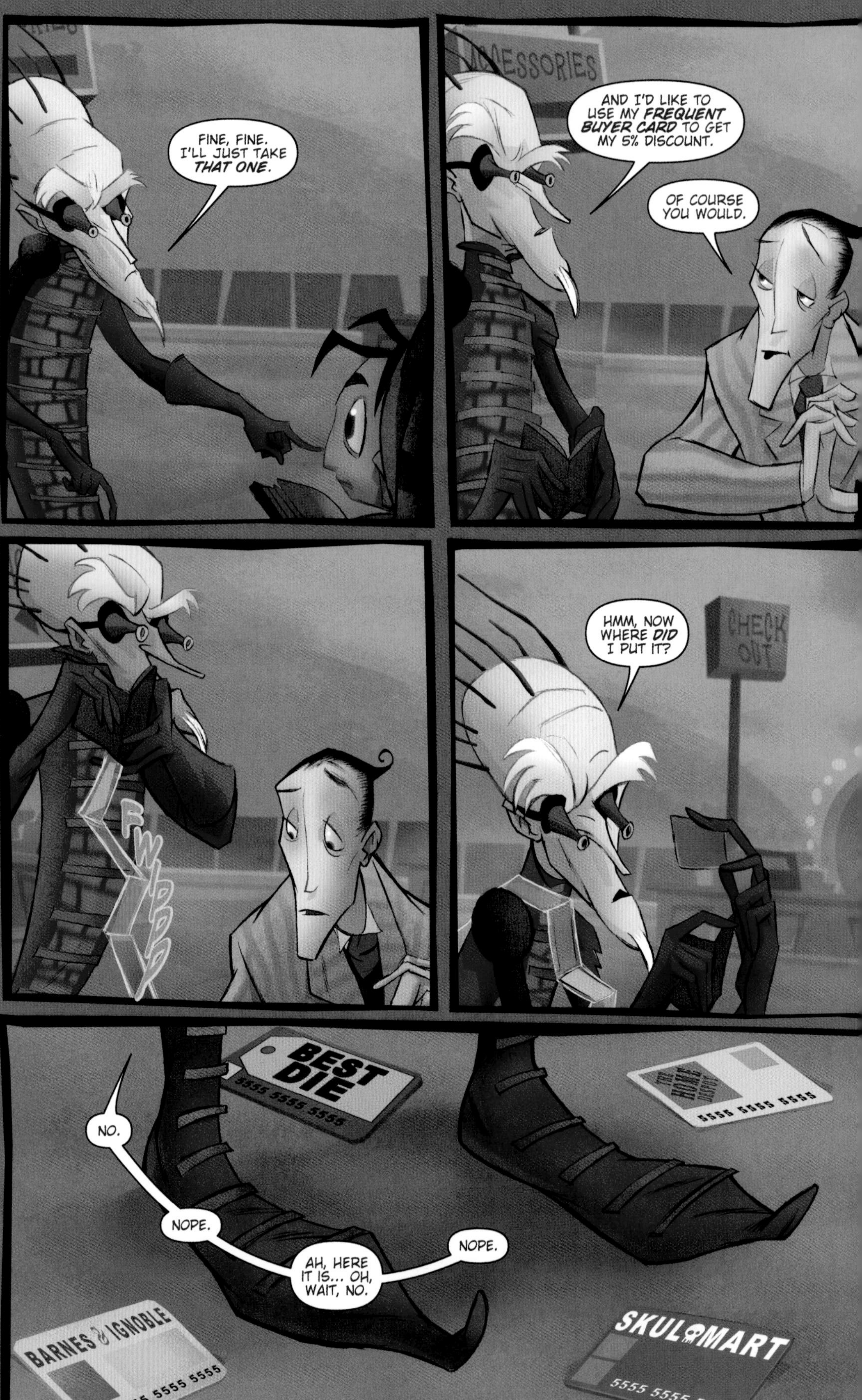
FINE, FINE. I'LL JUST TAKE ***THAT ONE***.
ACCESSORIES
AND I'D LIKE TO USE MY ***FREQUENT BUYER CARD*** TO GET MY 5% DISCOUNT.
OF COURSE YOU WOULD.
FWIPPP
HMM, NOW WHERE ***DID*** I PUT IT?
CHECK OUT
BEST DIE
5555 5555 5555
THE HOME DESPOT
5555 5555 5555
NO.
NOPE.
AH, HERE IT IS... OH, WAIT, NO.
NOPE.
BARNES & IGNOBLE
5555 5555 5555
SKULMART
5555 5555 5555

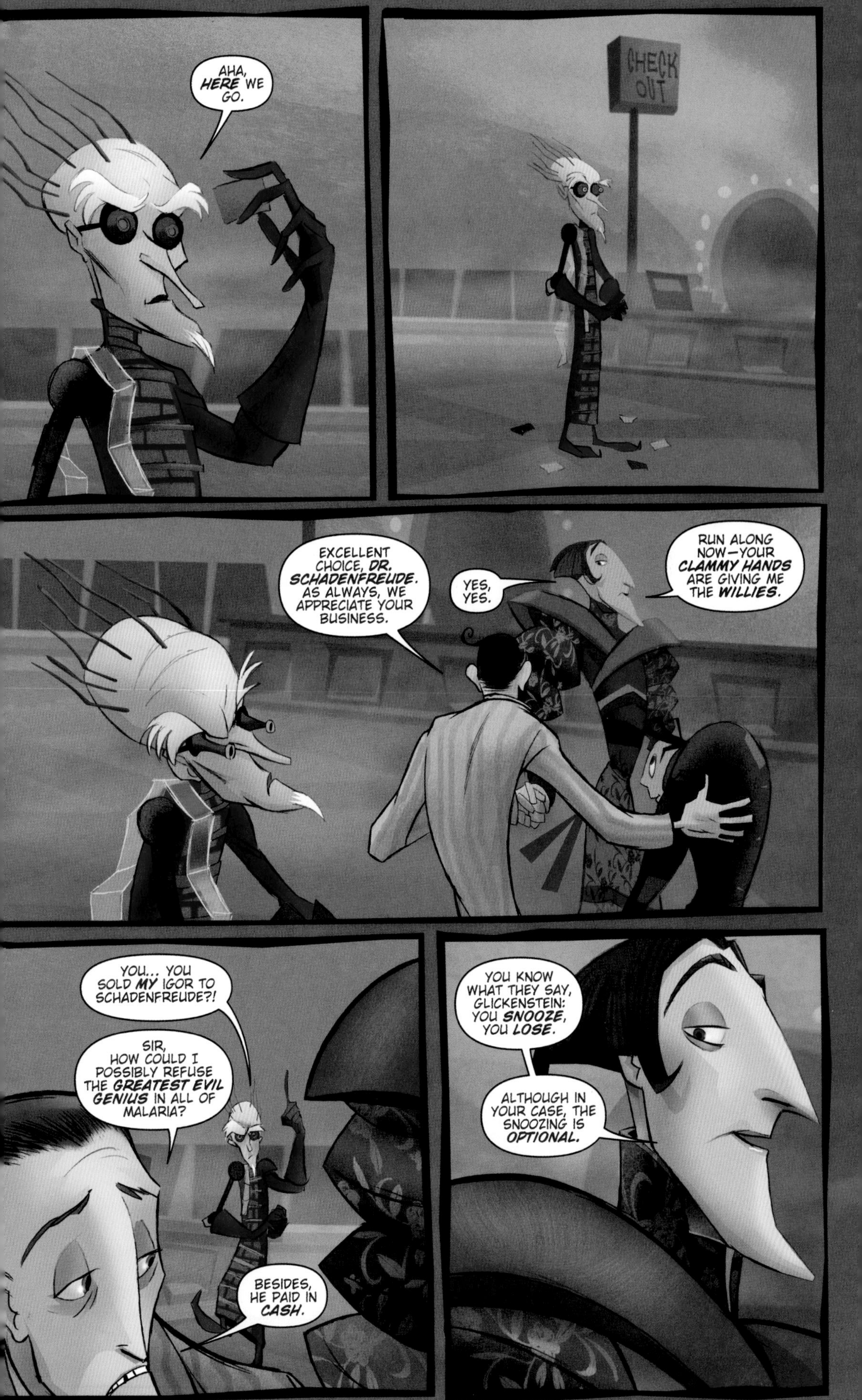
AHA, HERE WE GO.
CHECK OUT
EXCELLENT CHOICE, DR. SCHADENFREUDE. AS ALWAYS, WE APPRECIATE YOUR BUSINESS.
YES, YES.
RUN ALONG NOW—YOUR CLAMMY HANDS ARE GIVING ME THE WILLIES.
YOU... YOU SOLD MY IGOR TO SCHADENFREUDE?!
SIR, HOW COULD I POSSIBLY REFUSE THE GREATEST EVIL GENIUS IN ALL OF MALARIA?
BESIDES, HE PAID IN CASH.
YOU KNOW WHAT THEY SAY, GLICKENSTEIN: YOU SNOOZE, YOU LOSE.
ALTHOUGH IN YOUR CASE, THE SNOOZING IS OPTIONAL.

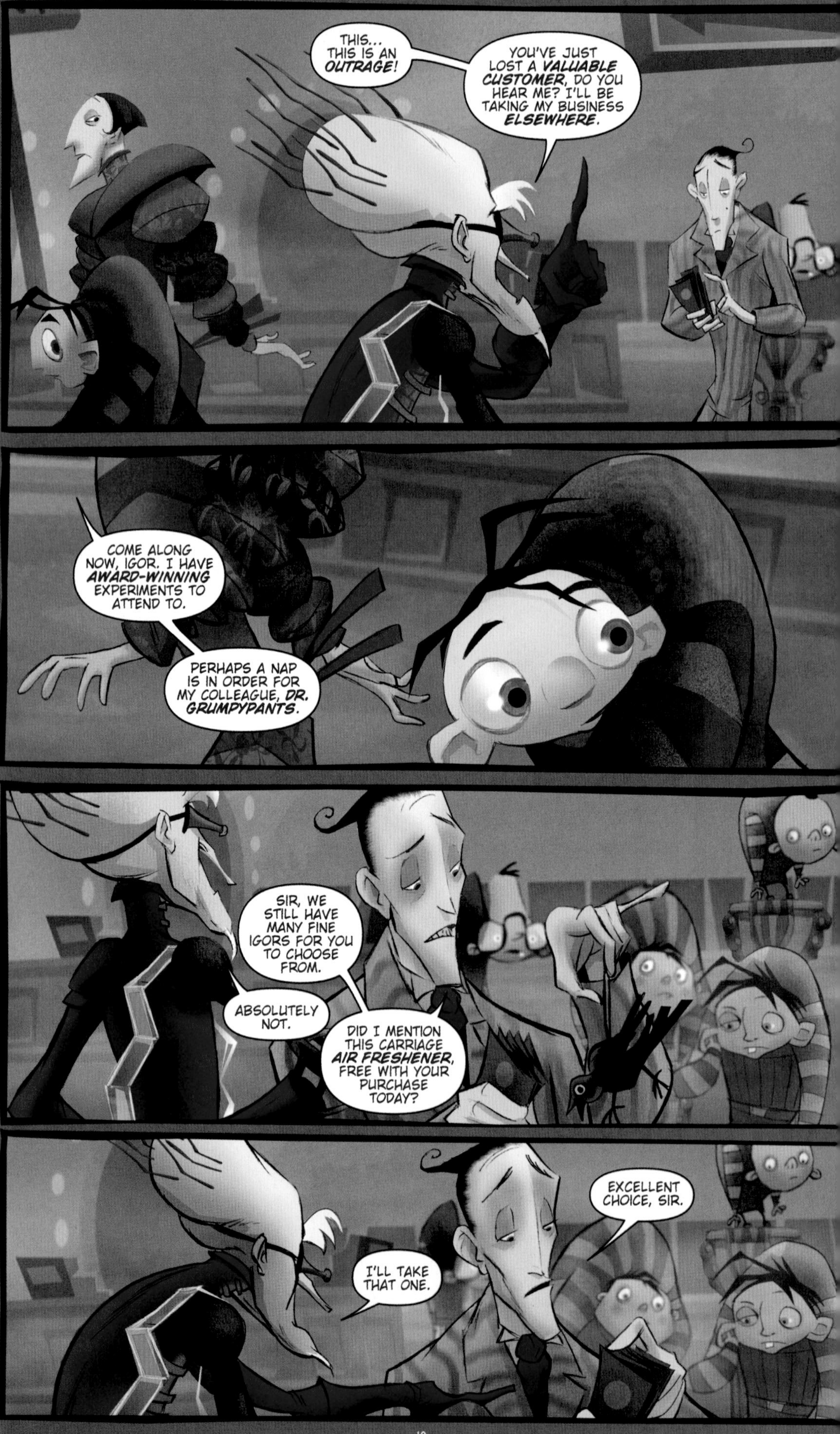
THIS... THIS IS AN OUTRAGE!
YOU'VE JUST LOST A VALUABLE CUSTOMER, DO YOU HEAR ME? I'LL BE TAKING MY BUSINESS ELSEWHERE.
COME ALONG NOW, IGOR. I HAVE AWARD-WINNING EXPERIMENTS TO ATTEND TO.
PERHAPS A NAP IS IN ORDER FOR MY COLLEAGUE, DR. GRUMPYPANTS.
SIR, WE STILL HAVE MANY FINE IGORS FOR YOU TO CHOOSE FROM.
ABSOLUTELY NOT.
DID I MENTION THIS CARRIAGE AIR FRESHENER, FREE WITH YOUR PURCHASE TODAY?
I'LL TAKE THAT ONE.
EXCELLENT CHOICE, SIR.

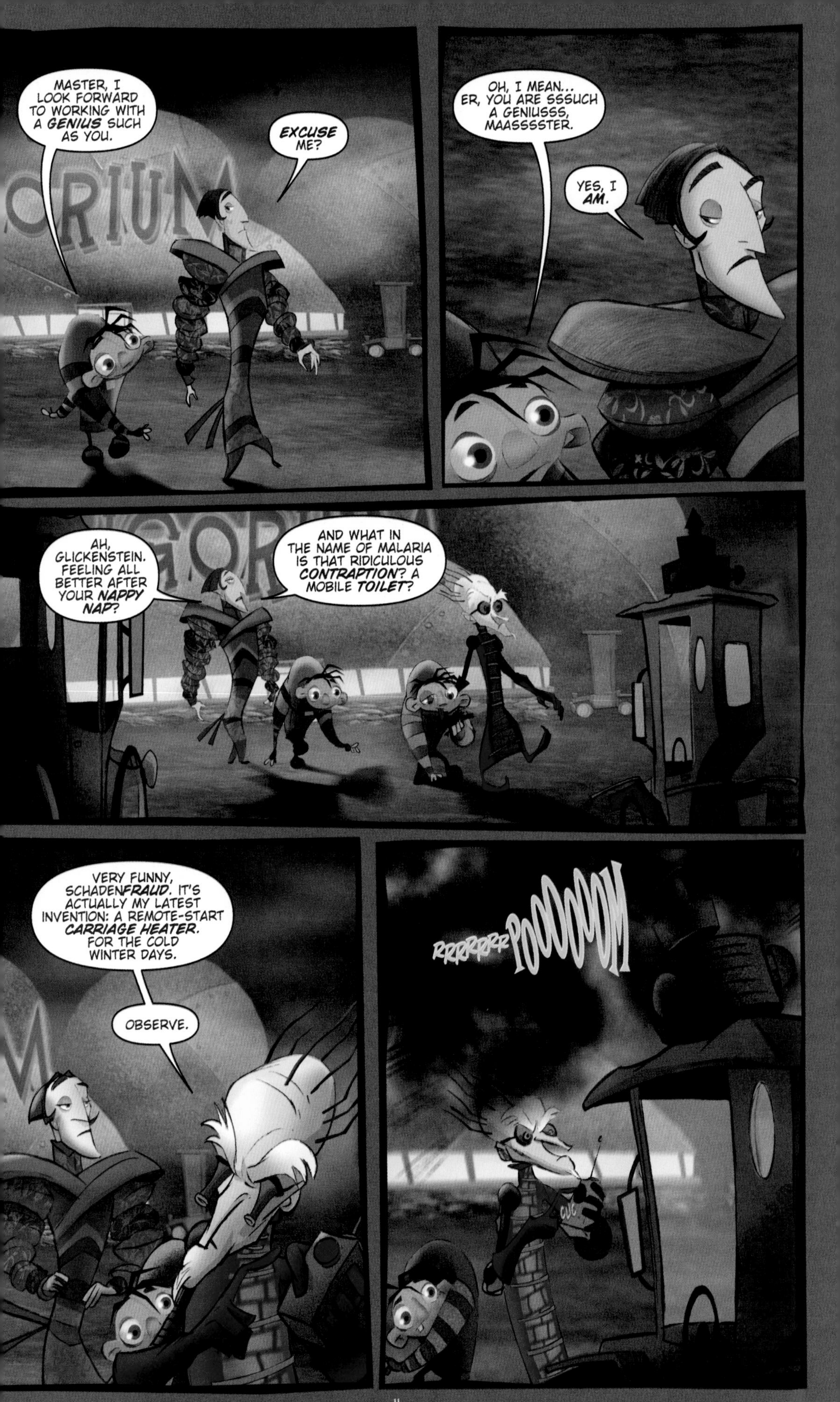

MASTER, I LOOK FORWARD TO WORKING WITH A GENIUS SUCH AS YOU.
EXCUSE ME?
ORIUM
OH, I MEAN... ER, YOU ARE SSSUCH A GENIUSSS, MAASSSSTER.
YES, I AM.
AH, GLICKENSTEIN. FEELING ALL BETTER AFTER YOUR NAPPY NAP?
AND WHAT IN THE NAME OF MALARIA IS THAT RIDICULOUS CONTRAPTION? A MOBILE TOILET?
VERY FUNNY, SCHADENFRAUD. IT'S ACTUALLY MY LATEST INVENTION: A REMOTE-START CARRIAGE HEATER. FOR THE COLD WINTER DAYS.
OBSERVE.
RRRRRRRR POOOOOOM

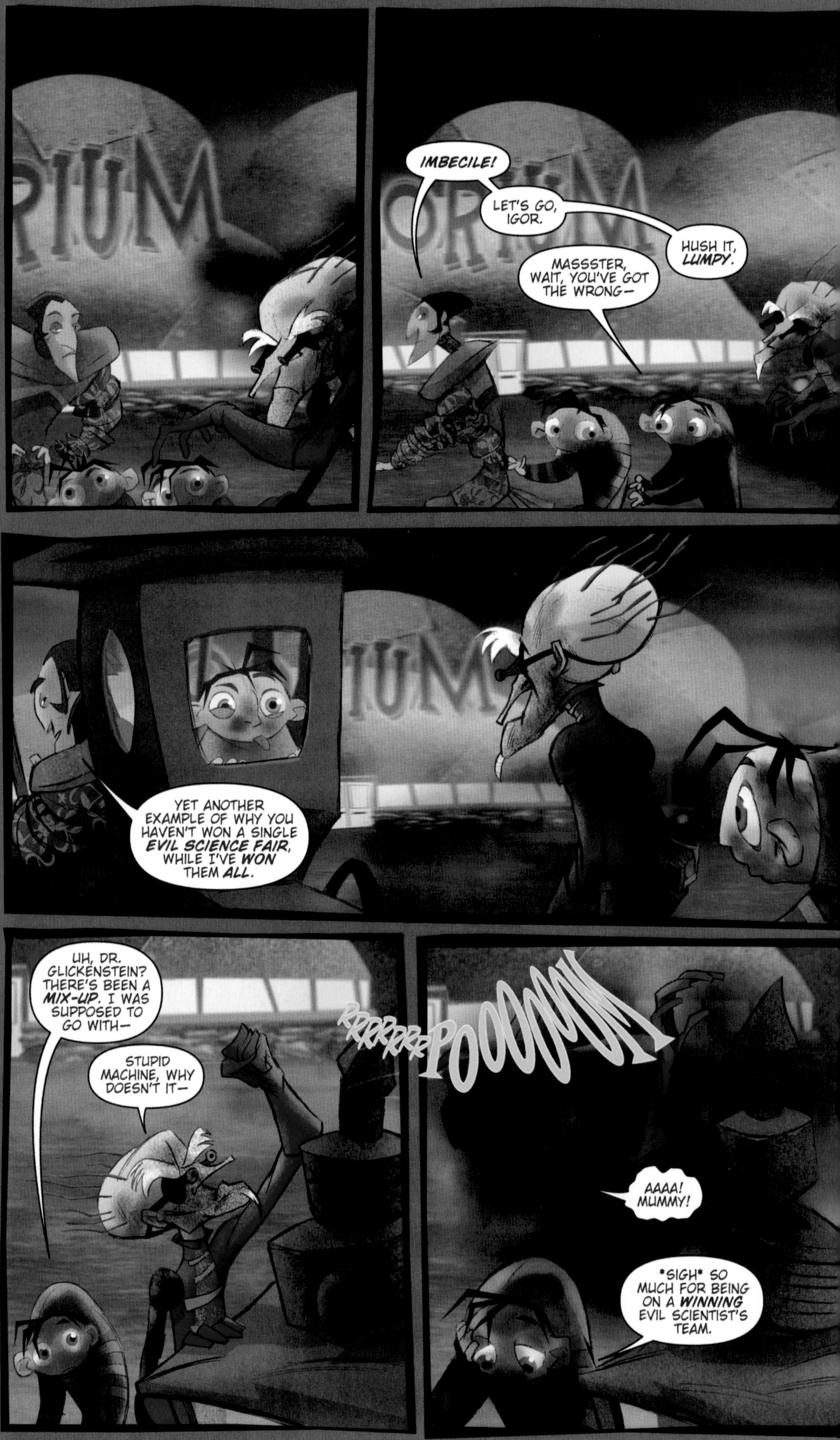
IMBECILE!
LET'S GO, IGOR.
HUSH IT, **LUMPY**.
MASSSTER, WAIT, YOU'VE GOT THE WRONG—
YET ANOTHER EXAMPLE OF WHY YOU HAVEN'T WON A SINGLE **EVIL SCIENCE FAIR**, WHILE I'VE **WON** THEM **ALL**.
UH, DR. GLICKENSTEIN? THERE'S BEEN A **MIX-UP**. I WAS SUPPOSED TO GO WITH—
STUPID MACHINE, WHY DOESN'T IT—
RRRRRRPOOOOOM
AAAA! MUMMY!
SIGH SO MUCH FOR BEING ON A **WINNING** EVIL SCIENTIST'S TEAM.

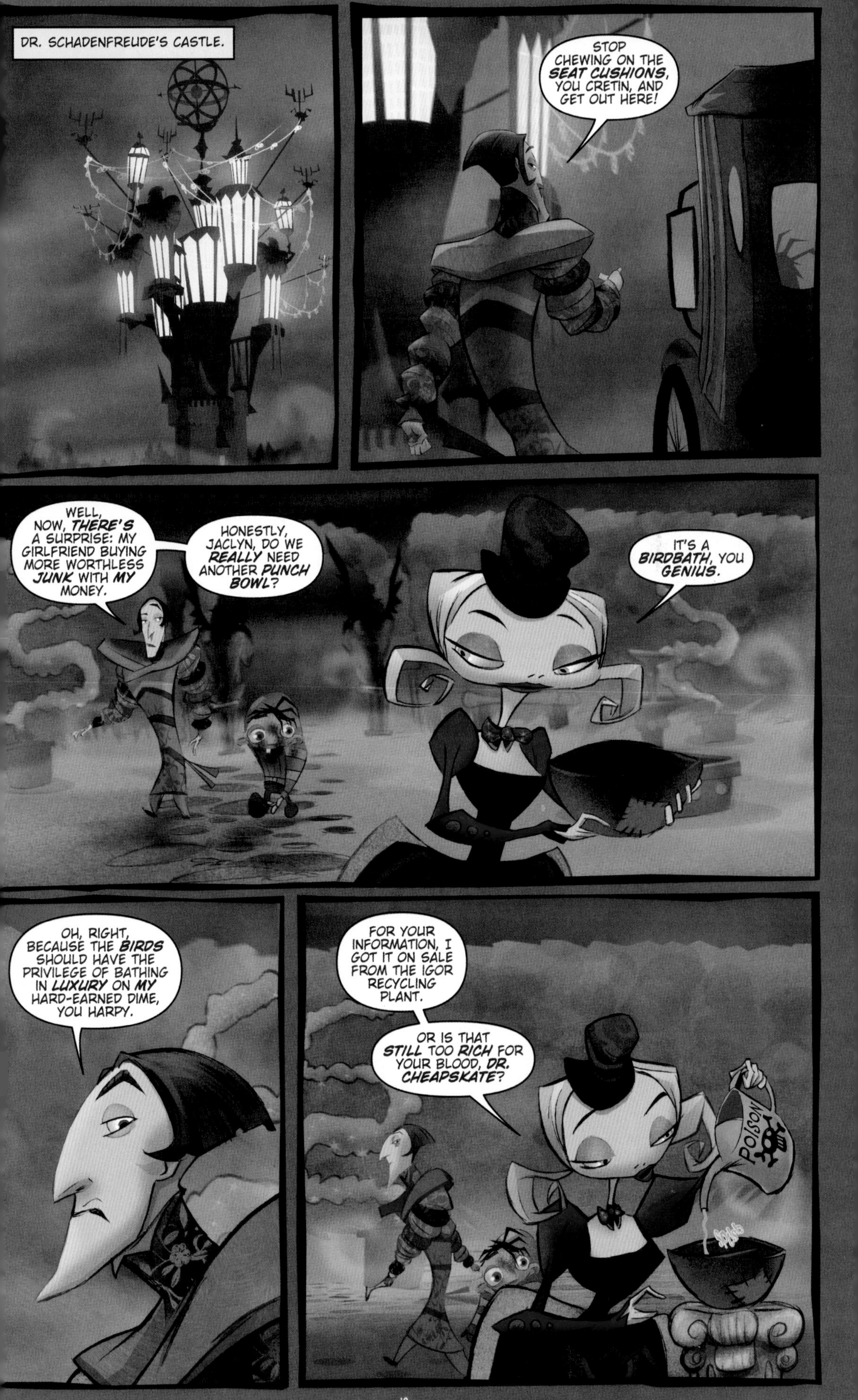
DR. SCHADENFREUDE'S CASTLE.
STOP CHEWING ON THE SEAT CUSHIONS, YOU CRETIN, AND GET OUT HERE!
WELL, NOW, THERE'S A SURPRISE: MY GIRLFRIEND BUYING MORE WORTHLESS JUNK WITH MY MONEY.
HONESTLY, JACLYN, DO WE REALLY NEED ANOTHER PUNCH BOWL?
IT'S A BIRDBATH, YOU GENIUS.
OH, RIGHT, BECAUSE THE BIRDS SHOULD HAVE THE PRIVILEGE OF BATHING IN LUXURY ON MY HARD-EARNED DIME, YOU HARPY.
FOR YOUR INFORMATION, I GOT IT ON SALE FROM THE IGOR RECYCLING PLANT.
OR IS THAT STILL TOO RICH FOR YOUR BLOOD, DR. CHEAPSKATE?
POISON

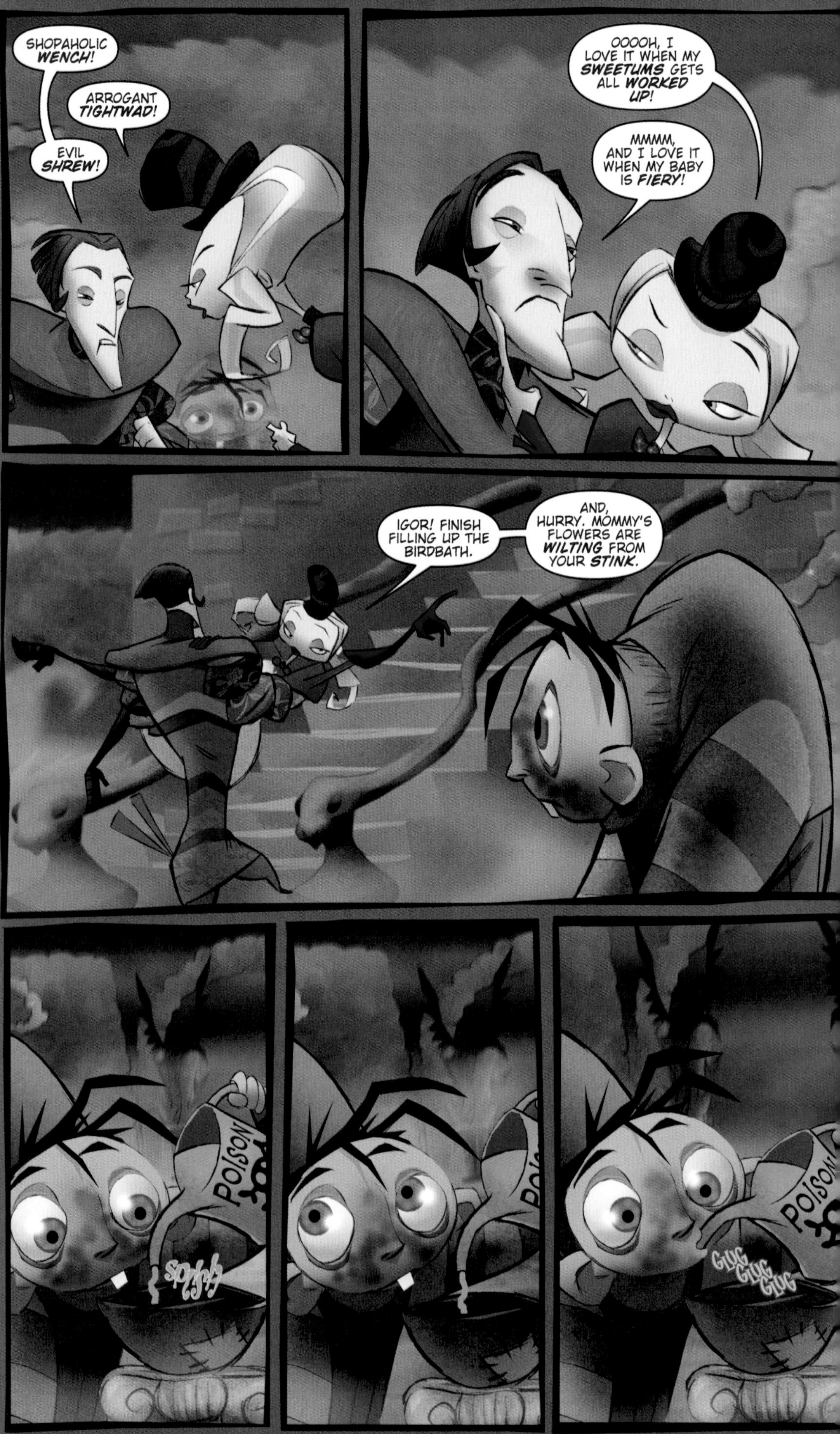
SHOPAHOLIC WENCH!
ARROGANT TIGHTWAD!
EVIL SHREW!
OOOOH, I LOVE IT WHEN MY SWEETUMS GETS ALL WORKED UP!
MMMM, AND I LOVE IT WHEN MY BABY IS FIERY!
IGOR! FINISH FILLING UP THE BIRDBATH.
AND, HURRY. MOMMY'S FLOWERS ARE WILTING FROM YOUR STINK.
POISON
splash
POISON
POISON
GLUG GLUG GLUG

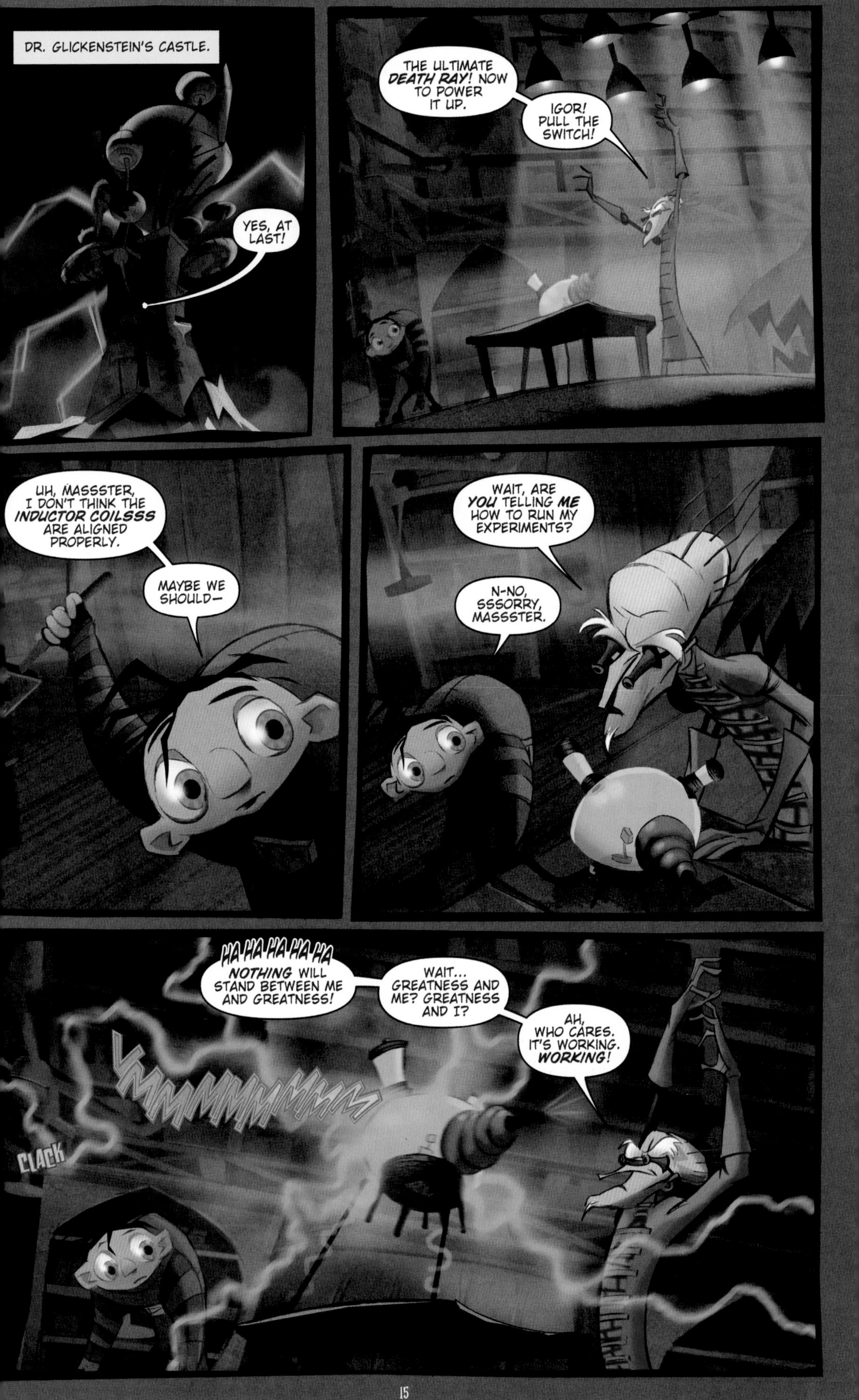

DR. GLICKENSTEIN'S CASTLE.
YES, AT LAST!
THE ULTIMATE DEATH RAY! NOW TO POWER IT UP.
IGOR! PULL THE SWITCH!
UH, MASSSTER, I DON'T THINK THE INDUCTOR COILSSS ARE ALIGNED PROPERLY.
MAYBE WE SHOULD—
WAIT, ARE YOU TELLING ME HOW TO RUN MY EXPERIMENTS?
N-NO, SSSORRY, MASSSTER.
HA HA HA HA HA
NOTHING WILL STAND BETWEEN ME AND GREATNESS!
WAIT... GREATNESS AND ME? GREATNESS AND I?
AH, WHO CARES. IT'S WORKING. WORKING!
VMMMMMMMMM
CLACK

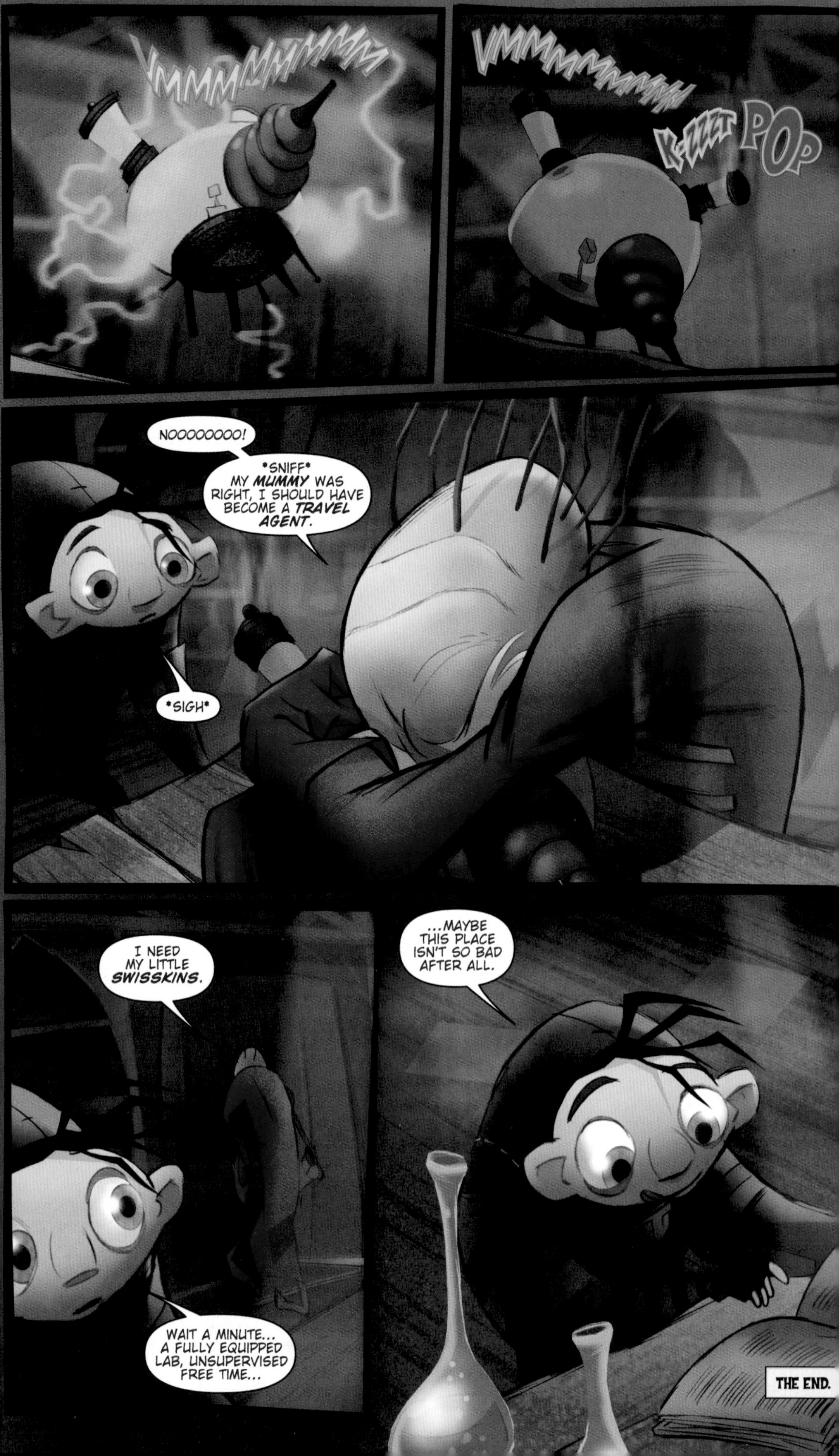
VMMMMMMMMM
VMMMMMMMMMM
K-ZZZT POP
NOOOOOOOO!
SNIFF MY MUMMY WAS RIGHT, I SHOULD HAVE BECOME A TRAVEL AGENT.
SIGH
I NEED MY LITTLE SWISSKINS.
WAIT A MINUTE... A FULLY EQUIPPED LAB, UNSUPERVISED FREE TIME...
...MAYBE THIS PLACE ISN'T SO BAD AFTER ALL.
THE END.

"The Life and Death (and Life) of Scamper"

by Dara Naraghi (writer)
& Grant Bond (artist)

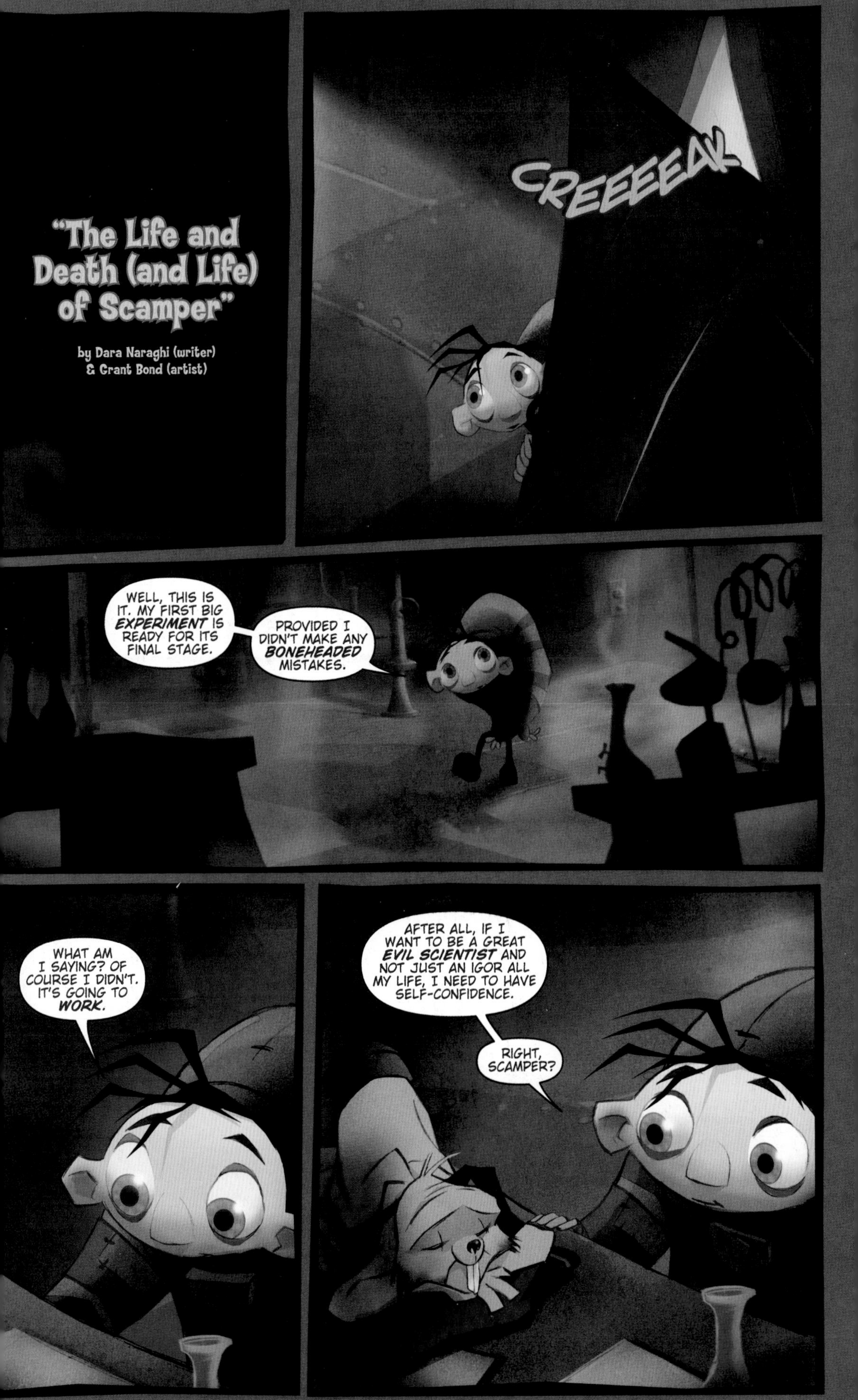
CREEEEAK
WELL, THIS IS IT. MY FIRST BIG EXPERIMENT IS READY FOR ITS FINAL STAGE.
PROVIDED I DIDN'T MAKE ANY BONEHEADED MISTAKES.
WHAT AM I SAYING? OF COURSE I DIDN'T. IT'S GOING TO WORK.
AFTER ALL, IF I WANT TO BE A GREAT EVIL SCIENTIST AND NOT JUST AN IGOR ALL MY LIFE, I NEED TO HAVE SELF-CONFIDENCE.
RIGHT, SCAMPER?

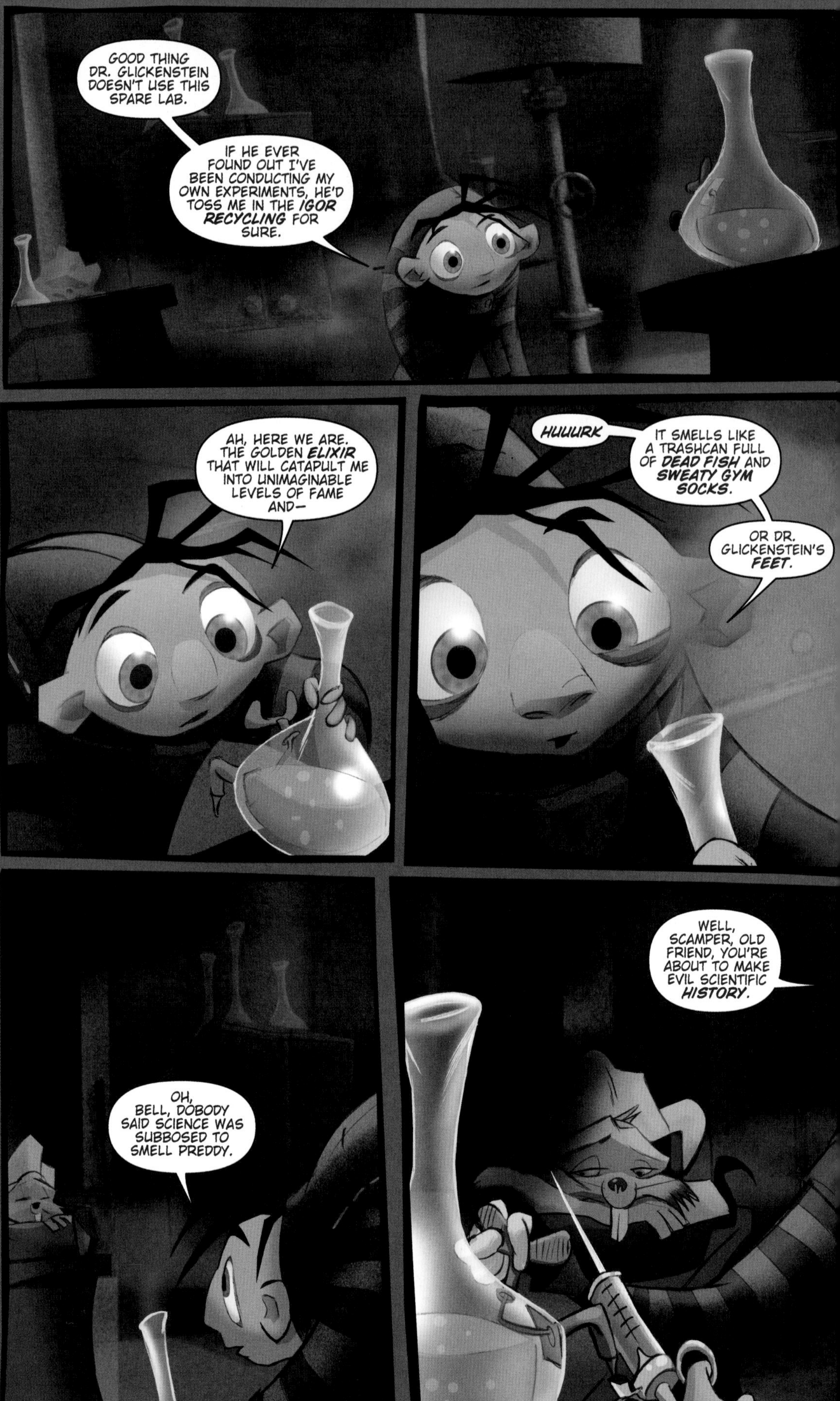
GOOD THING DR. GLICKENSTEIN DOESN'T USE THIS SPARE LAB.
IF HE EVER FOUND OUT I'VE BEEN CONDUCTING MY OWN EXPERIMENTS, HE'D TOSS ME IN THE IGOR RECYCLING FOR SURE.
AH, HERE WE ARE. THE GOLDEN ELIXIR THAT WILL CATAPULT ME INTO UNIMAGINABLE LEVELS OF FAME AND—
HUUURK
IT SMELLS LIKE A TRASHCAN FULL OF DEAD FISH AND SWEATY GYM SOCKS.
OR DR. GLICKENSTEIN'S FEET.
OH, BELL, DOBODY SAID SCIENCE WAS SUBBOSED TO SMELL PREDDY.
WELL, SCAMPER, OLD FRIEND, YOU'RE ABOUT TO MAKE EVIL SCIENTIFIC HISTORY.

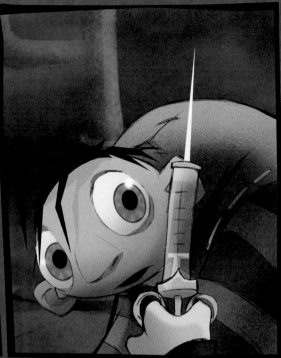

SIGH. HOW AM I *EVER* GOING TO BE AN EVIL SCIENTIST IF I CAN'T EVEN BRING MYSELF TO GIVE A LAB RABBIT A HORRIBLE, PAINFUL SHOT?

IT'S OK, I'LL WORK MY WAY UP TO IT. BUT FOR NOW—

—HERE YOU GO, *WIDDLE BUNNY*. IGOR'S GOT A NUMMY TWEAT FOR YOU!

AWWWWWW.

MUNCH MUNCH MUNCH

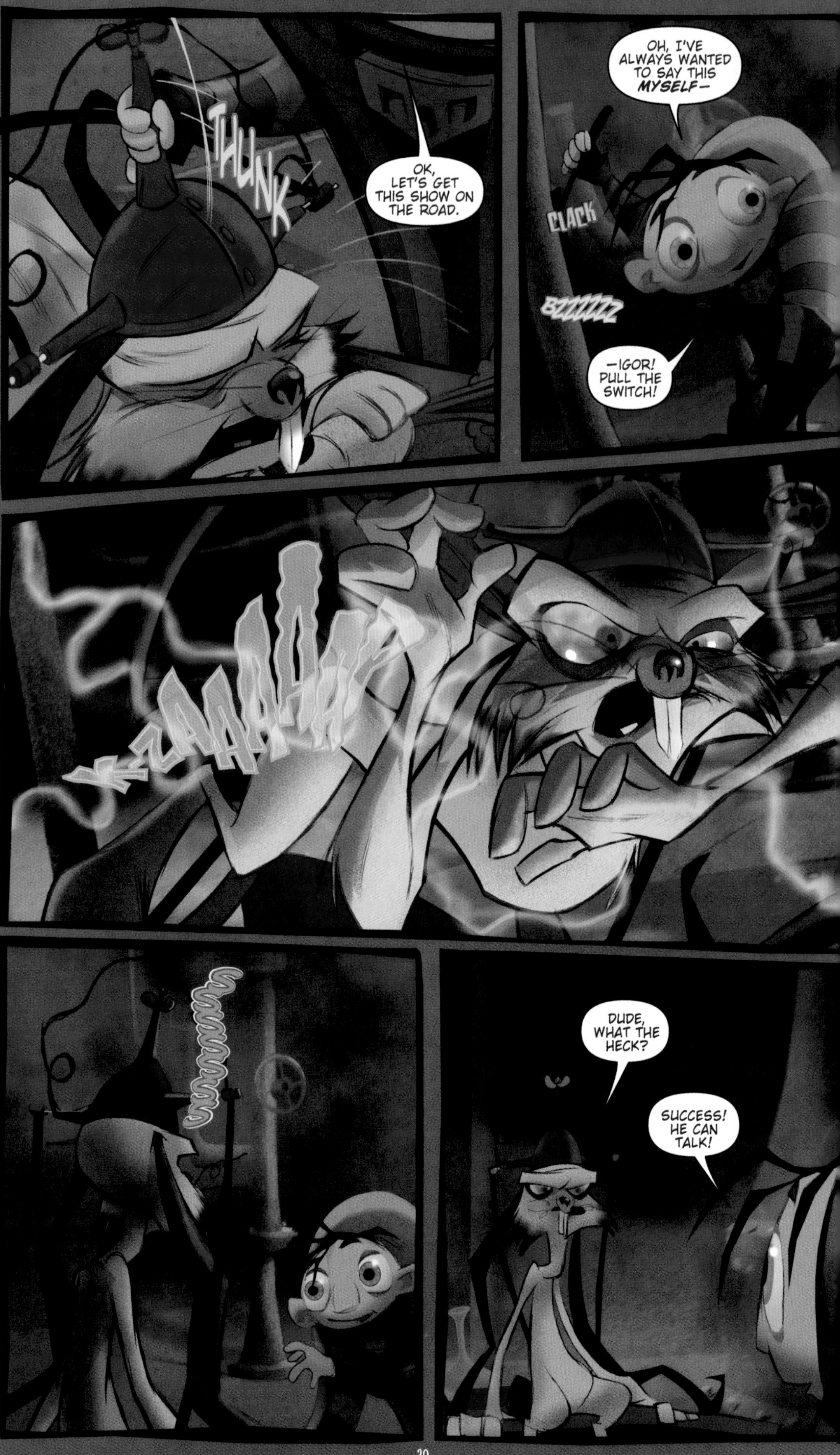
THUNK
OK, LET'S GET THIS SHOW ON THE ROAD.
OH, I'VE ALWAYS WANTED TO SAY THIS *MYSELF*—
CLACK
BZZZZZZ
—IGOR! PULL THE SWITCH!
K-ZAAAAAP
DUDE, WHAT THE HECK?
SUCCESS! HE CAN TALK!

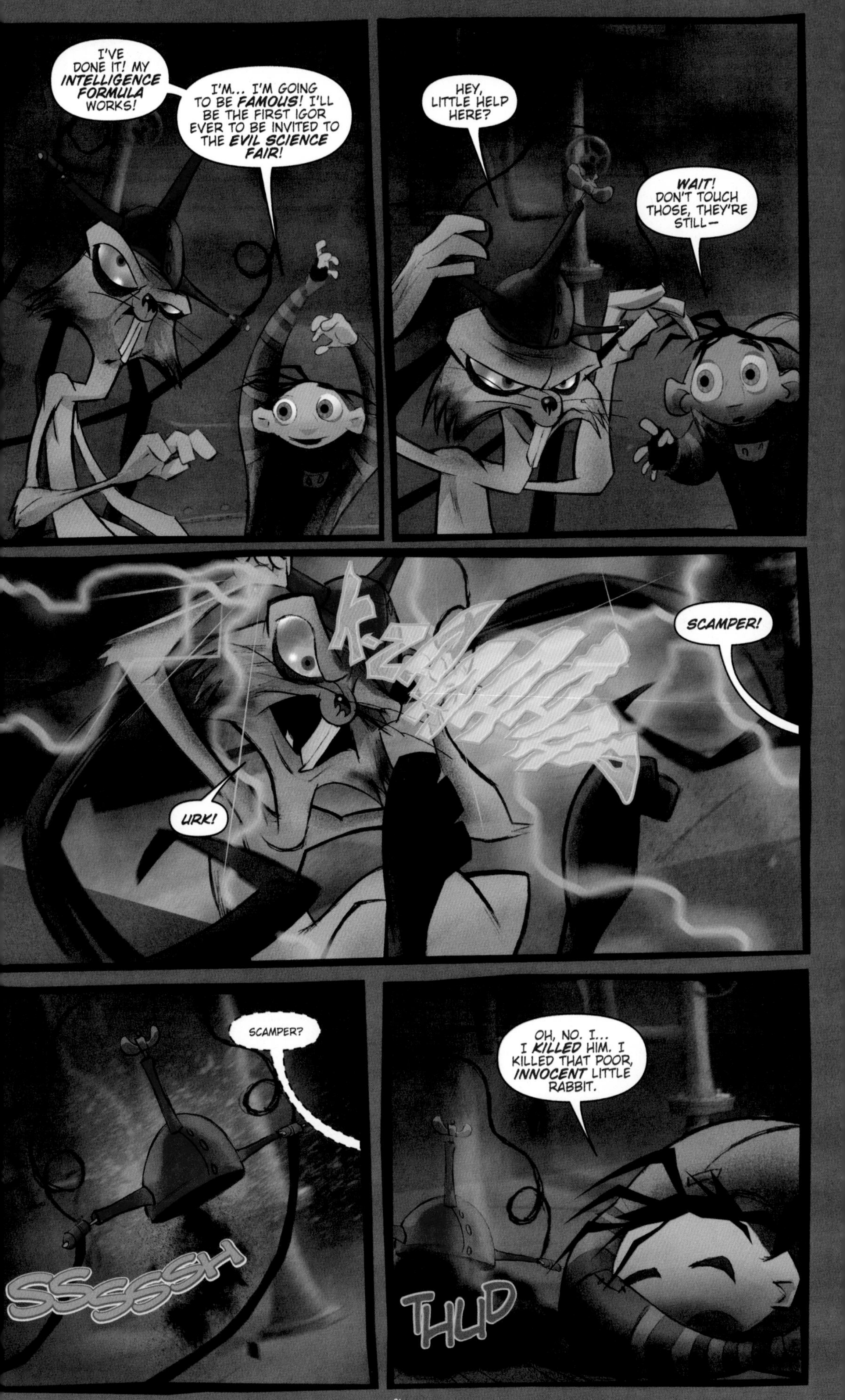
I'VE DONE IT! MY *INTELLIGENCE FORMULA* WORKS!
I'M... I'M GOING TO BE *FAMOUS*! I'LL BE THE FIRST IGOR EVER TO BE INVITED TO THE *EVIL SCIENCE FAIR*!
HEY, LITTLE HELP HERE?
WAIT! DON'T TOUCH THOSE, THEY'RE STILL—
K-ZAAAAP
SCAMPER!
URK!
SCAMPER?
SSSSSSH
OH, NO. I... I *KILLED* HIM. I KILLED THAT POOR, *INNOCENT* LITTLE RABBIT.
THUD

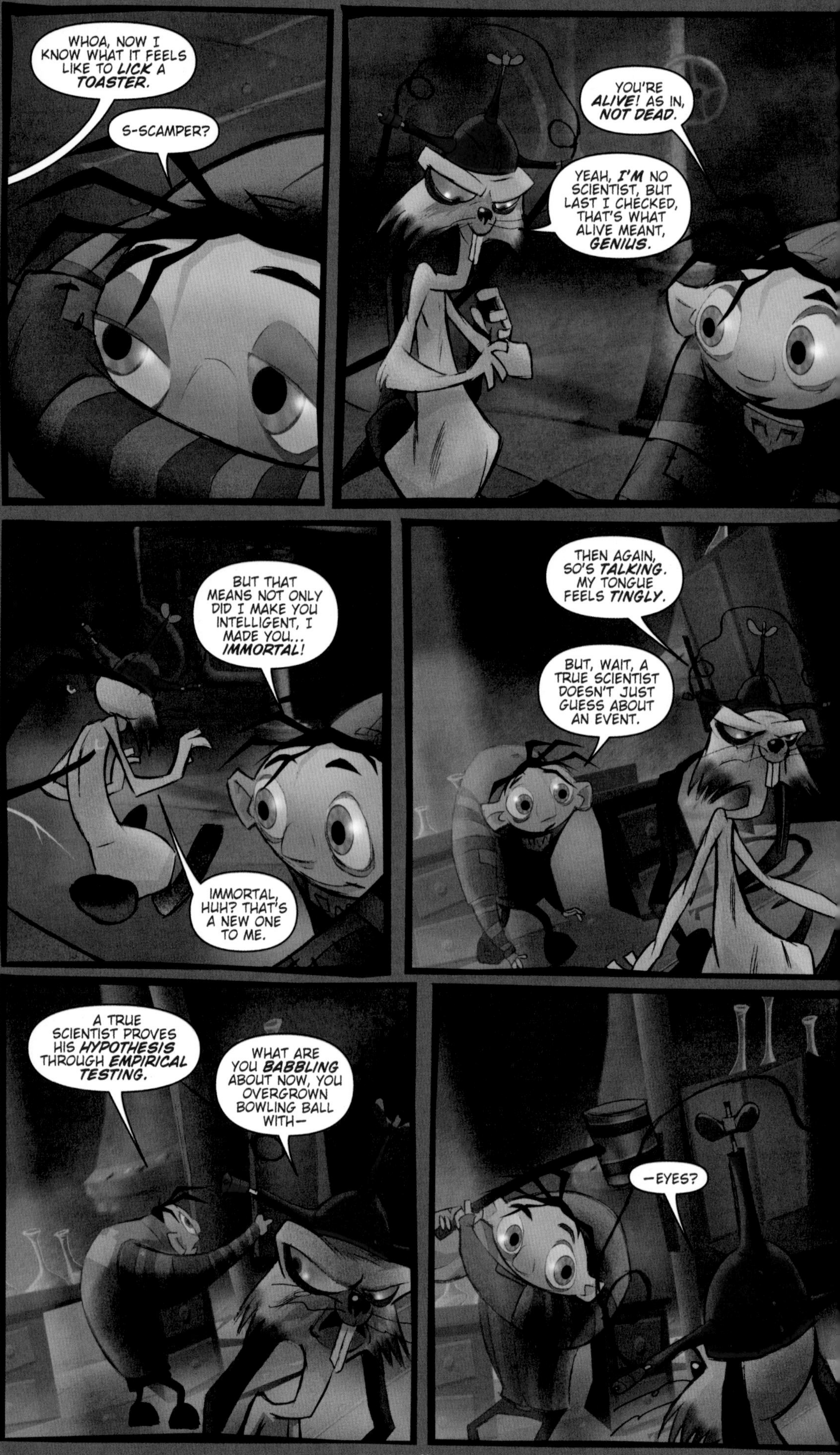
WHOA, NOW I KNOW WHAT IT FEELS LIKE TO LICK A TOASTER.
S-SCAMPER?
YOU'RE ALIVE! AS IN, NOT DEAD.
YEAH, I'M NO SCIENTIST, BUT LAST I CHECKED, THAT'S WHAT ALIVE MEANT, GENIUS.
BUT THAT MEANS NOT ONLY DID I MAKE YOU INTELLIGENT, I MADE YOU... IMMORTAL!
IMMORTAL, HUH? THAT'S A NEW ONE TO ME.
THEN AGAIN, SO'S TALKING. MY TONGUE FEELS TINGLY.
BUT, WAIT, A TRUE SCIENTIST DOESN'T JUST GUESS ABOUT AN EVENT.
A TRUE SCIENTIST PROVES HIS HYPOTHESIS THROUGH EMPIRICAL TESTING.
WHAT ARE YOU BABBLING ABOUT NOW, YOU OVERGROWN BOWLING BALL WITH—
—EYES?

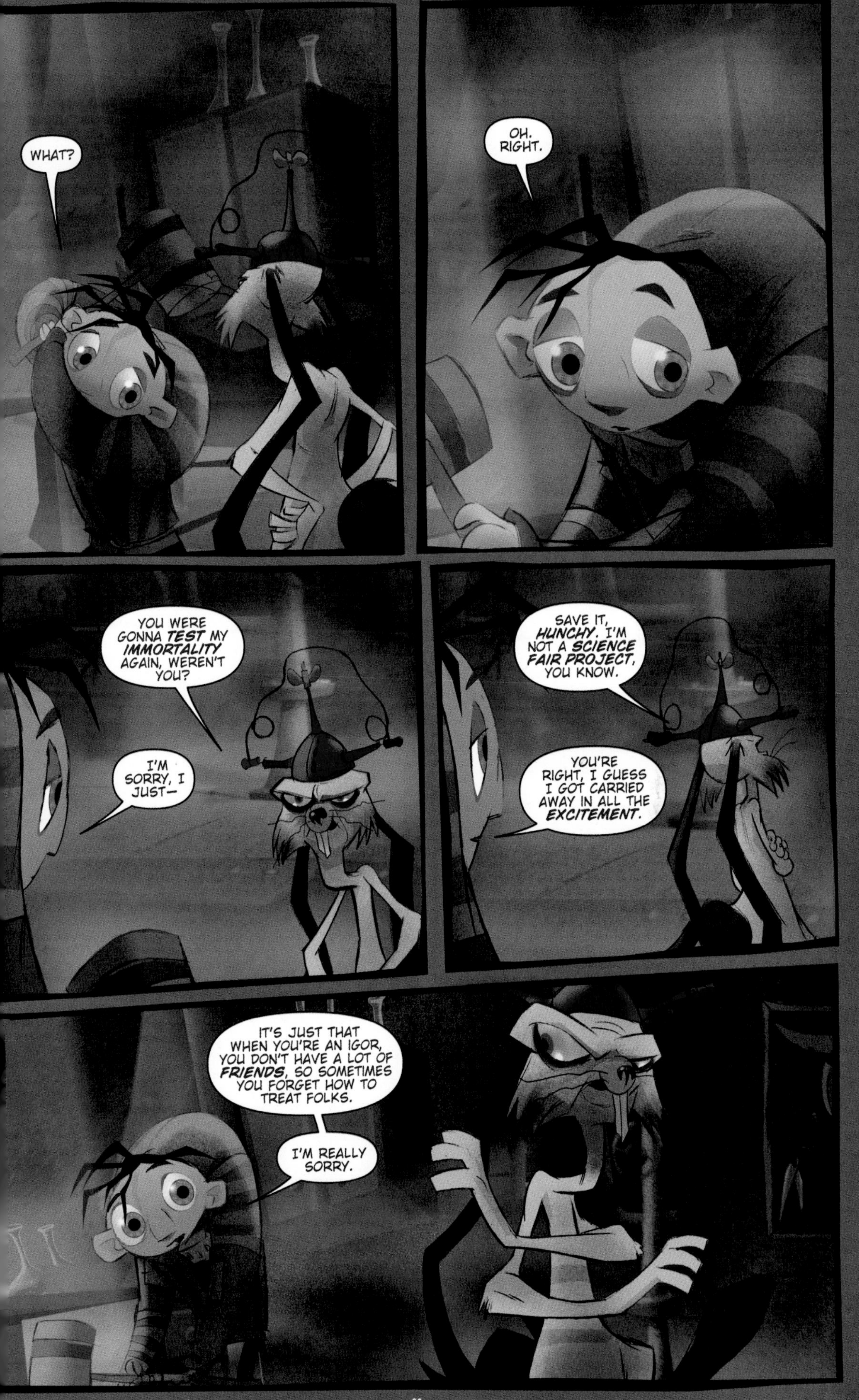

WHAT?
OH. RIGHT.
YOU WERE GONNA TEST MY IMMORTALITY AGAIN, WEREN'T YOU?
I'M SORRY, I JUST—
SAVE IT, HUNCHY. I'M NOT A SCIENCE FAIR PROJECT, YOU KNOW.
YOU'RE RIGHT, I GUESS I GOT CARRIED AWAY IN ALL THE EXCITEMENT.
IT'S JUST THAT WHEN YOU'RE AN IGOR, YOU DON'T HAVE A LOT OF FRIENDS, SO SOMETIMES YOU FORGET HOW TO TREAT FOLKS.
I'M REALLY SORRY.

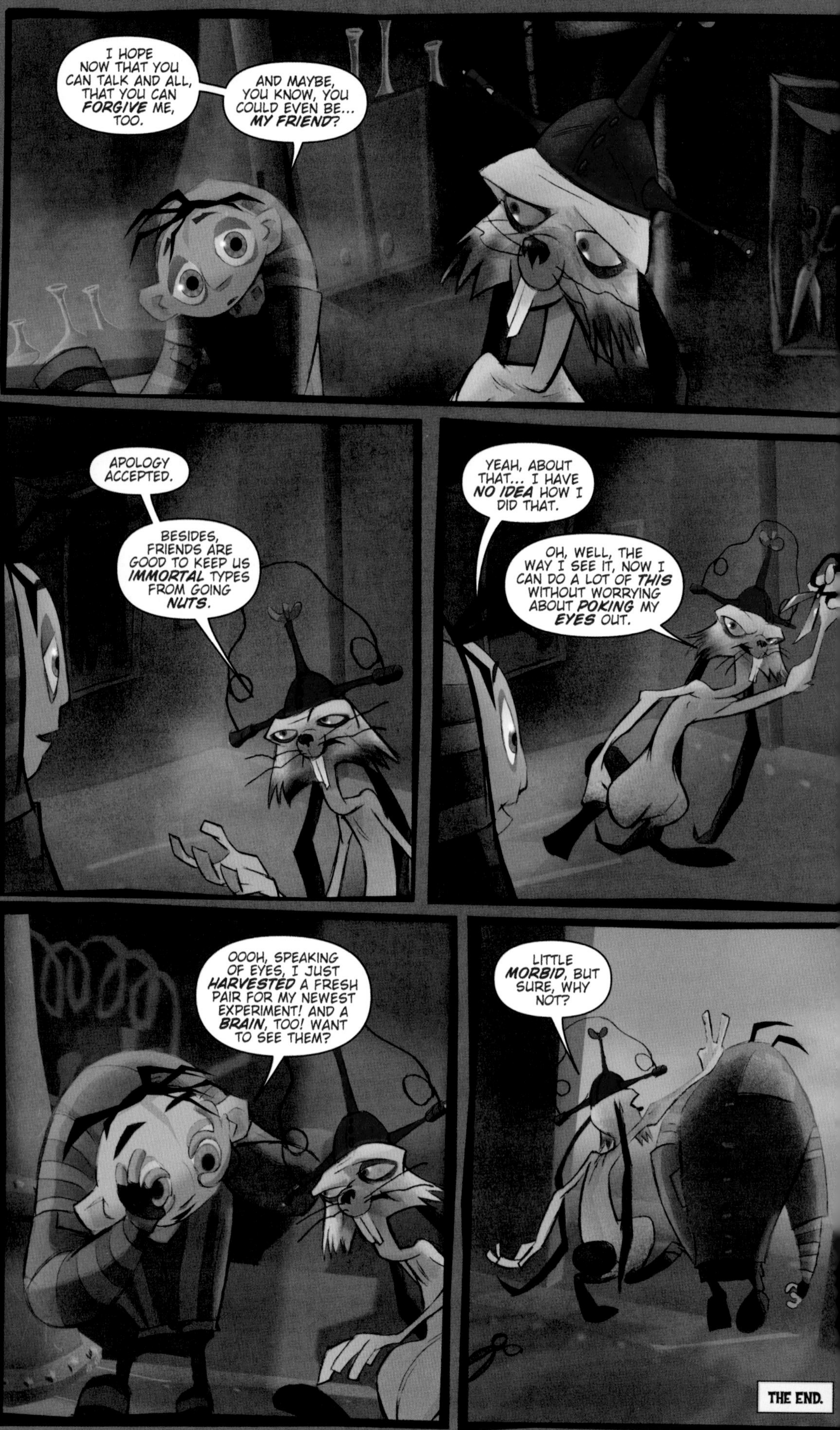
I HOPE NOW THAT YOU CAN TALK AND ALL, THAT YOU CAN FORGIVE ME, TOO.
AND MAYBE, YOU KNOW, YOU COULD EVEN BE... MY FRIEND?
APOLOGY ACCEPTED.
BESIDES, FRIENDS ARE GOOD TO KEEP US IMMORTAL TYPES FROM GOING NUTS.
YEAH, ABOUT THAT... I HAVE NO IDEA HOW I DID THAT.
OH, WELL, THE WAY I SEE IT, NOW I CAN DO A LOT OF THIS WITHOUT WORRYING ABOUT POKING MY EYES OUT.
OOOH, SPEAKING OF EYES, I JUST HARVESTED A FRESH PAIR FOR MY NEWEST EXPERIMENT! AND A BRAIN, TOO! WANT TO SEE THEM?
LITTLE MORBID, BUT SURE, WHY NOT?
THE END.

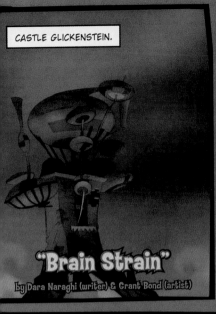

CASTLE GLICKENSTEIN.

"Brain Strain"

by Dara Naraghi (writer) & Grant Bond (artist)

I JUST NEED A FEW MORE PIECES TO FINISH MY LATEST *INVENTION*.

THERE SURE IS A LOT OF *JUNK* HERE, IGOR.

YEAH, WELL, LET'S JUST SAY DR. GLICKENSTEIN ISN'T THE MOST *SUCCESSFUL* EVIL SCIENTIST OF THE BUNCH.

WHAT THE HECK IS THIS?

DON'T KNOW. IT'S FROM *BEFORE* MY TIME HERE.

HUH.

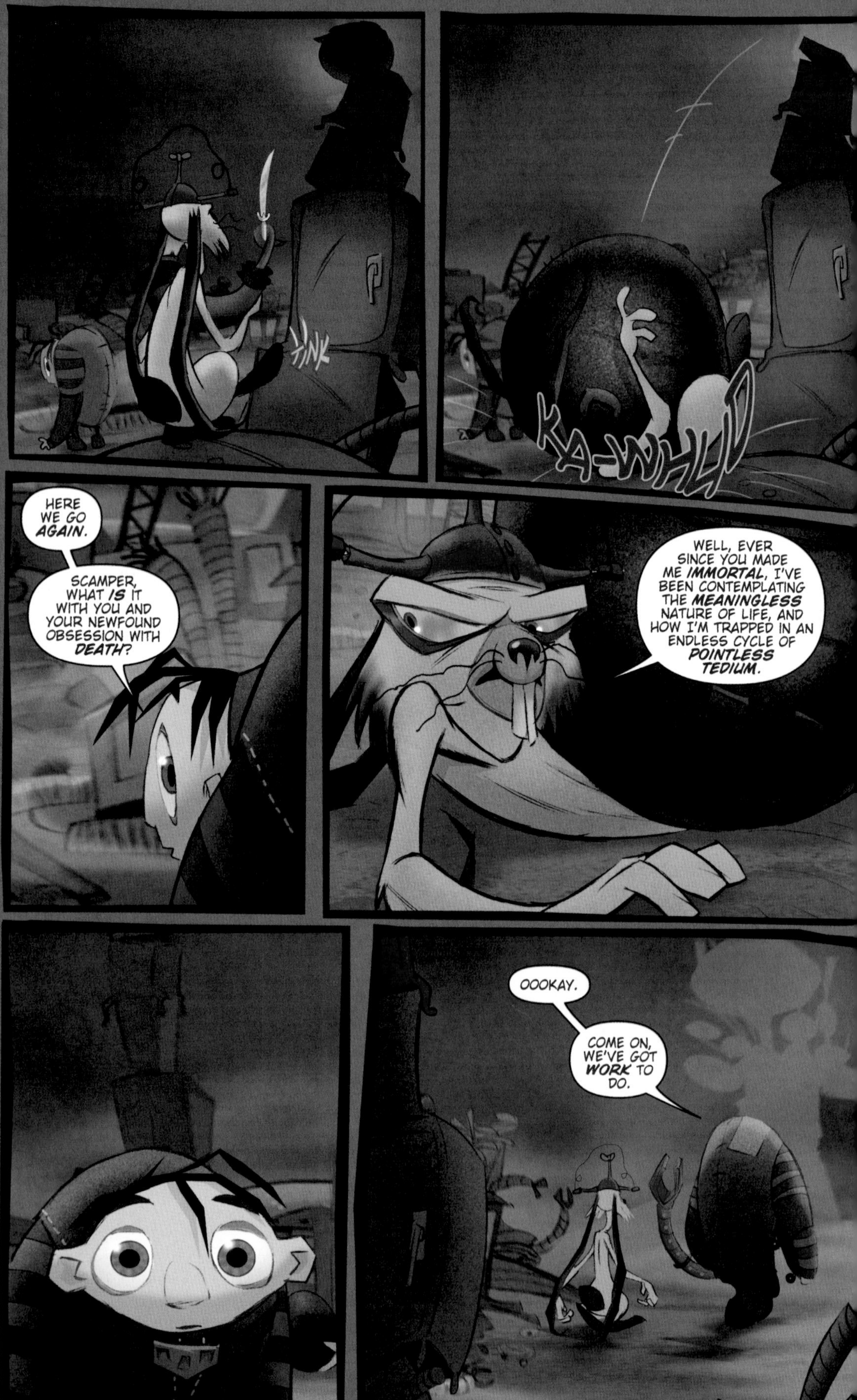

TINK
KA-WHUD
HERE WE GO AGAIN.
SCAMPER, WHAT IS IT WITH YOU AND YOUR NEWFOUND OBSESSION WITH DEATH?
WELL, EVER SINCE YOU MADE ME IMMORTAL, I'VE BEEN CONTEMPLATING THE MEANINGLESS NATURE OF LIFE, AND HOW I'M TRAPPED IN AN ENDLESS CYCLE OF POINTLESS TEDIUM.
OOOKAY.
COME ON, WE'VE GOT WORK TO DO.

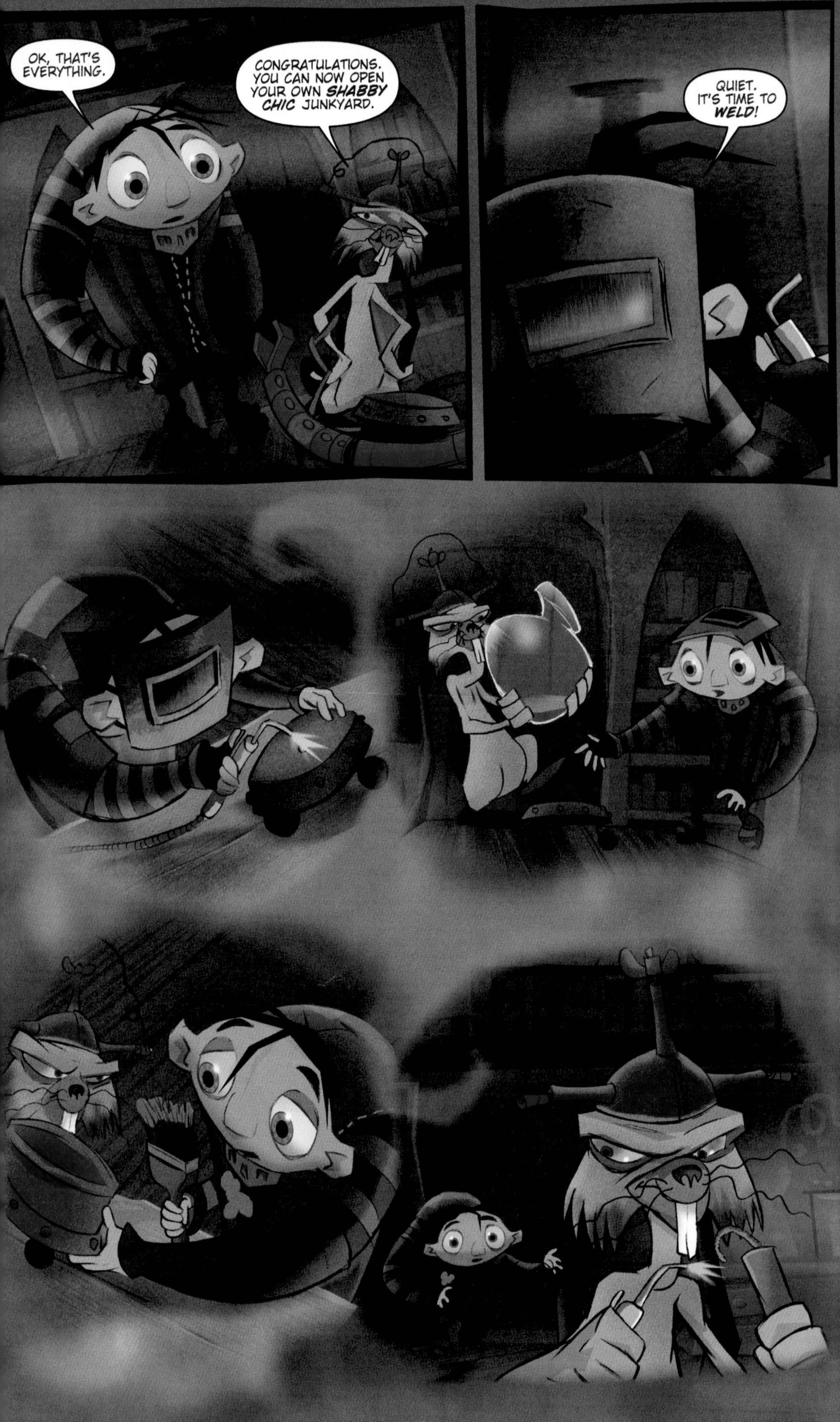
OK, THAT'S EVERYTHING.
CONGRATULATIONS. YOU CAN NOW OPEN YOUR OWN SHABBY CHIC JUNKYARD.
QUIET. IT'S TIME TO WELD!

THERE! IT'S *DONE!*

YEAH, THAT'S NOT *CREEPY* OR ANYTHING.

WHAT EXACTLY *IS* IT?

IT'S MY LATEST INVENTION: A MECHANICAL *KILLING DEVICE* CONTROLLED BY AN *EVIL HUMAN BRAIN.*

I DUG THIS ONE UP *FRESH* THIS MORNING!

NOW TO INSTALL IT AND—

OOPS!

SHLOOP

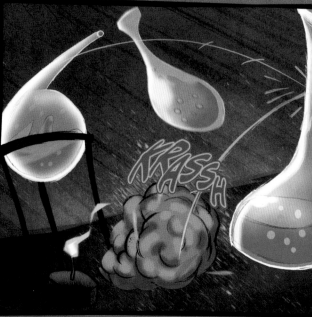

KRASSH

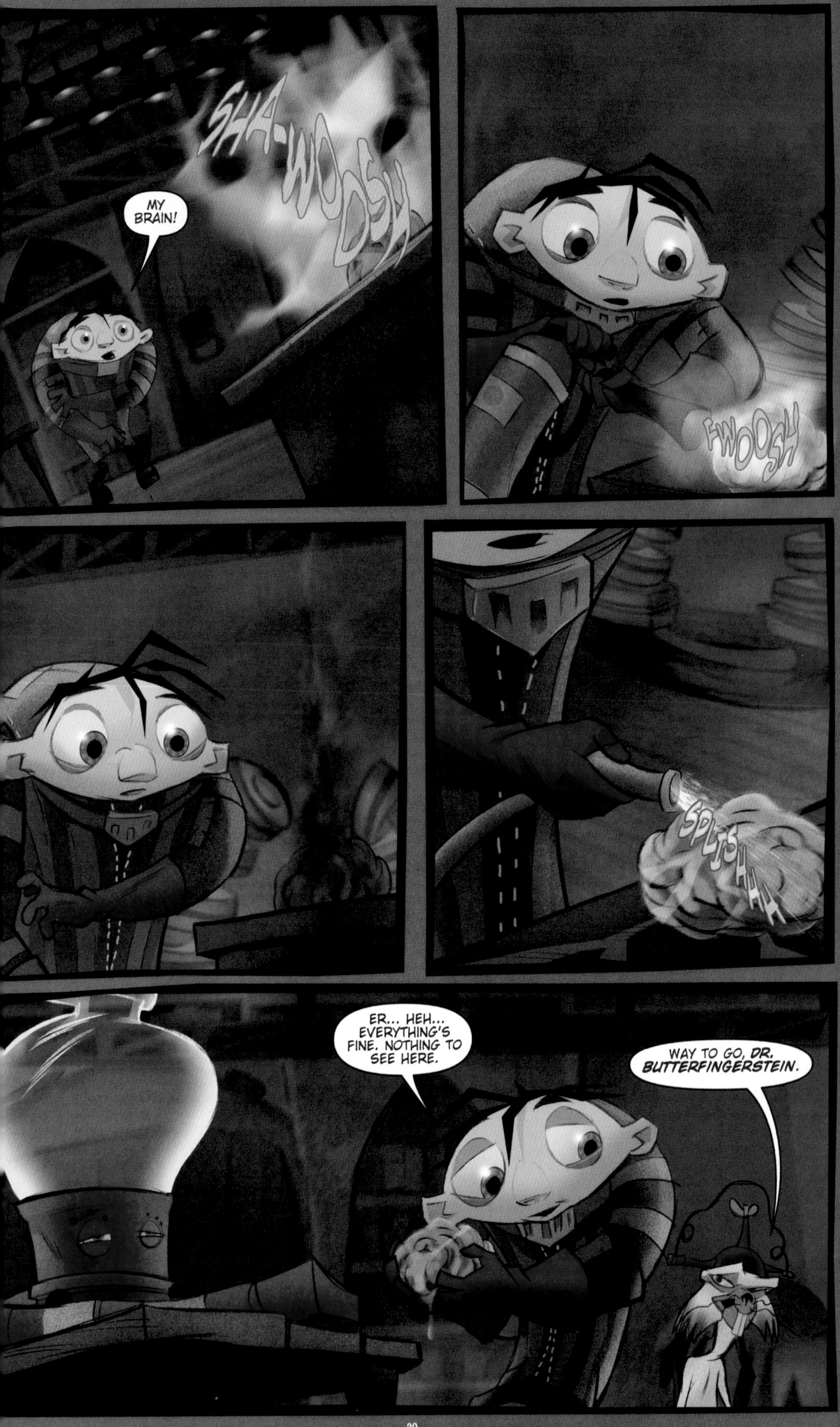
SHA-WOOSH
MY BRAIN!
FWOOSH
SPLISHHH
ER... HEH... EVERYTHING'S FINE. NOTHING TO SEE HERE.
WAY TO GO, DR. BUTTERFINGERSTEIN.

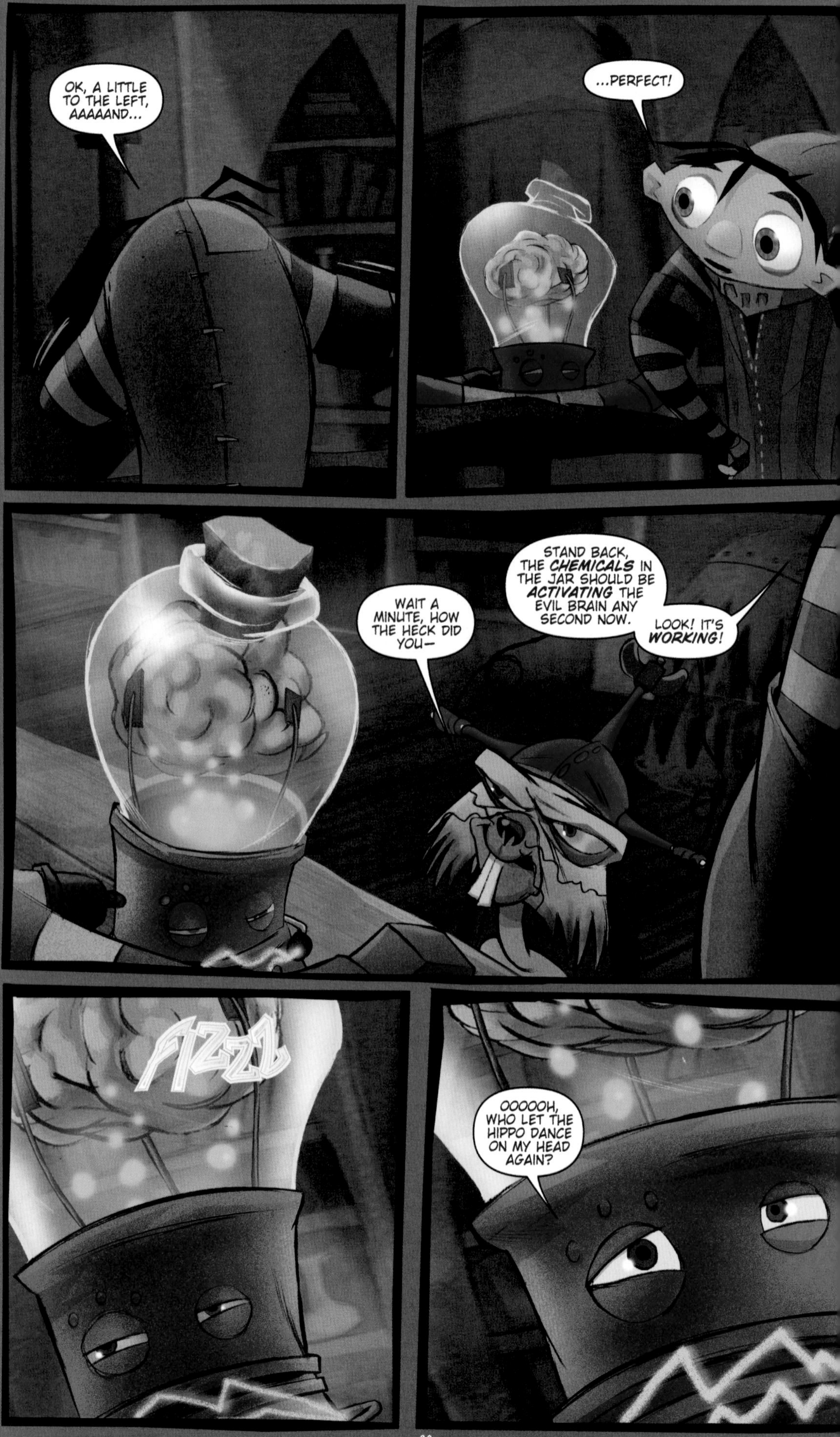
OK, A LITTLE TO THE LEFT, AAAAAND...
...PERFECT!
WAIT A MINUTE, HOW THE HECK DID YOU—
STAND BACK, THE CHEMICALS IN THE JAR SHOULD BE ACTIVATING THE EVIL BRAIN ANY SECOND NOW.
LOOK! IT'S WORKING!
FIZZ
OOOOOH, WHO LET THE HIPPO DANCE ON MY HEAD AGAIN?

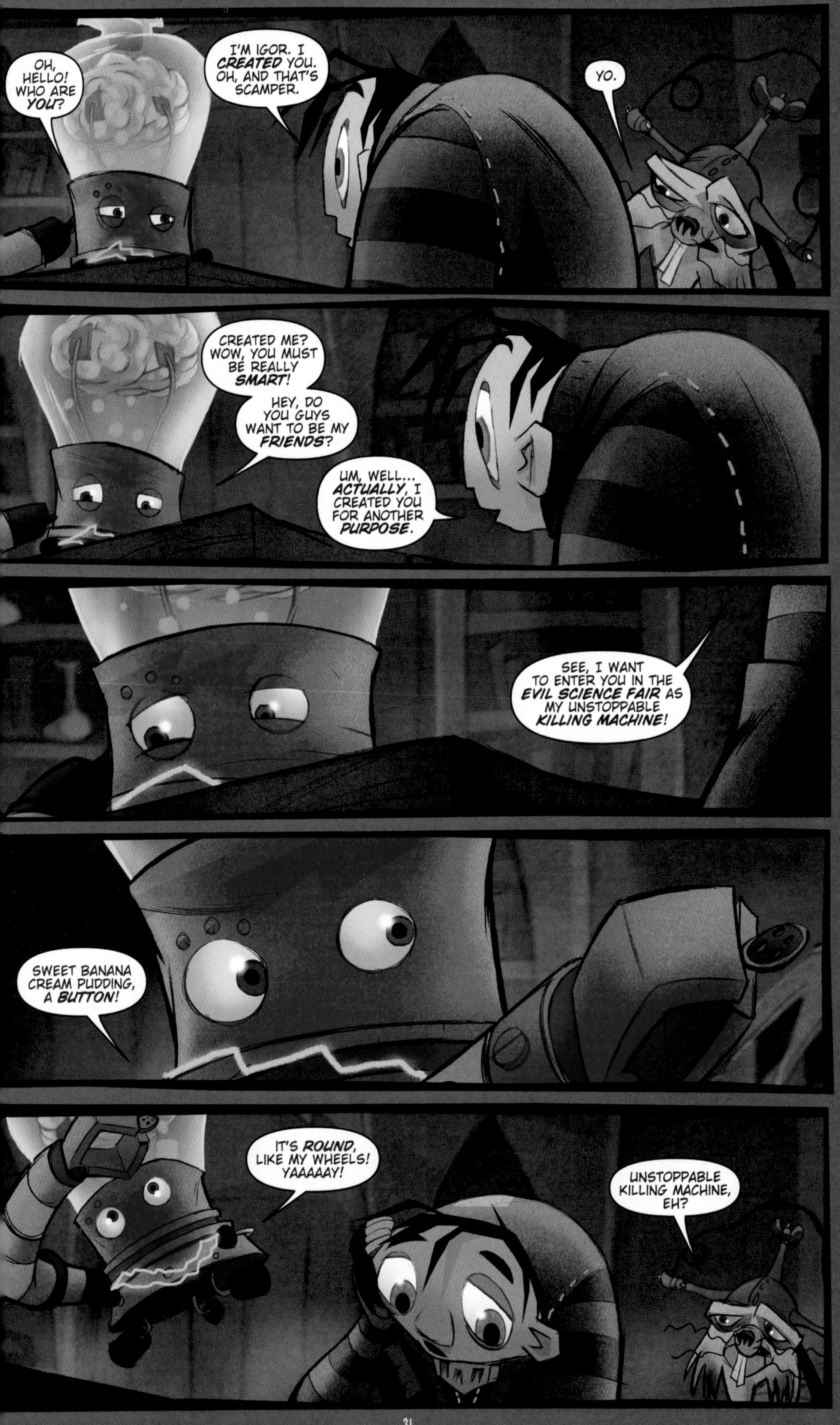
OH, HELLO! WHO ARE YOU?
I'M IGOR. I CREATED YOU. OH, AND THAT'S SCAMPER.
YO.
CREATED ME? WOW, YOU MUST BE REALLY SMART!
HEY, DO YOU GUYS WANT TO BE MY FRIENDS?
UM, WELL... ACTUALLY, I CREATED YOU FOR ANOTHER PURPOSE.
SEE, I WANT TO ENTER YOU IN THE EVIL SCIENCE FAIR AS MY UNSTOPPABLE KILLING MACHINE!
SWEET BANANA CREAM PUDDING, A BUTTON!
IT'S ROUND, LIKE MY WHEELS! YAAAAAY!
UNSTOPPABLE KILLING MACHINE, EH?

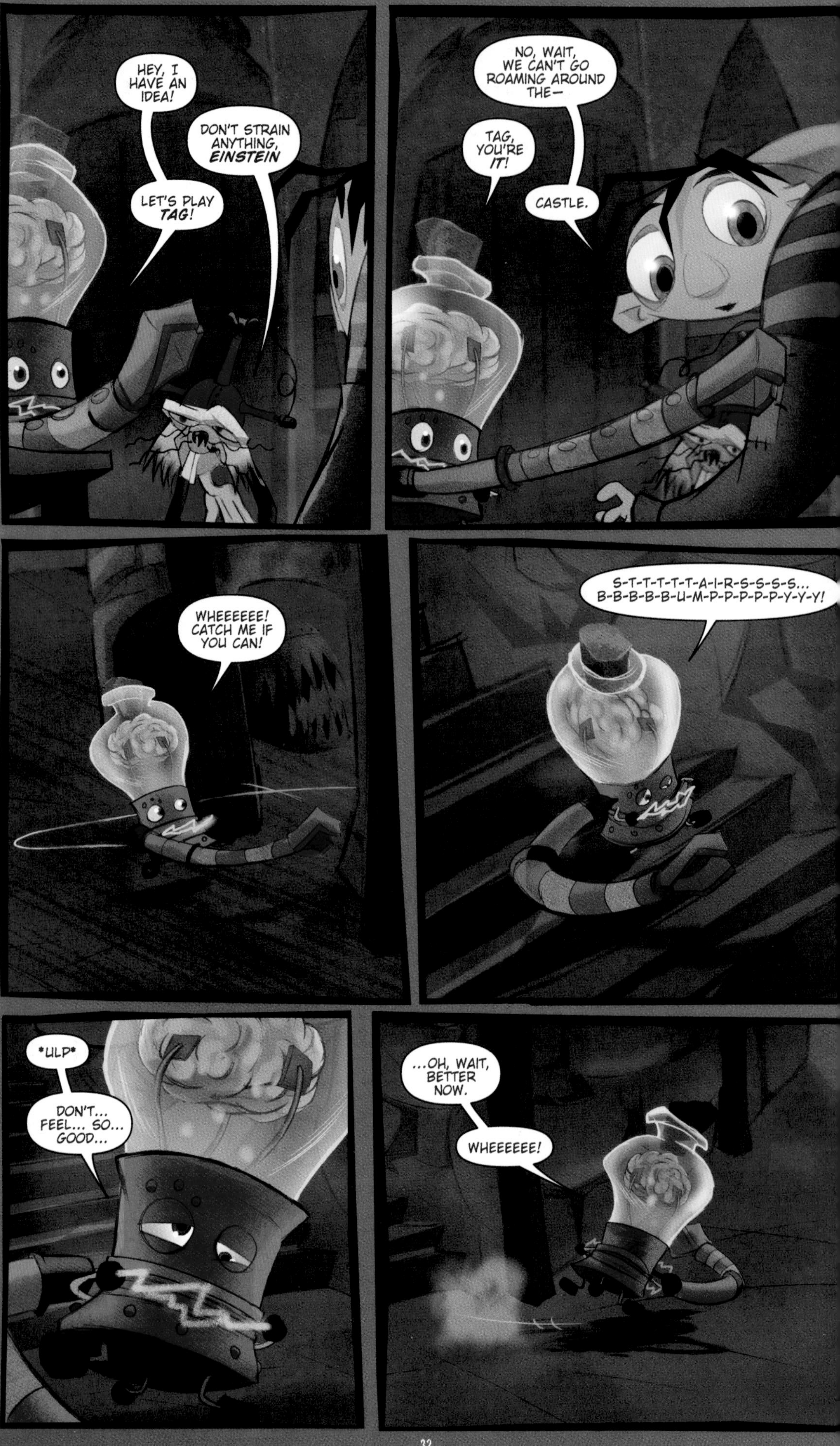

HEY, I HAVE AN IDEA!
DON'T STRAIN ANYTHING, *EINSTEIN*
LET'S PLAY *TAG*!
NO, WAIT, WE CAN'T GO ROAMING AROUND THE—
TAG, YOU'RE *IT*!
CASTLE.
WHEEEEEE! CATCH ME IF YOU CAN!
S-T-T-T-T-T-A-I-R-S-S-S-S-S... B-B-B-B-B-U-M-P-P-P-P-P-Y-Y-Y!
ULP
DON'T... FEEL... SO... GOOD...
...OH, WAIT, BETTER NOW.
WHEEEEEE!

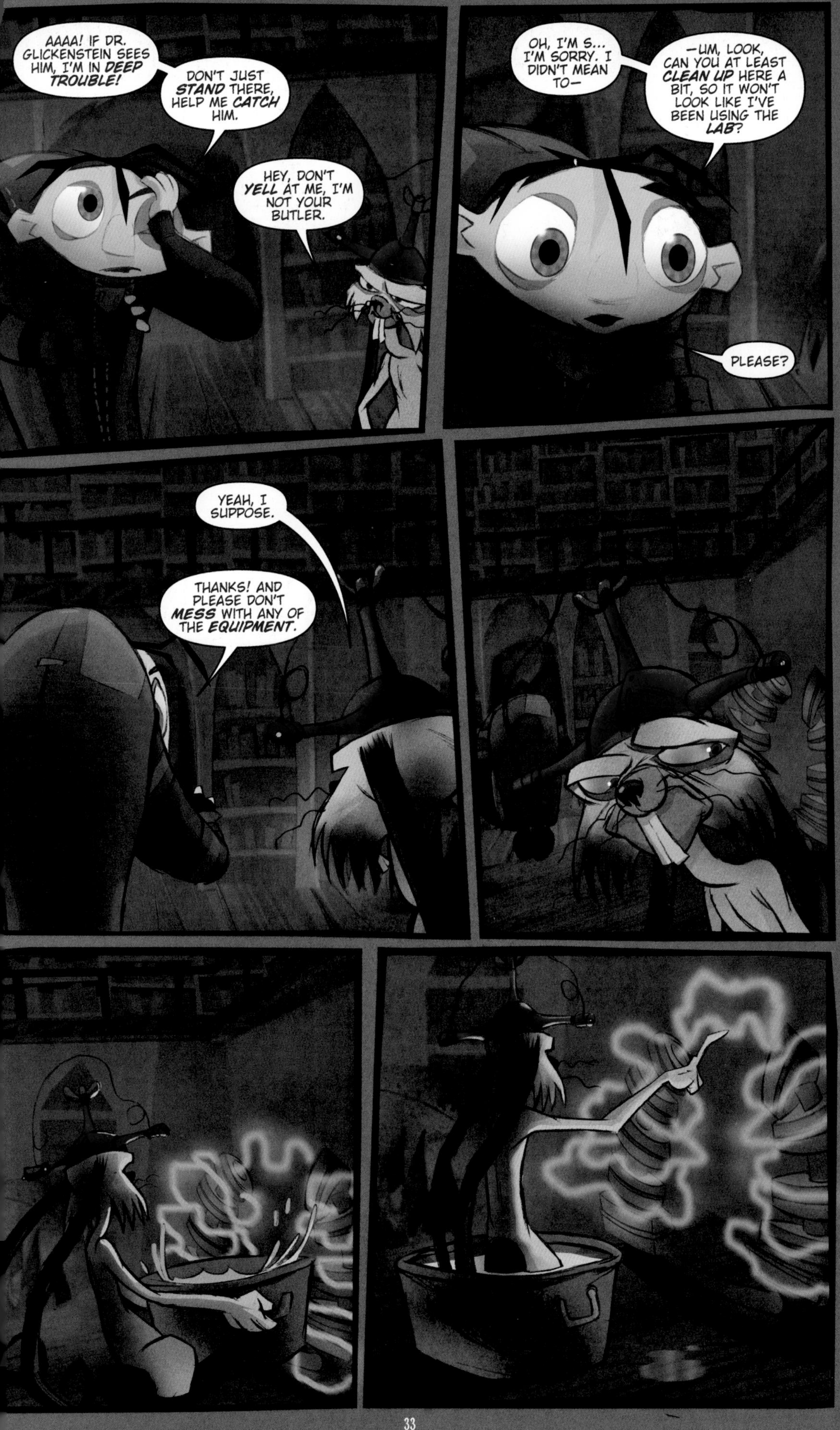
AAAA! IF DR. GLICKENSTEIN SEES HIM, I'M IN DEEP TROUBLE!
DON'T JUST STAND THERE, HELP ME CATCH HIM.
HEY, DON'T YELL AT ME, I'M NOT YOUR BUTLER.
OH, I'M S... I'M SORRY. I DIDN'T MEAN TO—
—UM, LOOK, CAN YOU AT LEAST CLEAN UP HERE A BIT, SO IT WON'T LOOK LIKE I'VE BEEN USING THE LAB?
PLEASE?
YEAH, I SUPPOSE.
THANKS! AND PLEASE DON'T MESS WITH ANY OF THE EQUIPMENT.

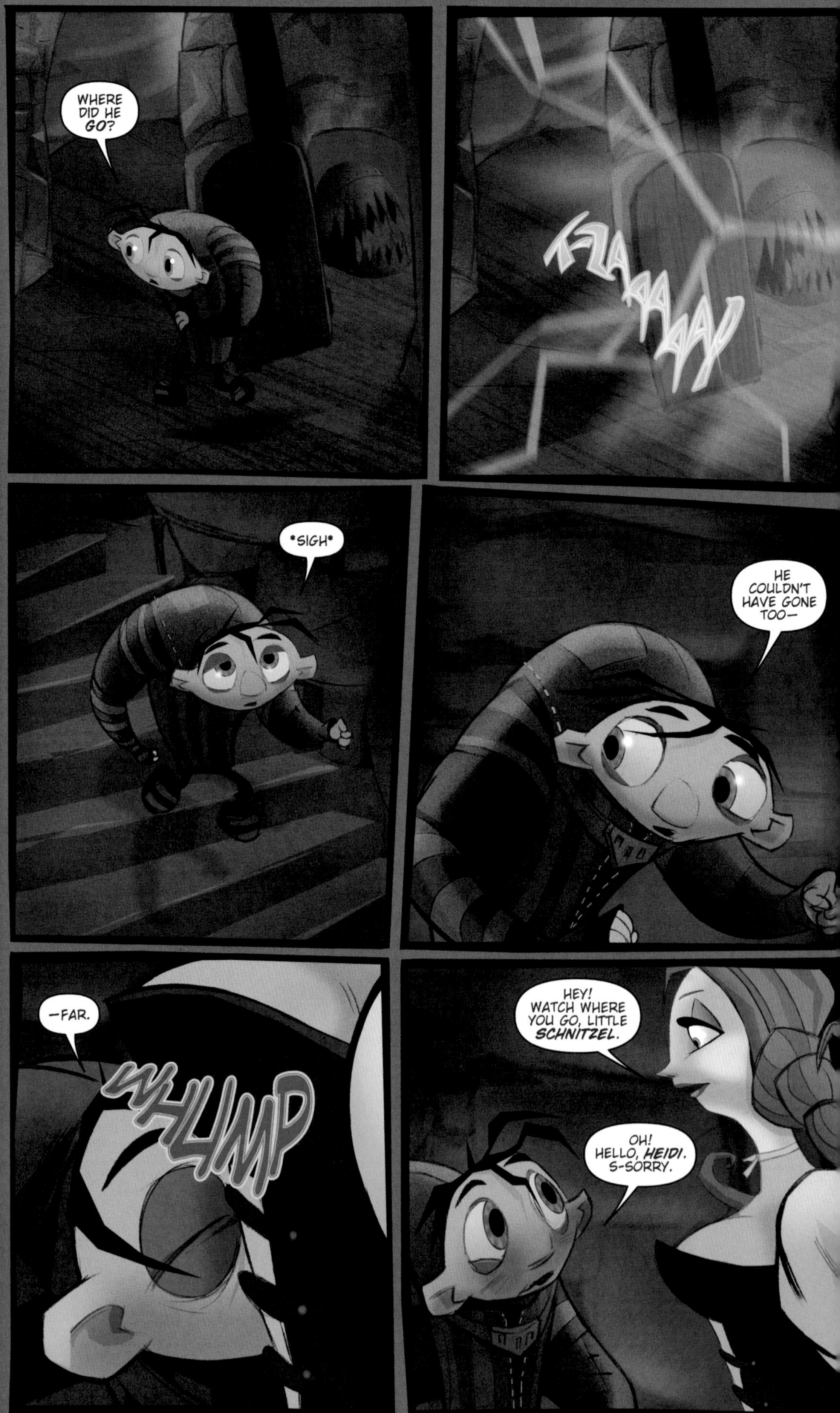
WHERE DID HE GO?
T-ZAAAAAAP
SIGH
HE COULDN'T HAVE GONE TOO—
—FAR.
WHUMP
HEY! WATCH WHERE YOU GO, LITTLE SCHNITZEL.
OH! HELLO, HEIDI. S-SORRY.

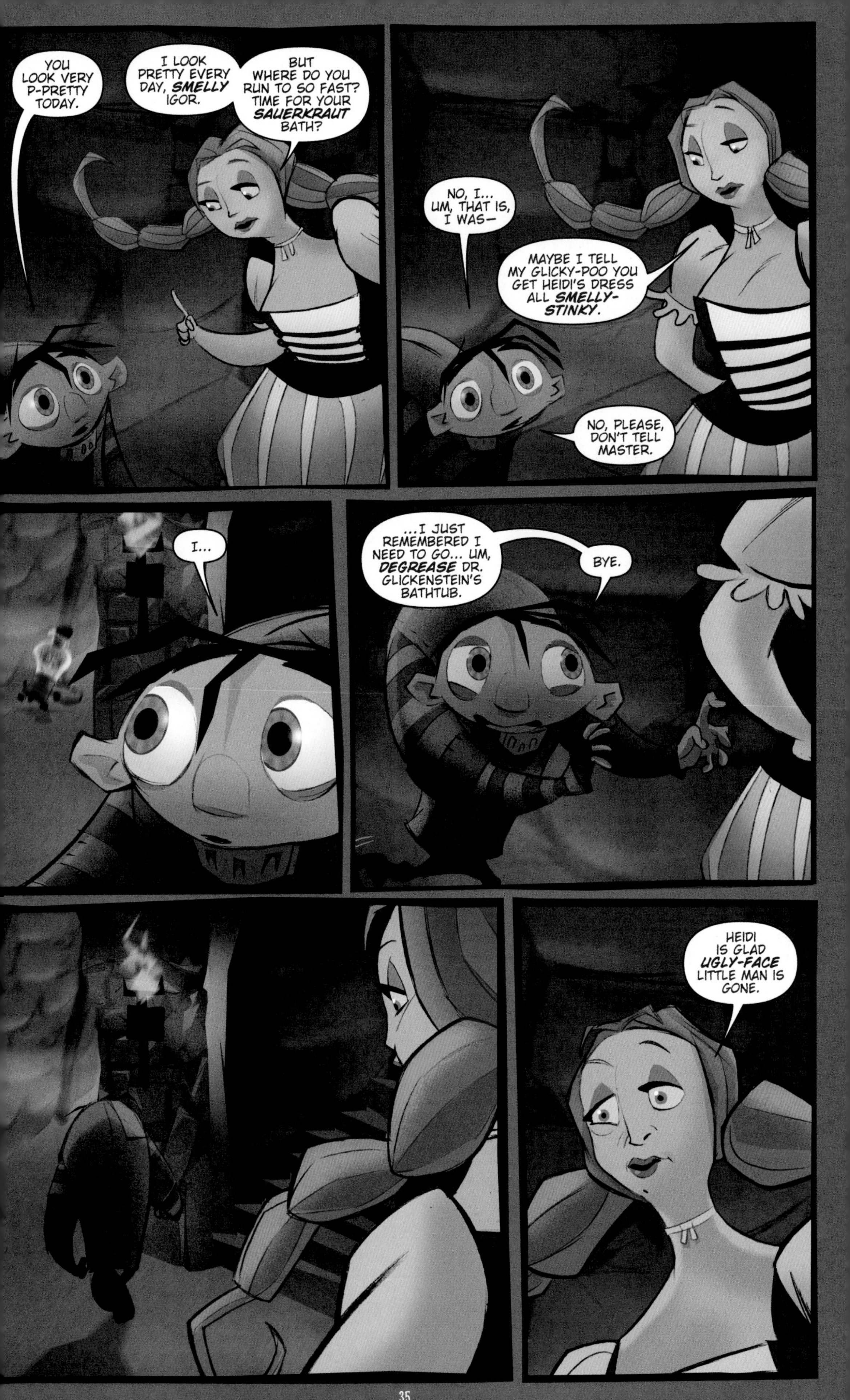

YOU LOOK VERY P-PRETTY TODAY.
I LOOK PRETTY EVERY DAY, SMELLY IGOR.
BUT WHERE DO YOU RUN TO SO FAST? TIME FOR YOUR SAUERKRAUT BATH?
NO, I... UM, THAT IS, I WAS—
MAYBE I TELL MY GLICKY-POO YOU GET HEIDI'S DRESS ALL SMELLY-STINKY.
NO, PLEASE, DON'T TELL MASTER.
I...
...I JUST REMEMBERED I NEED TO GO... UM, DEGREASE DR. GLICKENSTEIN'S BATHTUB.
BYE.
HEIDI IS GLAD UGLY-FACE LITTLE MAN IS GONE.

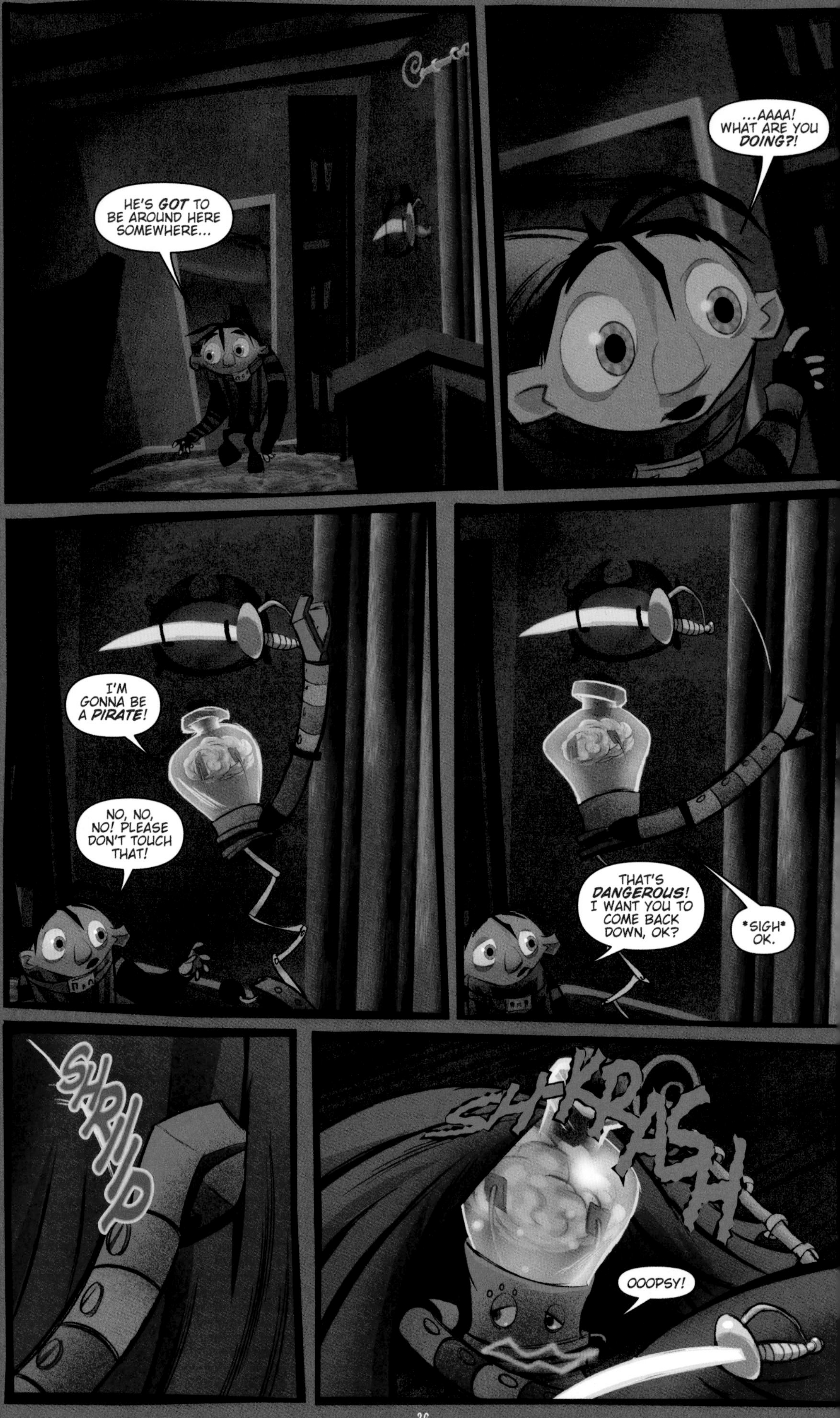
HE'S GOT TO BE AROUND HERE SOMEWHERE...
...AAAA! WHAT ARE YOU DOING?!
I'M GONNA BE A PIRATE!
NO, NO, NO! PLEASE DON'T TOUCH THAT!
THAT'S DANGEROUS! I WANT YOU TO COME BACK DOWN, OK?
SIGH OK.
SHRIIP
SHKRASH
OOOPSY!

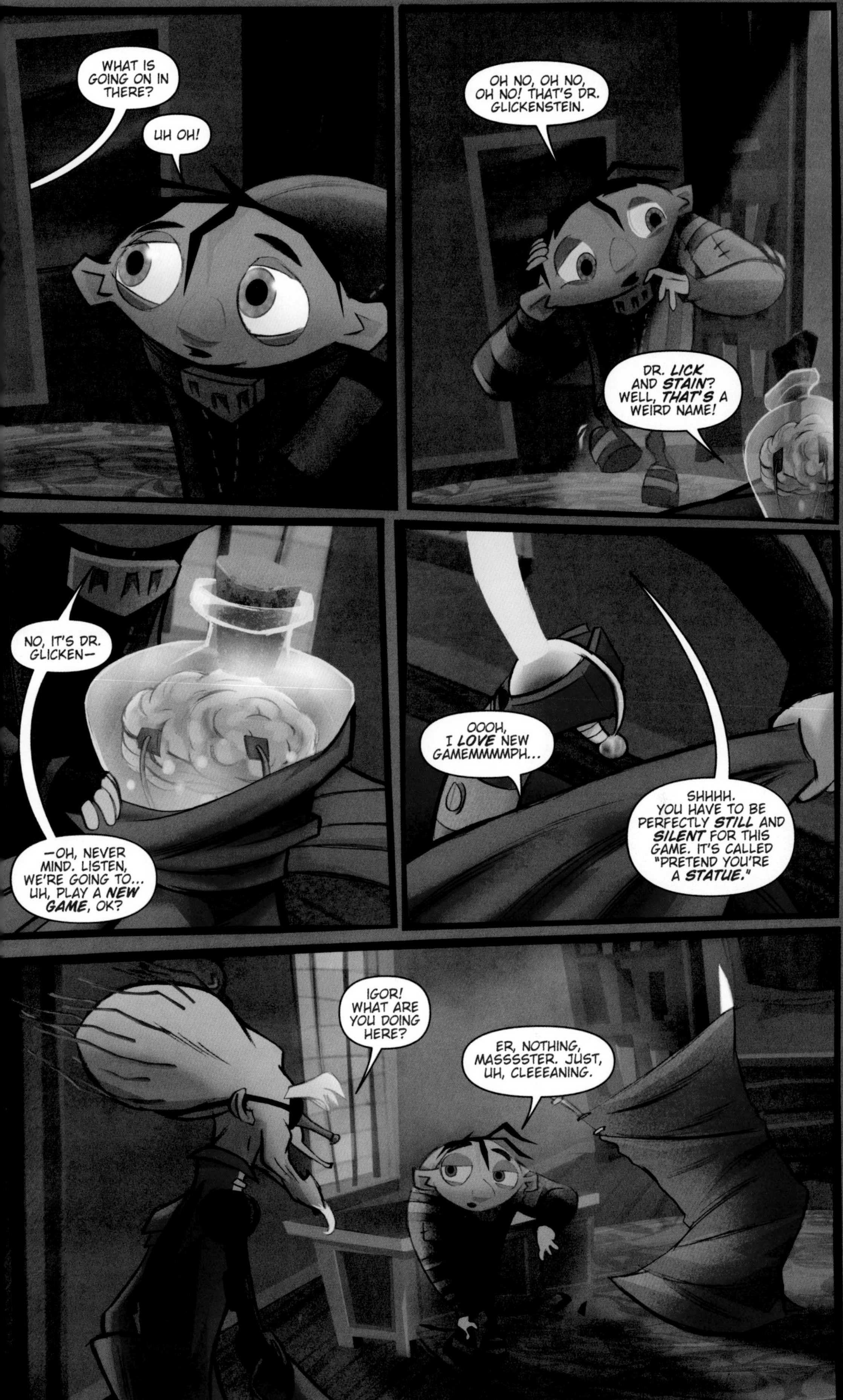
WHAT IS GOING ON IN THERE?
UH OH!
OH NO, OH NO, OH NO! THAT'S DR. GLICKENSTEIN.
DR. LICK AND STAIN? WELL, THAT'S A WEIRD NAME!
NO, IT'S DR. GLICKEN—
—OH, NEVER MIND. LISTEN, WE'RE GOING TO... UH, PLAY A NEW GAME, OK?
OOOH, I LOVE NEW GAMEMMMMPH...
SHHHH. YOU HAVE TO BE PERFECTLY STILL AND SILENT FOR THIS GAME. IT'S CALLED "PRETEND YOU'RE A STATUE."
IGOR! WHAT ARE YOU DOING HERE?
ER, NOTHING, MASSSSTER. JUST, UH, CLEEEANING.

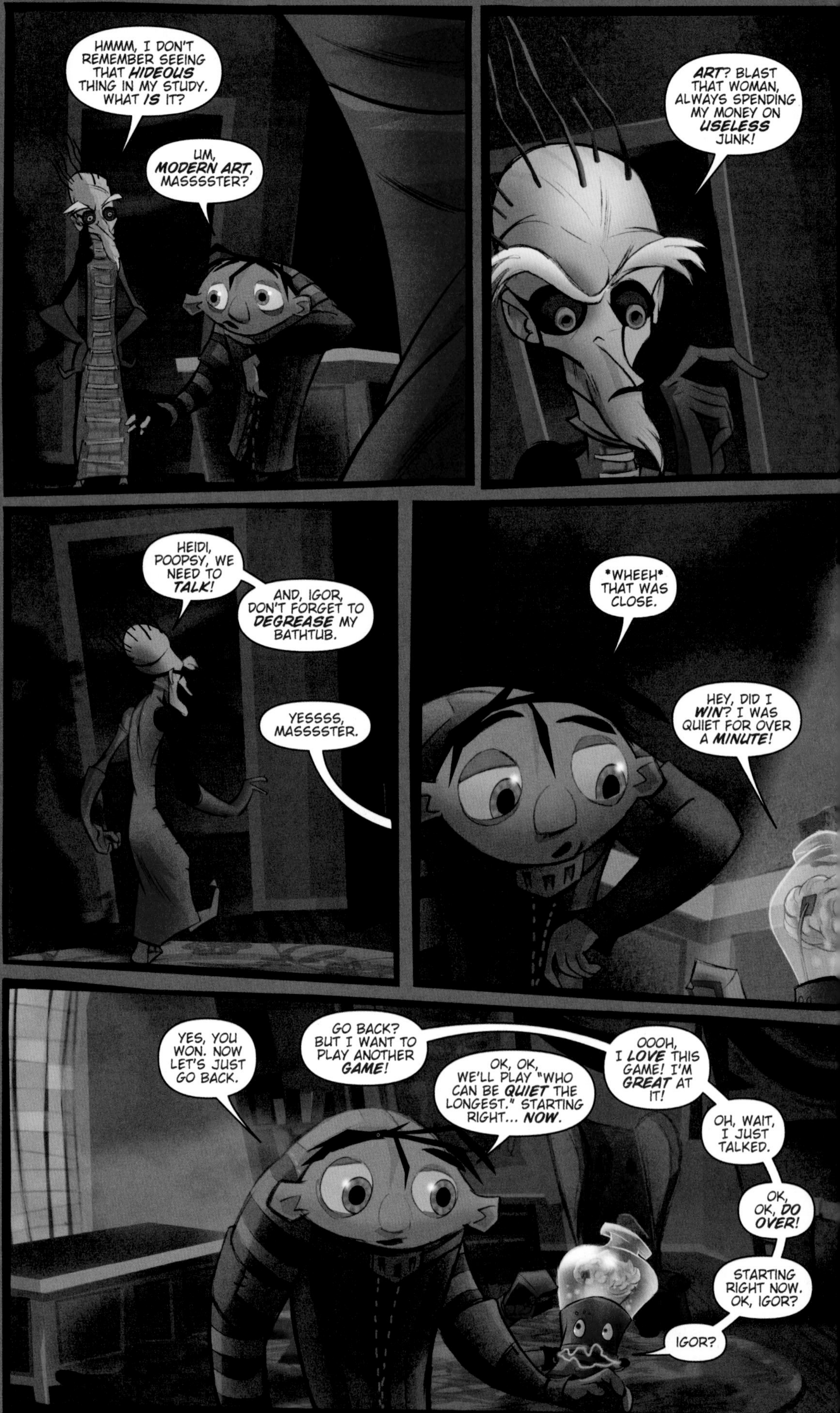
HMMM, I DON'T REMEMBER SEEING THAT HIDEOUS THING IN MY STUDY. WHAT IS IT?
UM, MODERN ART, MASSSSTER?
ART? BLAST THAT WOMAN, ALWAYS SPENDING MY MONEY ON USELESS JUNK!
HEIDI, POOPSY, WE NEED TO TALK!
AND, IGOR, DON'T FORGET TO DEGREASE MY BATHTUB.
YESSSS, MASSSSTER.
WHEEH THAT WAS CLOSE.
HEY, DID I WIN? I WAS QUIET FOR OVER A MINUTE!
YES, YOU WON. NOW LET'S JUST GO BACK.
GO BACK? BUT I WANT TO PLAY ANOTHER GAME!
OK, OK, WE'LL PLAY "WHO CAN BE QUIET THE LONGEST." STARTING RIGHT... NOW.
OOOH, I LOVE THIS GAME! I'M GREAT AT IT!
OH, WAIT, I JUST TALKED.
OK, OK, DO OVER!
STARTING RIGHT NOW. OK, IGOR?
IGOR?

I JUST DON'T GET IT, SCAMPER. HE'S NOT EVEN A *TINY* BIT *EVIL*. HE'S JUST... *DUMB*.

AND REALLY *HYPER*.

WHERE DID I GO WRONG?

GEE, I DON'T KNOW. MAYBE IT WAS WHEN YOU PLAYED *DEMOLITION DERBY* WITH HIS BRAIN.

UGH. DON'T REMIND ME.

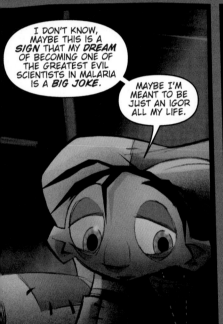

I DON'T KNOW, MAYBE THIS IS A *SIGN* THAT MY *DREAM* OF BECOMING ONE OF THE GREATEST EVIL SCIENTISTS IN MALARIA IS A *BIG JOKE*.

MAYBE I'M MEANT TO BE JUST AN IGOR ALL MY LIFE.

AW, DON'T SAY THAT. YOU'LL GET IT RIGHT... EVENTUALLY.

AFTER ALL, YOU *MADE* ME INTELLIGENT AND IMMORTAL, RIGHT? JUST THINK OF *WHAT'S-HIS-FACE* AS ANOTHER PRACTICE ROUND.

YOU MEAN *BRAIN*?

THAT'S HIS *NAME*?

YEAH. HE DECIDED TO NAME HIMSELF.

WE WERE WALKING BY A *MIRROR* AT THE TIME.

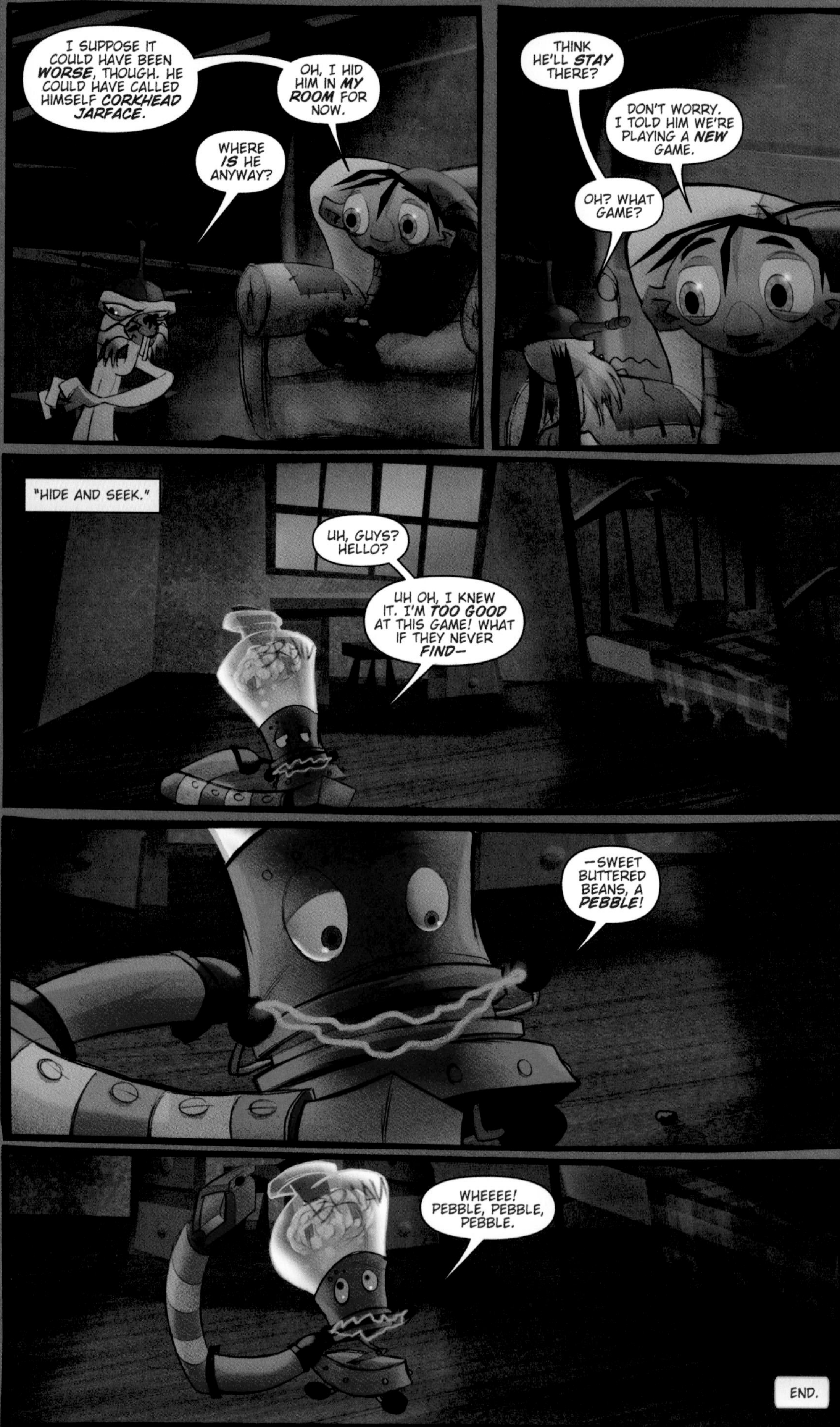
I SUPPOSE IT COULD HAVE BEEN WORSE, THOUGH. HE COULD HAVE CALLED HIMSELF CORKHEAD JARFACE.
WHERE IS HE ANYWAY?
OH, I HID HIM IN MY ROOM FOR NOW.
THINK HE'LL STAY THERE?
DON'T WORRY. I TOLD HIM WE'RE PLAYING A NEW GAME.
OH? WHAT GAME?
"HIDE AND SEEK."
UH, GUYS? HELLO?
UH OH, I KNEW IT. I'M TOO GOOD AT THIS GAME! WHAT IF THEY NEVER FIND—
—SWEET BUTTERED BEANS, A PEBBLE!
WHEEEE! PEBBLE, PEBBLE, PEBBLE.
END.

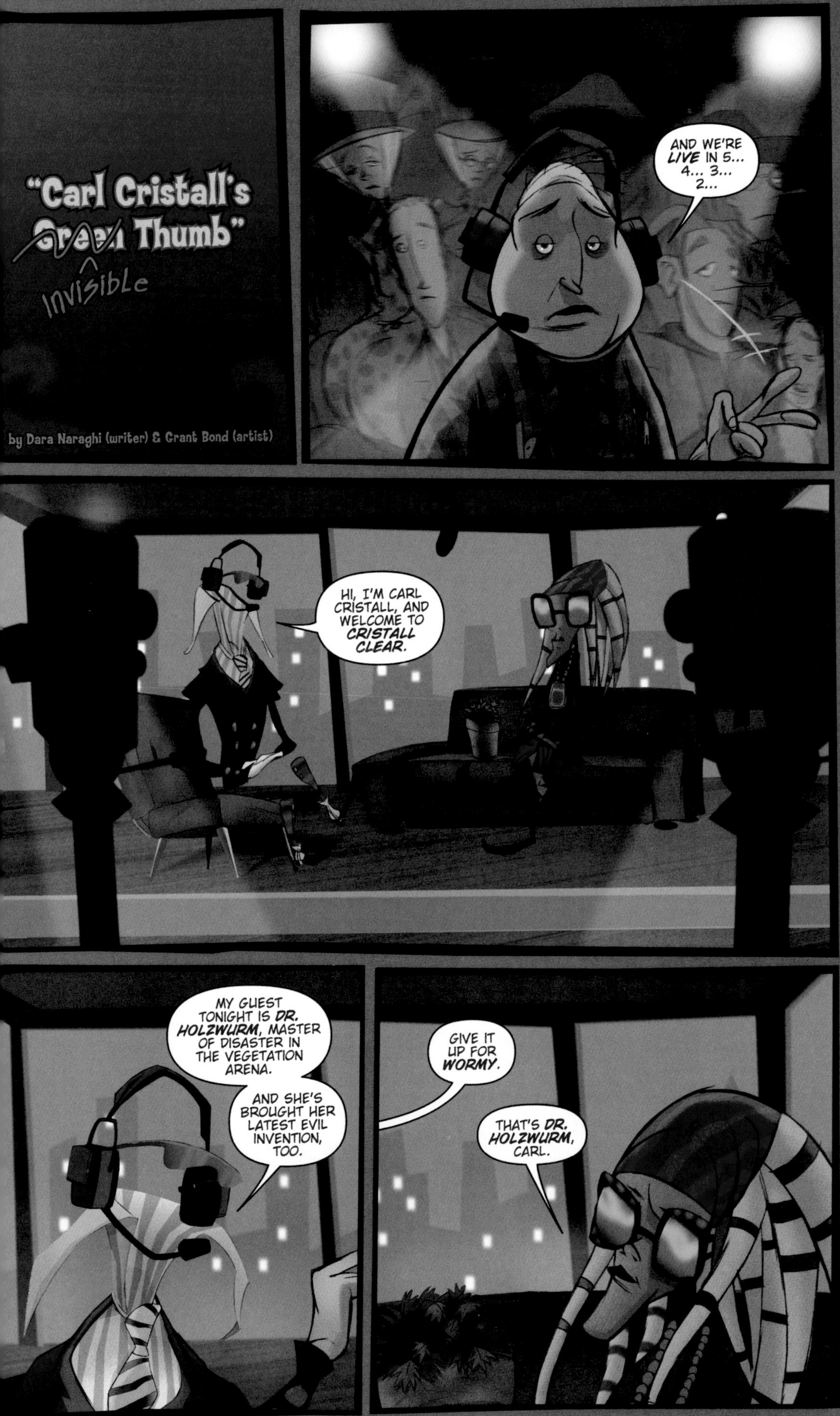
"Carl Cristall's Green Thumb"
invisible
by Dara Naraghi (writer) & Grant Bond (artist)
AND WE'RE LIVE IN 5... 4... 3... 2...
HI, I'M CARL CRISTALL, AND WELCOME TO CRISTALL CLEAR.
MY GUEST TONIGHT IS DR. HOLZWURM, MASTER OF DISASTER IN THE VEGETATION ARENA.
AND SHE'S BROUGHT HER LATEST EVIL INVENTION, TOO.
GIVE IT UP FOR WORMY.
THAT'S DR. HOLZWURM, CARL.

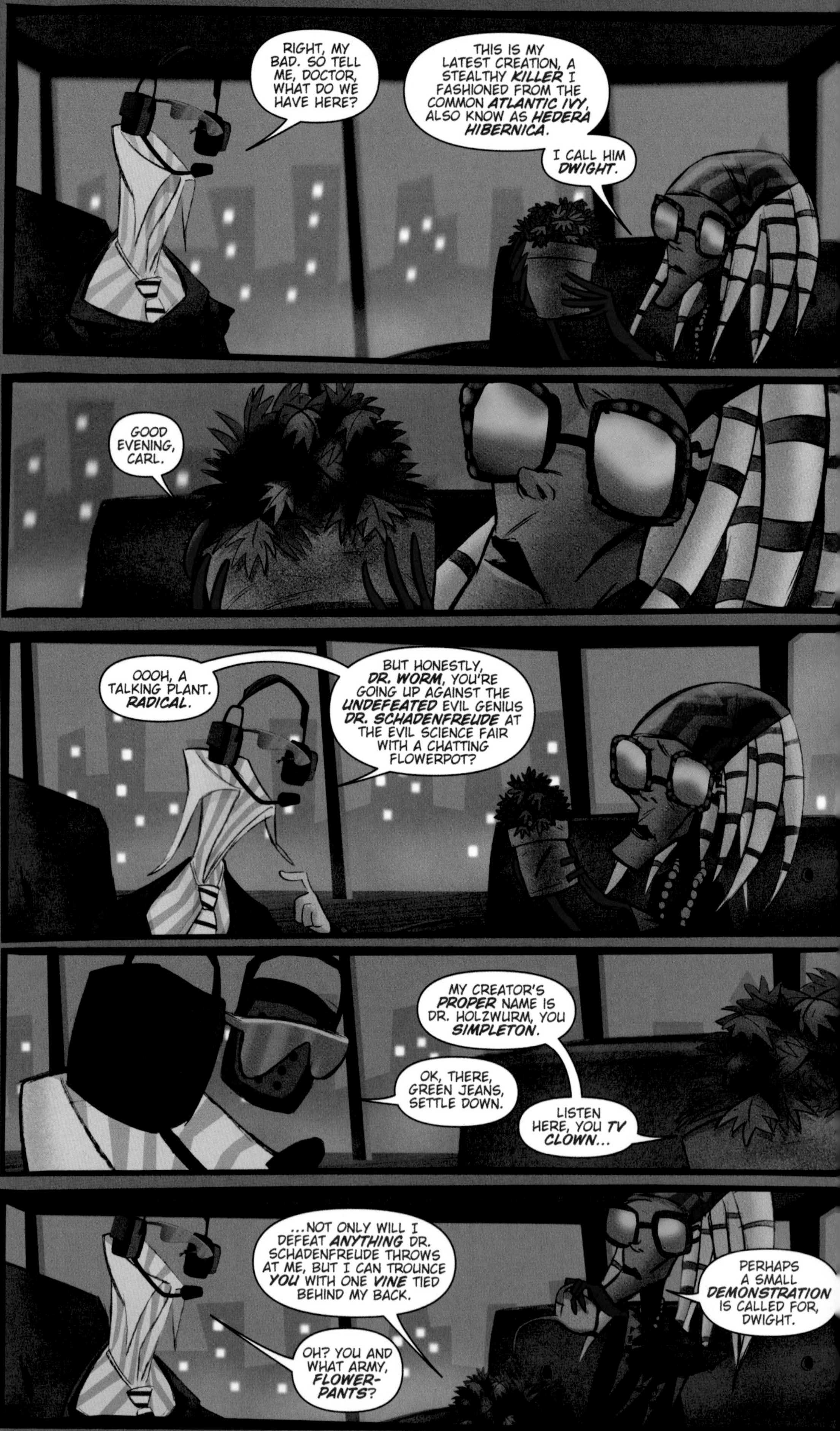
RIGHT, MY BAD. SO TELL ME, DOCTOR, WHAT DO WE HAVE HERE?
THIS IS MY LATEST CREATION, A STEALTHY KILLER I FASHIONED FROM THE COMMON ATLANTIC IVY, ALSO KNOW AS HEDERA HIBERNICA.
I CALL HIM DWIGHT.
GOOD EVENING, CARL.
OOOH, A TALKING PLANT. RADICAL.
BUT HONESTLY, DR. WORM, YOU'RE GOING UP AGAINST THE UNDEFEATED EVIL GENIUS DR. SCHADENFREUDE AT THE EVIL SCIENCE FAIR WITH A CHATTING FLOWERPOT?
MY CREATOR'S PROPER NAME IS DR. HOLZWURM, YOU SIMPLETON.
OK, THERE, GREEN JEANS, SETTLE DOWN.
LISTEN HERE, YOU TV CLOWN...
...NOT ONLY WILL I DEFEAT ANYTHING DR. SCHADENFREUDE THROWS AT ME, BUT I CAN TROUNCE YOU WITH ONE VINE TIED BEHIND MY BACK.
OH? YOU AND WHAT ARMY, FLOWER-PANTS?
PERHAPS A SMALL DEMONSTRATION IS CALLED FOR, DWIGHT.

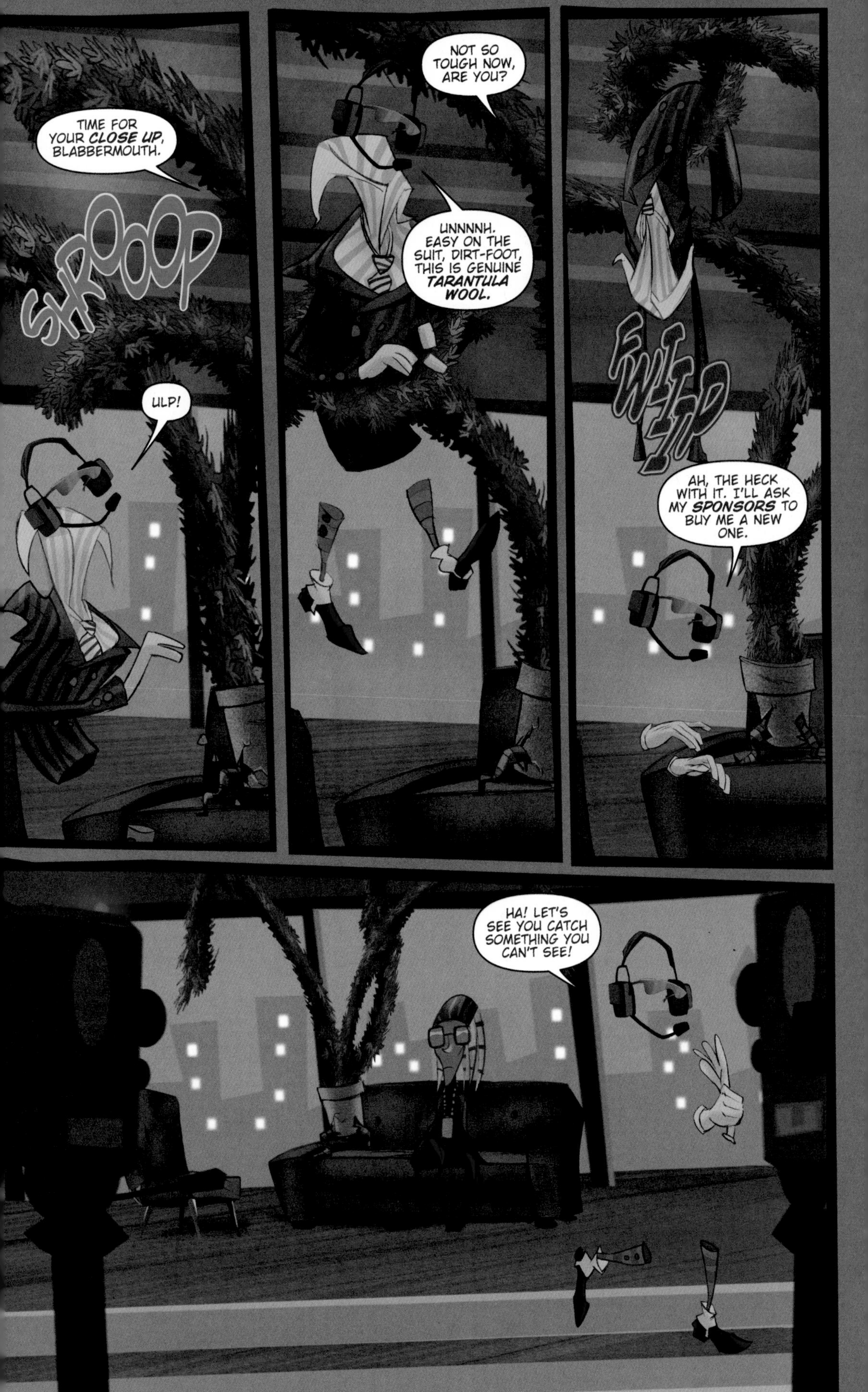
TIME FOR YOUR CLOSE UP, BLABBERMOUTH.
SHROOOP
ULP!
NOT SO TOUGH NOW, ARE YOU?
UNNNNH. EASY ON THE SUIT, DIRT-FOOT, THIS IS GENUINE TARANTULA WOOL.
FWIIIP
AH, THE HECK WITH IT. I'LL ASK MY SPONSORS TO BUY ME A NEW ONE.
HA! LET'S SEE YOU CATCH SOMETHING YOU CAN'T SEE!

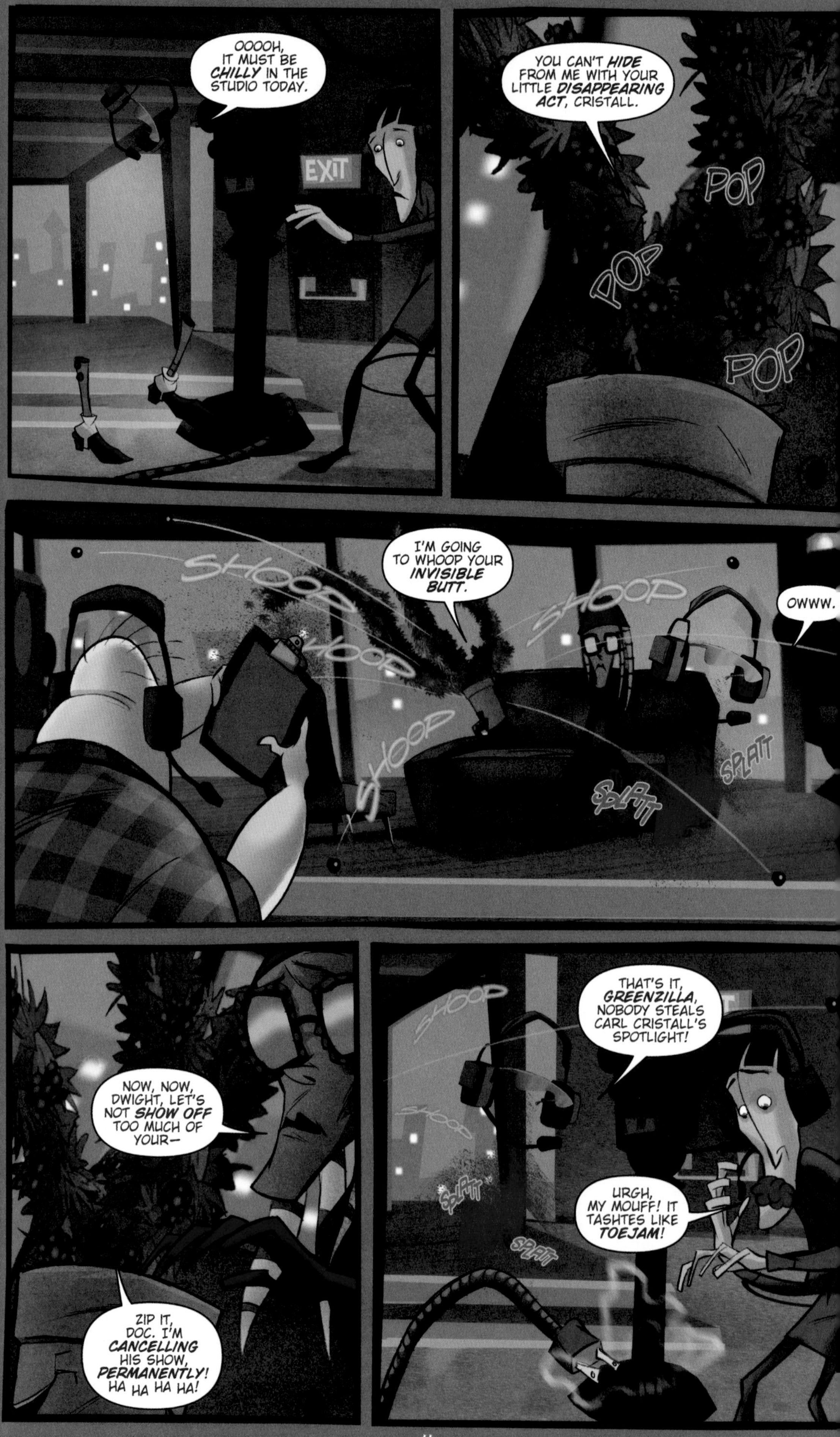
OOOOH, IT MUST BE CHILLY IN THE STUDIO TODAY.
EXIT
YOU CAN'T HIDE FROM ME WITH YOUR LITTLE DISAPPEARING ACT, CRISTALL.
POP
POP
POP
I'M GOING TO WHOOP YOUR INVISIBLE BUTT.
SHOOP
SHOOP
WHOOP
SHOOP
OWWW.
SPLATT
SPLATT
NOW, NOW, DWIGHT, LET'S NOT SHOW OFF TOO MUCH OF YOUR—
ZIP IT, DOC. I'M CANCELLING HIS SHOW, PERMANENTLY! HA HA HA HA!
THAT'S IT, GREENZILLA, NOBODY STEALS CARL CRISTALL'S SPOTLIGHT!
SHOOP
SHOOP
SPLATT
SPLATT
URGH, MY MOUFF! IT TASHTES LIKE TOEJAM!

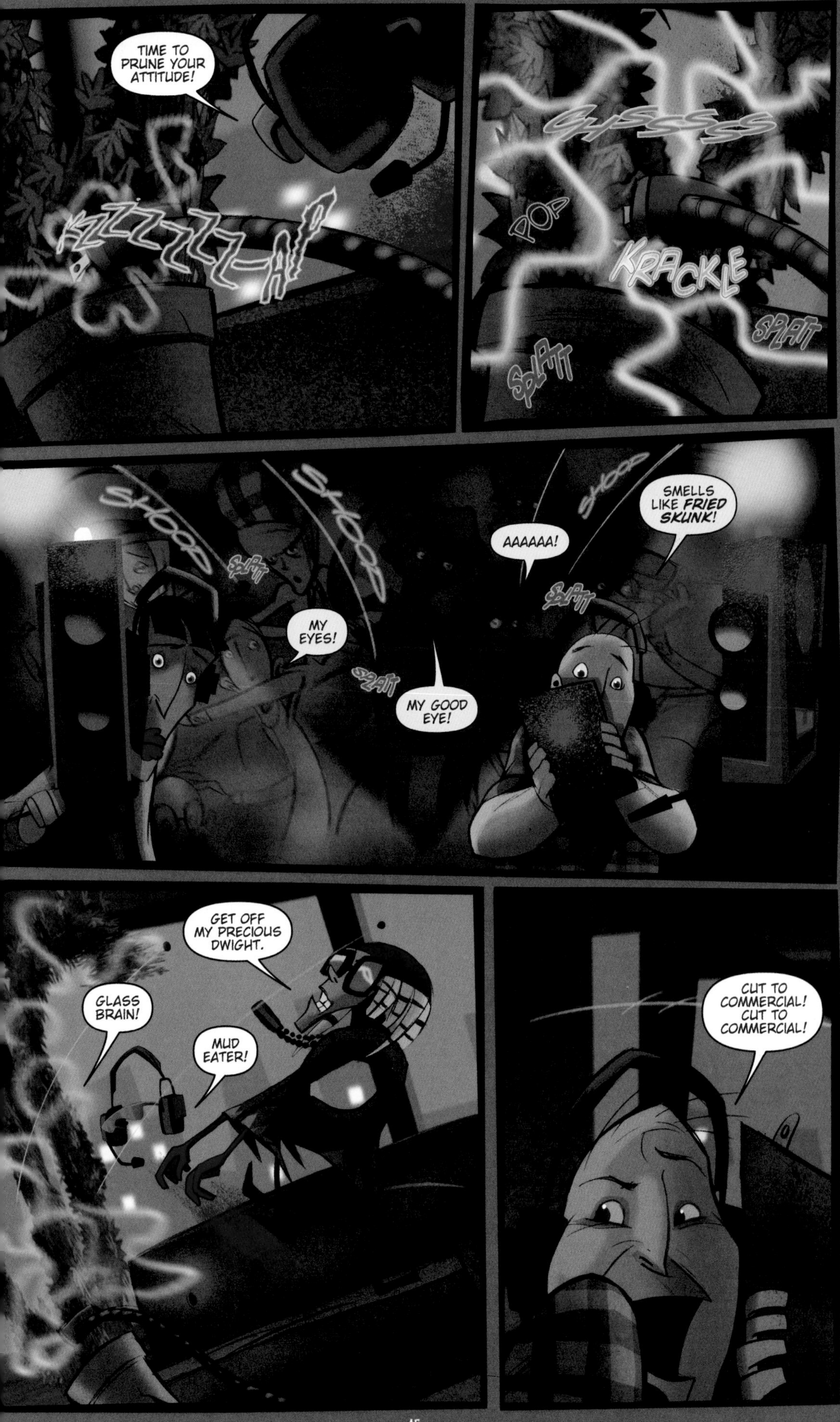
TIME TO PRUNE YOUR ATTITUDE!
KZZZZZZZ-AP
CHSSSSSS
POP
KRACKLE
SPLATT
SPLATT
SHOOP
SHOOP
SHOOP
SPLATT
SMELLS LIKE FRIED SKUNK!
AAAAAA!
SPLATT
MY EYES!
SPLATT
MY GOOD EYE!
GET OFF MY PRECIOUS DWIGHT.
GLASS BRAIN!
MUD EATER!
CUT TO COMMERCIAL! CUT TO COMMERCIAL!

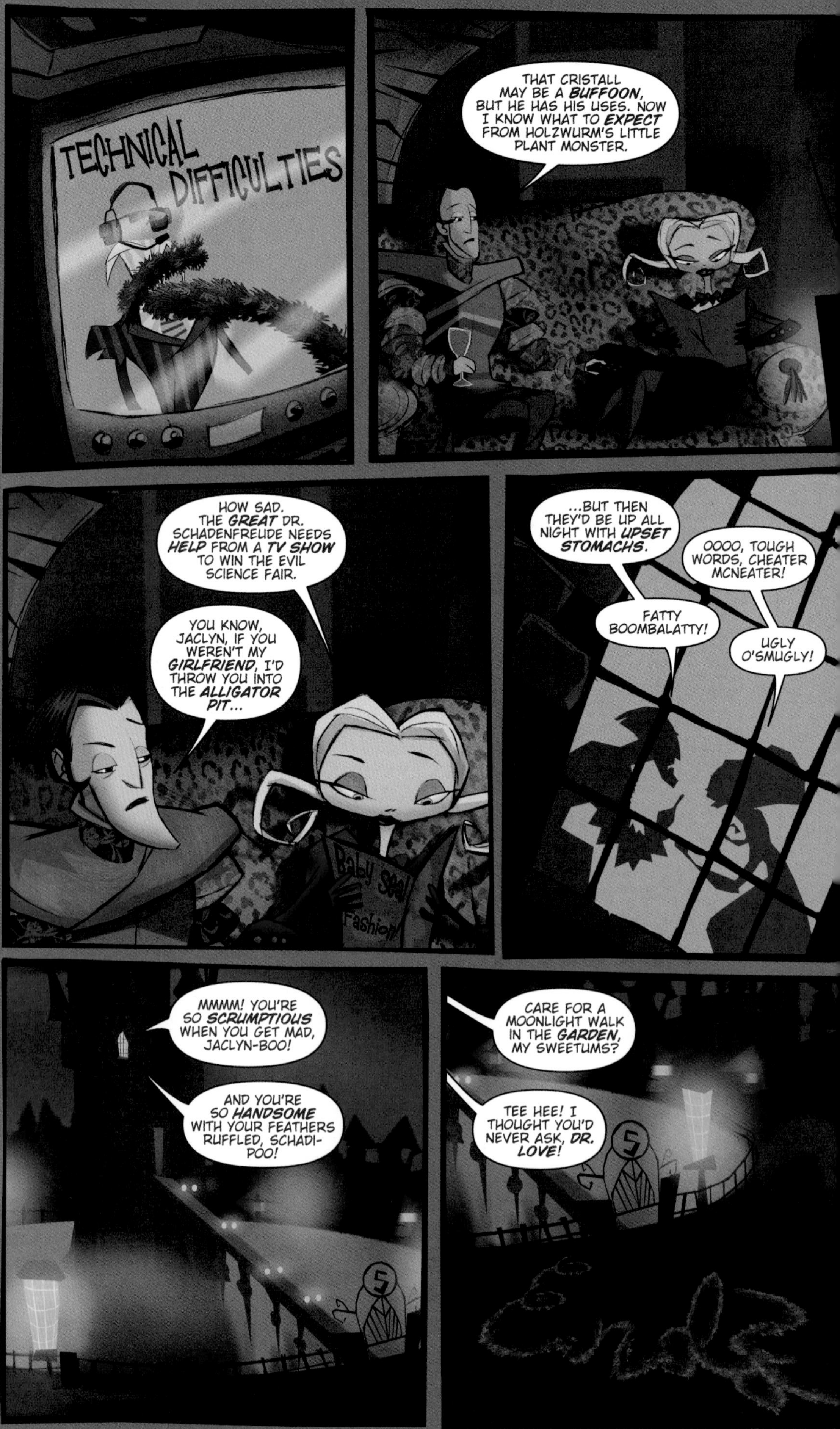
TECHNICAL DIFFICULTIES
THAT CRISTALL MAY BE A BUFFOON, BUT HE HAS HIS USES. NOW I KNOW WHAT TO EXPECT FROM HOLZWURM'S LITTLE PLANT MONSTER.
HOW SAD. THE GREAT DR. SCHADENFREUDE NEEDS HELP FROM A TV SHOW TO WIN THE EVIL SCIENCE FAIR.
YOU KNOW, JACLYN, IF YOU WEREN'T MY GIRLFRIEND, I'D THROW YOU INTO THE ALLIGATOR PIT...
Baby Seal Fashion
...BUT THEN THEY'D BE UP ALL NIGHT WITH UPSET STOMACHS.
OOOO, TOUGH WORDS, CHEATER MCNEATER!
FATTY BOOMBALATTY!
UGLY O'SMUGLY!
MMMM! YOU'RE SO SCRUMPTIOUS WHEN YOU GET MAD, JACLYN-BOO!
AND YOU'RE SO HANDSOME WITH YOUR FEATHERS RUFFLED, SCHADI-POO!
CARE FOR A MOONLIGHT WALK IN THE GARDEN, MY SWEETUMS?
TEE HEE! I THOUGHT YOU'D NEVER ASK, DR. LOVE!

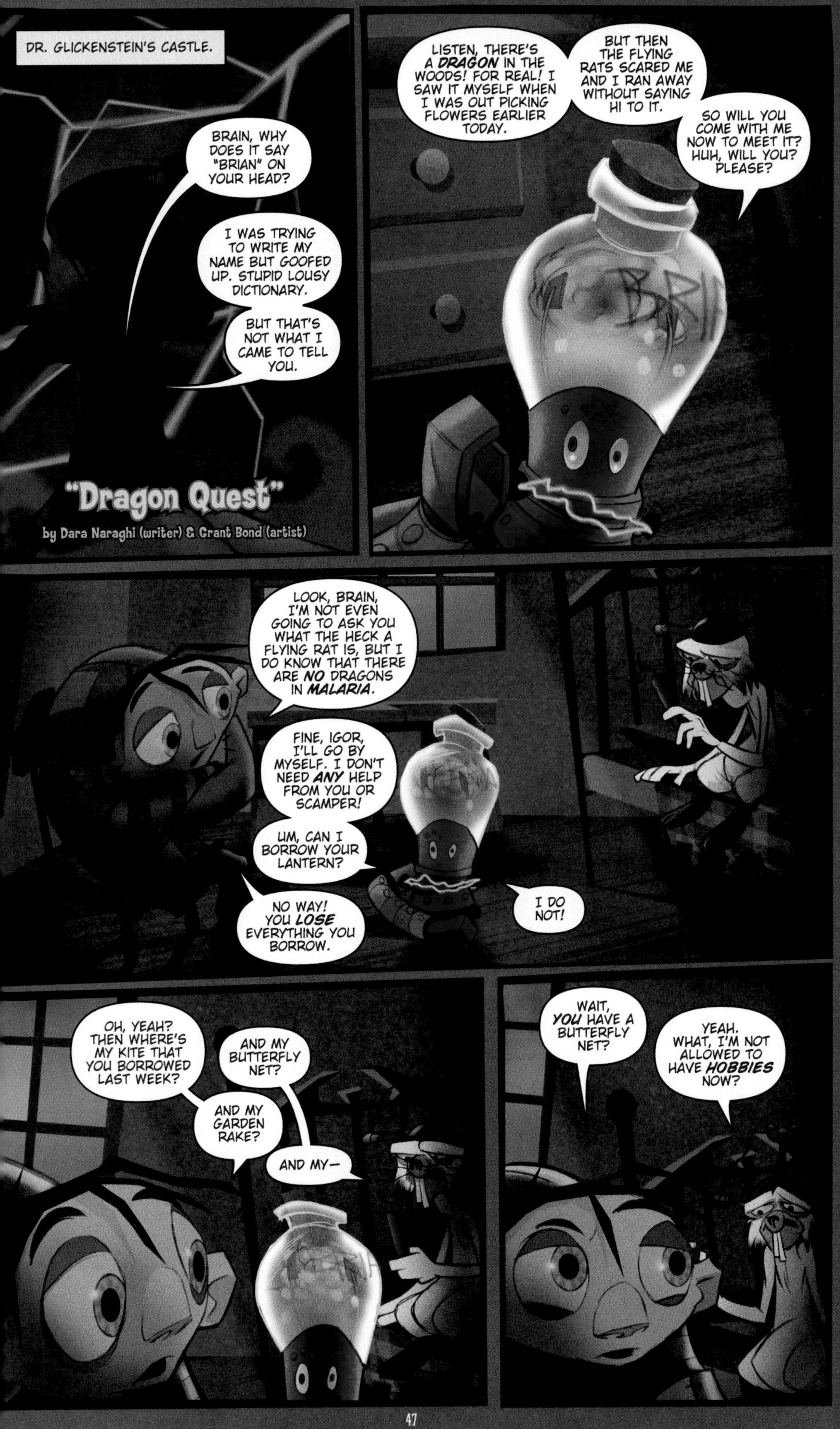
DR. GLICKENSTEIN'S CASTLE.
BRAIN, WHY DOES IT SAY "BRIAN" ON YOUR HEAD?
I WAS TRYING TO WRITE MY NAME BUT GOOFED UP. STUPID LOUSY DICTIONARY.
BUT THAT'S NOT WHAT I CAME TO TELL YOU.
"Dragon Quest"
by Dara Naraghi (writer) & Grant Bond (artist)
LISTEN, THERE'S A DRAGON IN THE WOODS! FOR REAL! I SAW IT MYSELF WHEN I WAS OUT PICKING FLOWERS EARLIER TODAY.
BUT THEN THE FLYING RATS SCARED ME AND I RAN AWAY WITHOUT SAYING HI TO IT.
SO WILL YOU COME WITH ME NOW TO MEET IT? HUH, WILL YOU? PLEASE?
LOOK, BRAIN, I'M NOT EVEN GOING TO ASK YOU WHAT THE HECK A FLYING RAT IS, BUT I DO KNOW THAT THERE ARE NO DRAGONS IN MALARIA.
FINE, IGOR, I'LL GO BY MYSELF. I DON'T NEED ANY HELP FROM YOU OR SCAMPER!
UM, CAN I BORROW YOUR LANTERN?
NO WAY! YOU LOSE EVERYTHING YOU BORROW.
I DO NOT!
OH, YEAH? THEN WHERE'S MY KITE THAT YOU BORROWED LAST WEEK?
AND MY BUTTERFLY NET?
AND MY GARDEN RAKE?
AND MY—
WAIT, YOU HAVE A BUTTERFLY NET?
YEAH. WHAT, I'M NOT ALLOWED TO HAVE HOBBIES NOW?

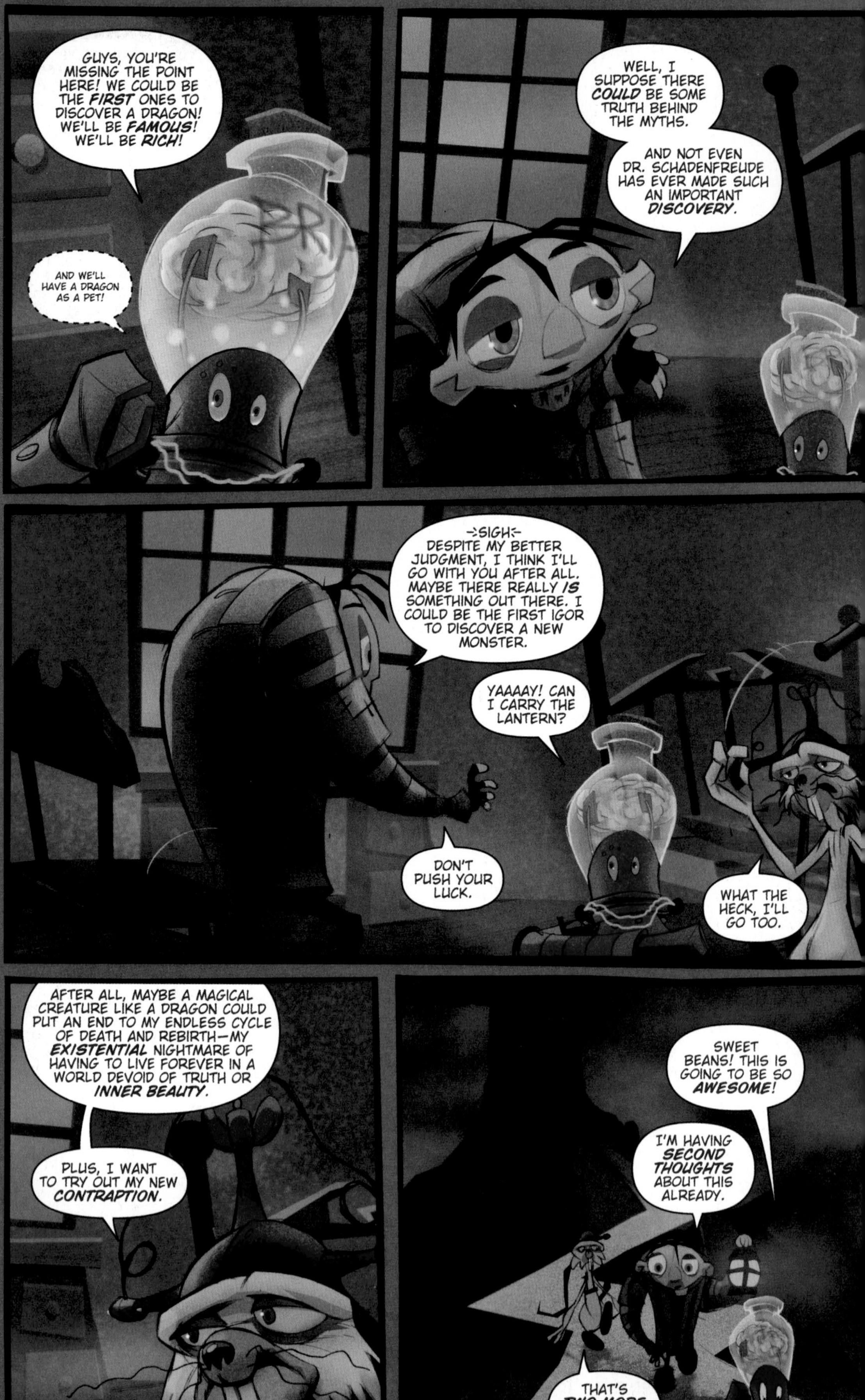
GUYS, YOU'RE MISSING THE POINT HERE! WE COULD BE THE FIRST ONES TO DISCOVER A DRAGON! WE'LL BE FAMOUS! WE'LL BE RICH!
AND WE'LL HAVE A DRAGON AS A PET!
WELL, I SUPPOSE THERE COULD BE SOME TRUTH BEHIND THE MYTHS.
AND NOT EVEN DR. SCHADENFREUDE HAS EVER MADE SUCH AN IMPORTANT DISCOVERY.
-SIGH- DESPITE MY BETTER JUDGMENT, I THINK I'LL GO WITH YOU AFTER ALL. MAYBE THERE REALLY IS SOMETHING OUT THERE. I COULD BE THE FIRST IGOR TO DISCOVER A NEW MONSTER.
YAAAAY! CAN I CARRY THE LANTERN?
DON'T PUSH YOUR LUCK.
WHAT THE HECK, I'LL GO TOO.
AFTER ALL, MAYBE A MAGICAL CREATURE LIKE A DRAGON COULD PUT AN END TO MY ENDLESS CYCLE OF DEATH AND REBIRTH—MY EXISTENTIAL NIGHTMARE OF HAVING TO LIVE FOREVER IN A WORLD DEVOID OF TRUTH OR INNER BEAUTY.
PLUS, I WANT TO TRY OUT MY NEW CONTRAPTION.
SWEET BEANS! THIS IS GOING TO BE SO AWESOME!
I'M HAVING SECOND THOUGHTS ABOUT THIS ALREADY.
THAT'S TWO MORE THAN BRAIN EVER HAD.

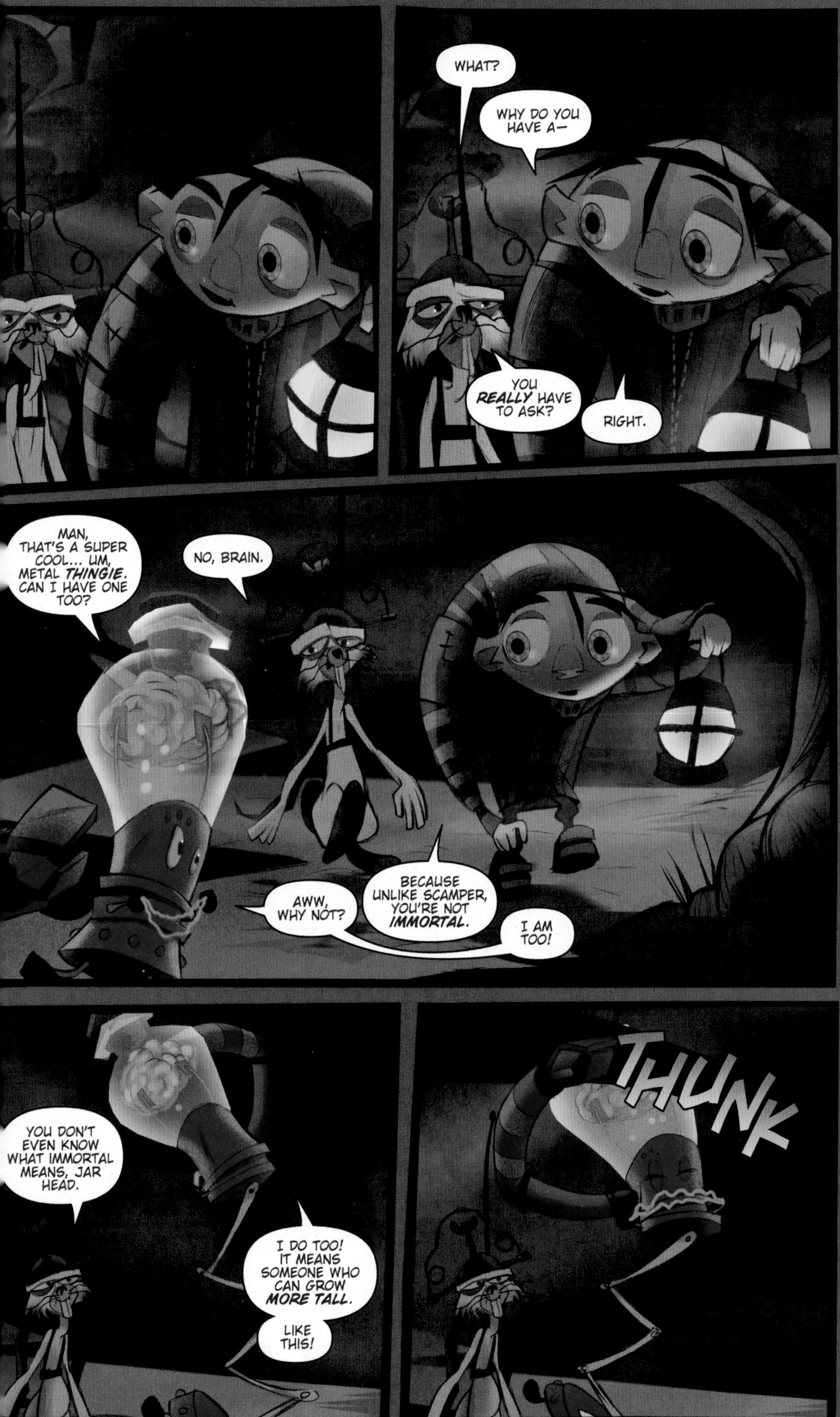

WHAT?
WHY DO YOU HAVE A—
YOU REALLY HAVE TO ASK?
RIGHT.
MAN, THAT'S A SUPER COOL... UM, METAL THINGIE. CAN I HAVE ONE TOO?
NO, BRAIN.
AWW, WHY NOT?
BECAUSE UNLIKE SCAMPER, YOU'RE NOT IMMORTAL.
I AM TOO!
YOU DON'T EVEN KNOW WHAT IMMORTAL MEANS, JAR HEAD.
I DO TOO! IT MEANS SOMEONE WHO CAN GROW MORE TALL.
LIKE THIS!
THUNK

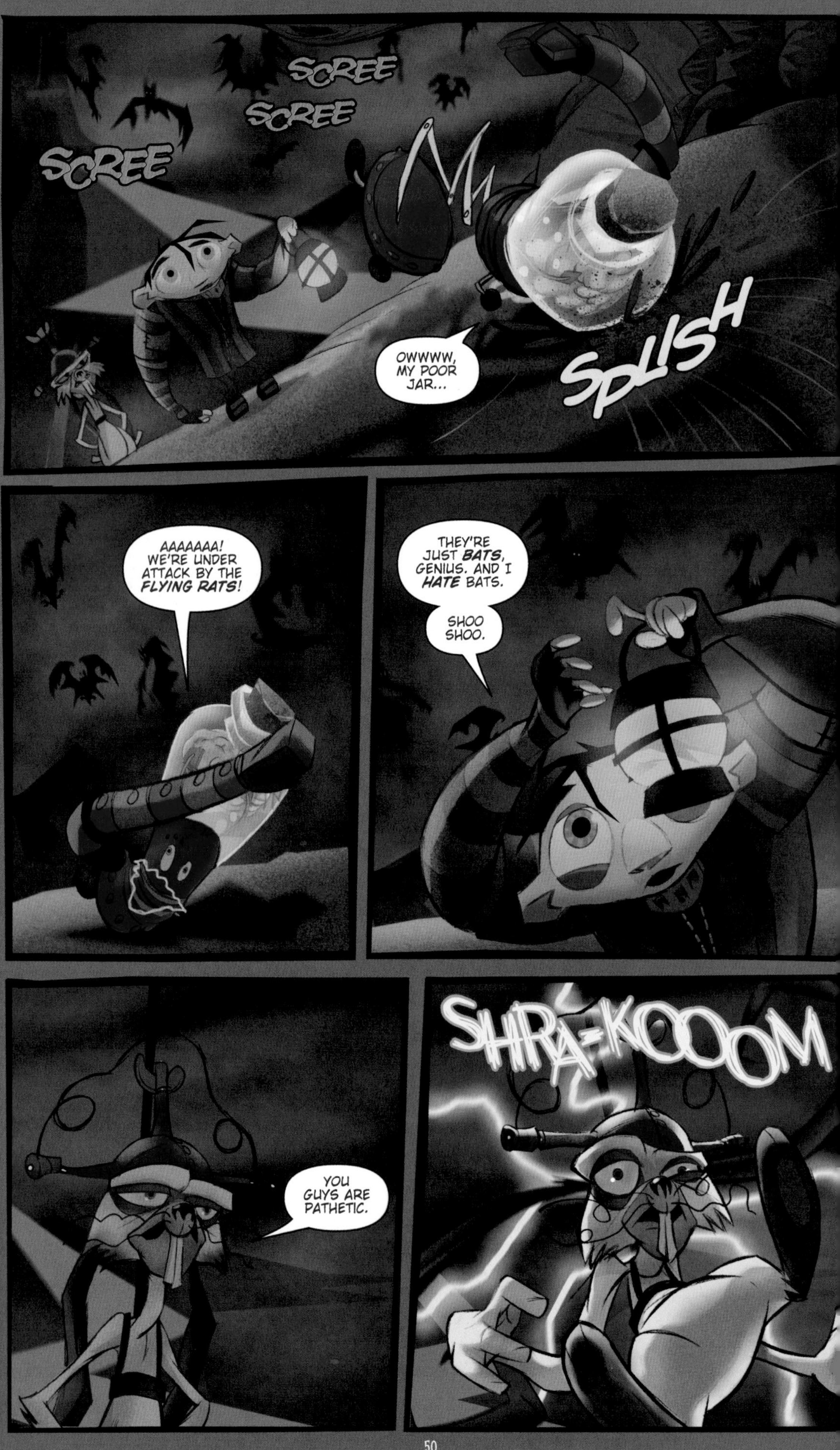
SCREE
SCREE
SCREE
OWWWW, MY POOR JAR...
SPLISH
AAAAAAA! WE'RE UNDER ATTACK BY THE FLYING RATS!
THEY'RE JUST BATS, GENIUS. AND I HATE BATS.
SHOO SHOO.
YOU GUYS ARE PATHETIC.
SHRA-KOOOOM

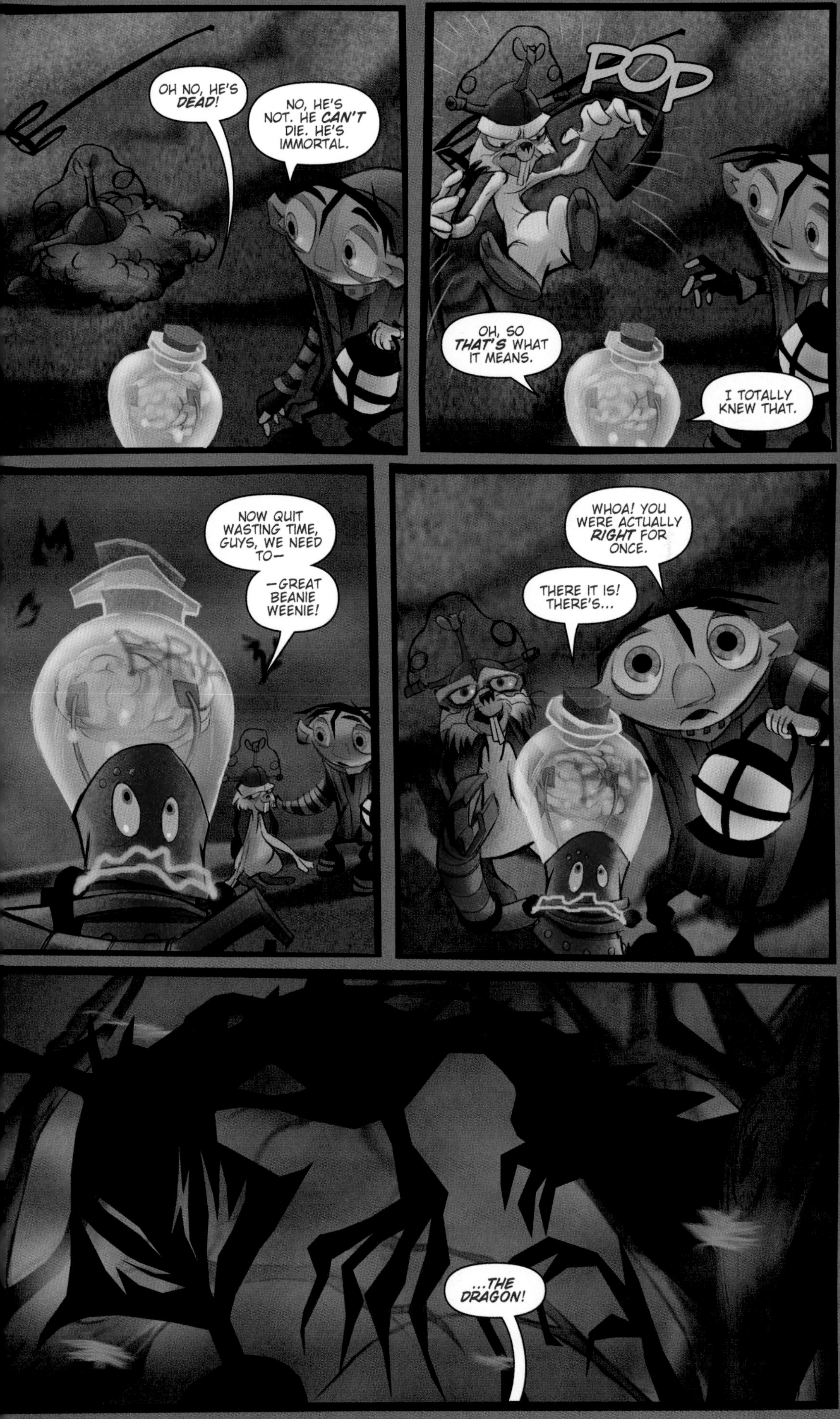
OH NO, HE'S DEAD!
NO, HE'S NOT. HE CAN'T DIE. HE'S IMMORTAL.
POP
OH, SO THAT'S WHAT IT MEANS.
I TOTALLY KNEW THAT.
NOW QUIT WASTING TIME, GUYS, WE NEED TO—
—GREAT BEANIE WEENIE!
WHOA! YOU WERE ACTUALLY RIGHT FOR ONCE.
THERE IT IS! THERE'S...
...THE DRAGON!

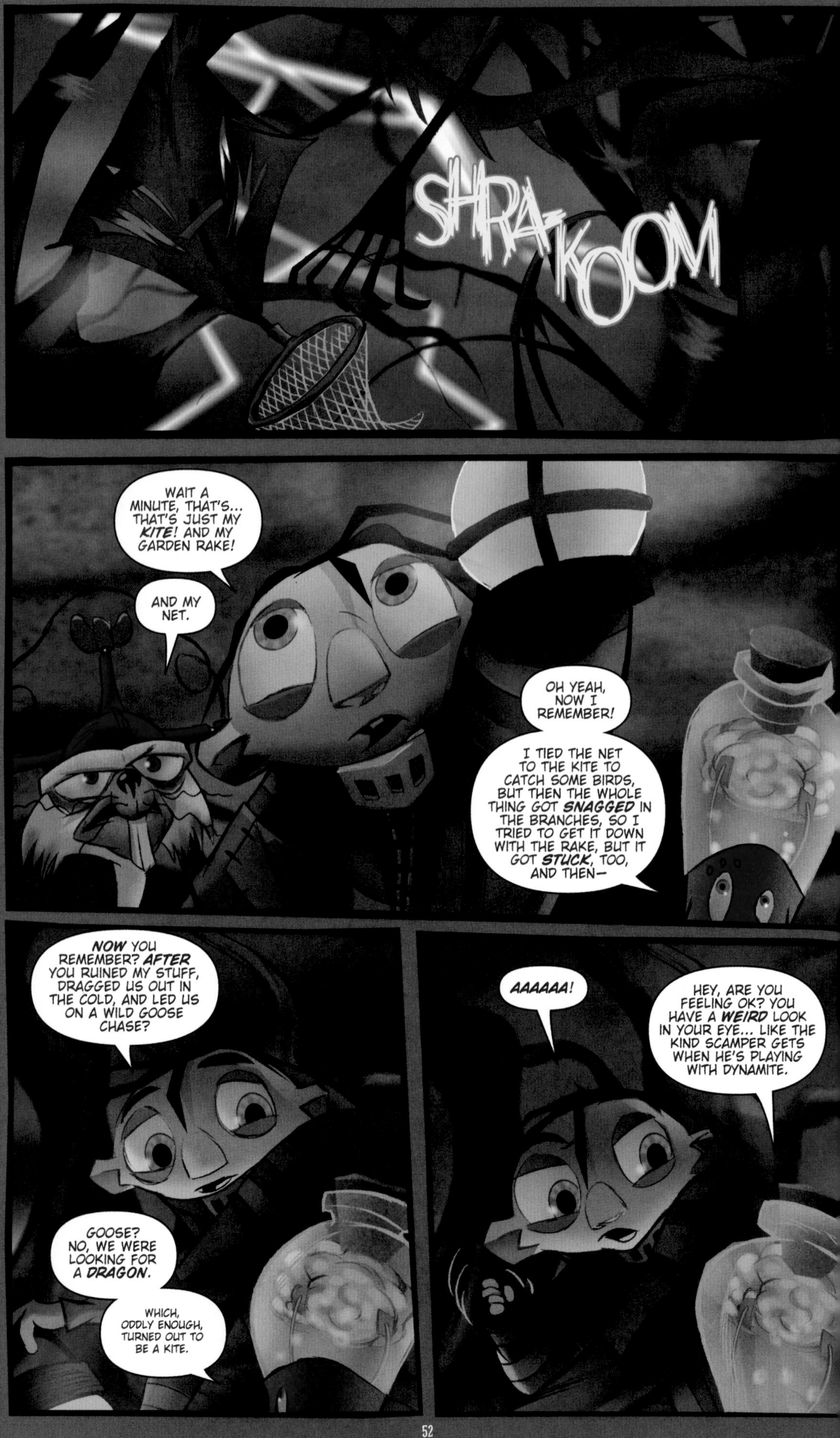
SHRA-KOOM
WAIT A MINUTE, THAT'S... THAT'S JUST MY KITE! AND MY GARDEN RAKE!
AND MY NET.
OH YEAH, NOW I REMEMBER!
I TIED THE NET TO THE KITE TO CATCH SOME BIRDS, BUT THEN THE WHOLE THING GOT SNAGGED IN THE BRANCHES, SO I TRIED TO GET IT DOWN WITH THE RAKE, BUT IT GOT STUCK, TOO, AND THEN—
NOW YOU REMEMBER? AFTER YOU RUINED MY STUFF, DRAGGED US OUT IN THE COLD, AND LED US ON A WILD GOOSE CHASE?
GOOSE? NO, WE WERE LOOKING FOR A DRAGON.
WHICH, ODDLY ENOUGH, TURNED OUT TO BE A KITE.
AAAAAA!
HEY, ARE YOU FEELING OK? YOU HAVE A WEIRD LOOK IN YOUR EYE... LIKE THE KIND SCAMPER GETS WHEN HE'S PLAYING WITH DYNAMITE.

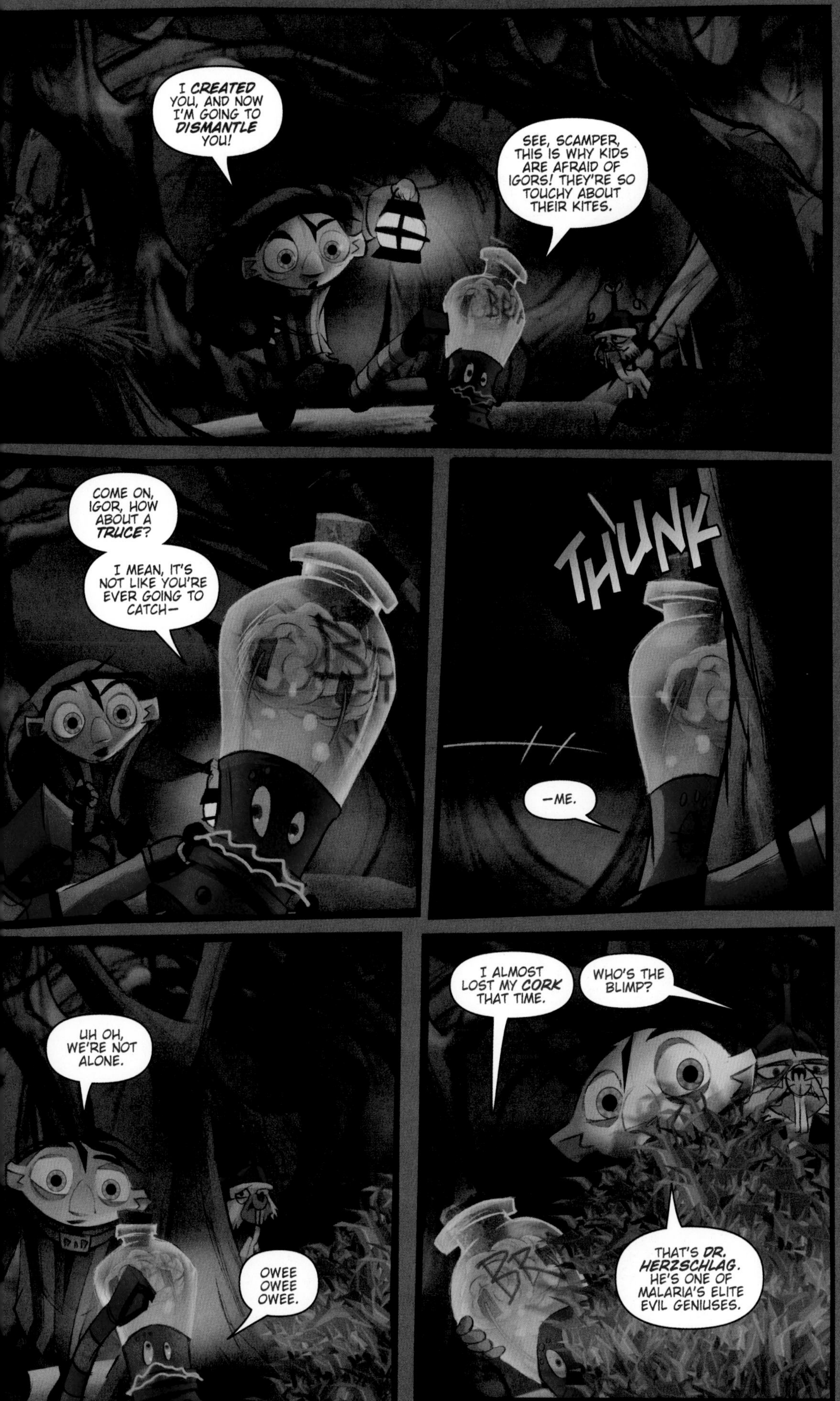
I **CREATED** YOU, AND NOW I'M GOING TO **DISMANTLE** YOU!
SEE, SCAMPER, THIS IS WHY KIDS ARE AFRAID OF IGORS! THEY'RE SO TOUCHY ABOUT THEIR KITES.
COME ON, IGOR, HOW ABOUT A **TRUCE**?
I MEAN, IT'S NOT LIKE YOU'RE EVER GOING TO CATCH—
THUNK
—ME.
UH OH, WE'RE NOT ALONE.
OWEE OWEE OWEE.
I ALMOST LOST MY **CORK** THAT TIME.
WHO'S THE BLIMP?
THAT'S **DR. HERZSCHLAG**. HE'S ONE OF MALARIA'S ELITE EVIL GENIUSES.

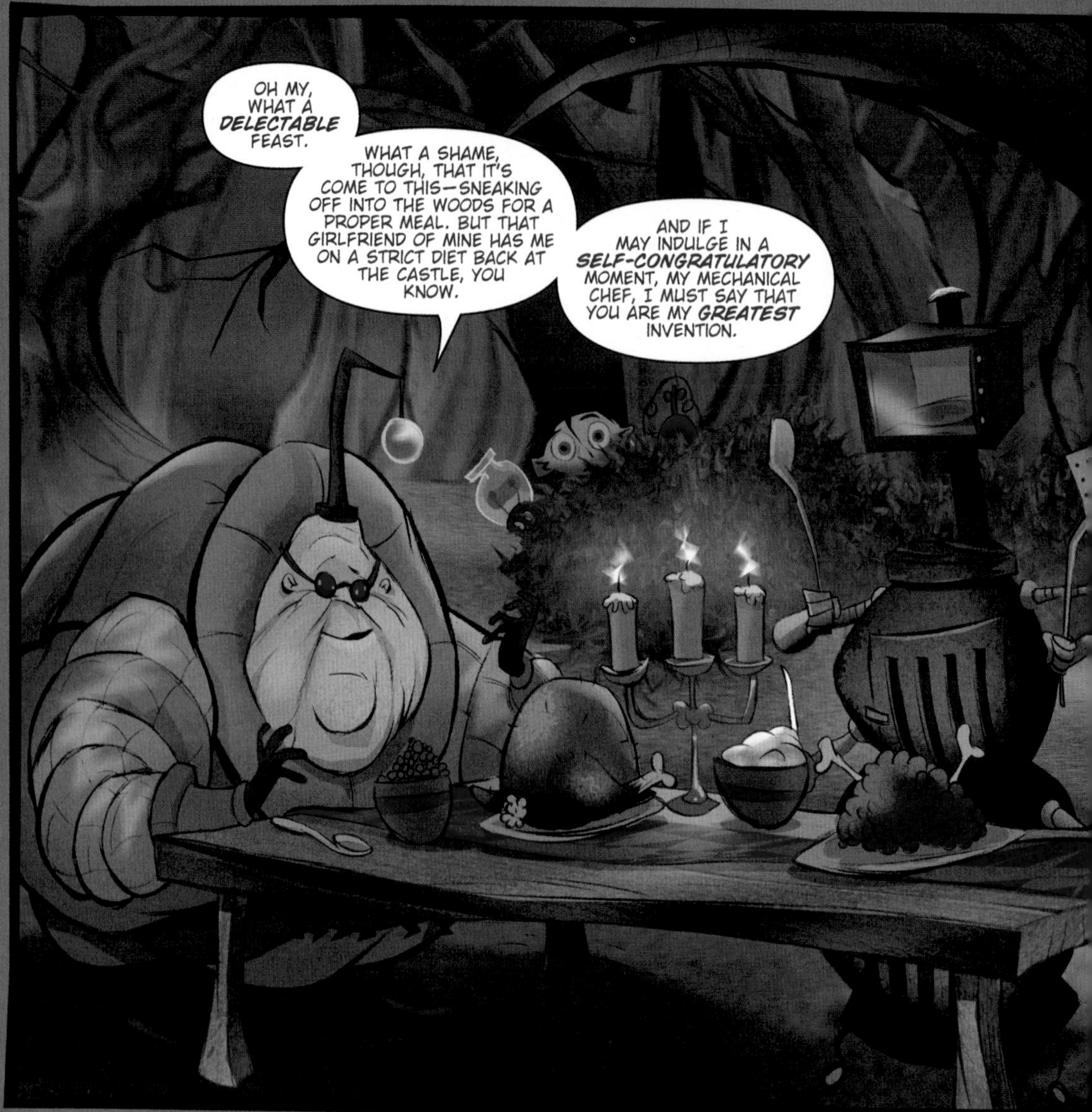
OH MY, WHAT A DELECTABLE FEAST.
WHAT A SHAME, THOUGH, THAT IT'S COME TO THIS—SNEAKING OFF INTO THE WOODS FOR A PROPER MEAL. BUT THAT GIRLFRIEND OF MINE HAS ME ON A STRICT DIET BACK AT THE CASTLE, YOU KNOW.
AND IF I MAY INDULGE IN A SELF-CONGRATULATORY MOMENT, MY MECHANICAL CHEF, I MUST SAY THAT YOU ARE MY GREATEST INVENTION.

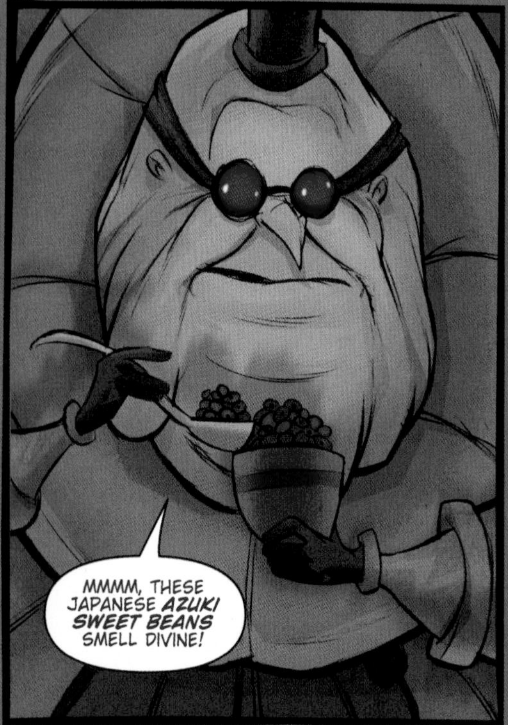
MMMM, THESE JAPANESE AZUKI SWEET BEANS SMELL DIVINE!

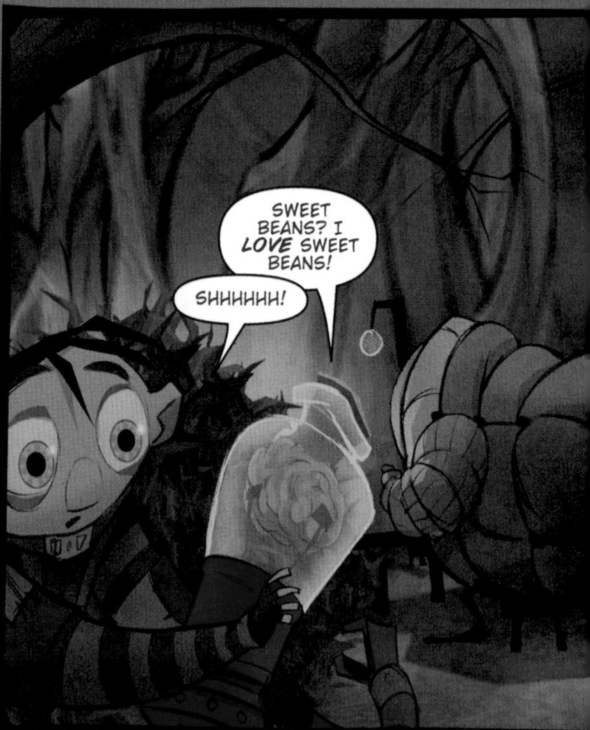
SWEET BEANS? I LOVE SWEET BEANS!
SHHHHHH!

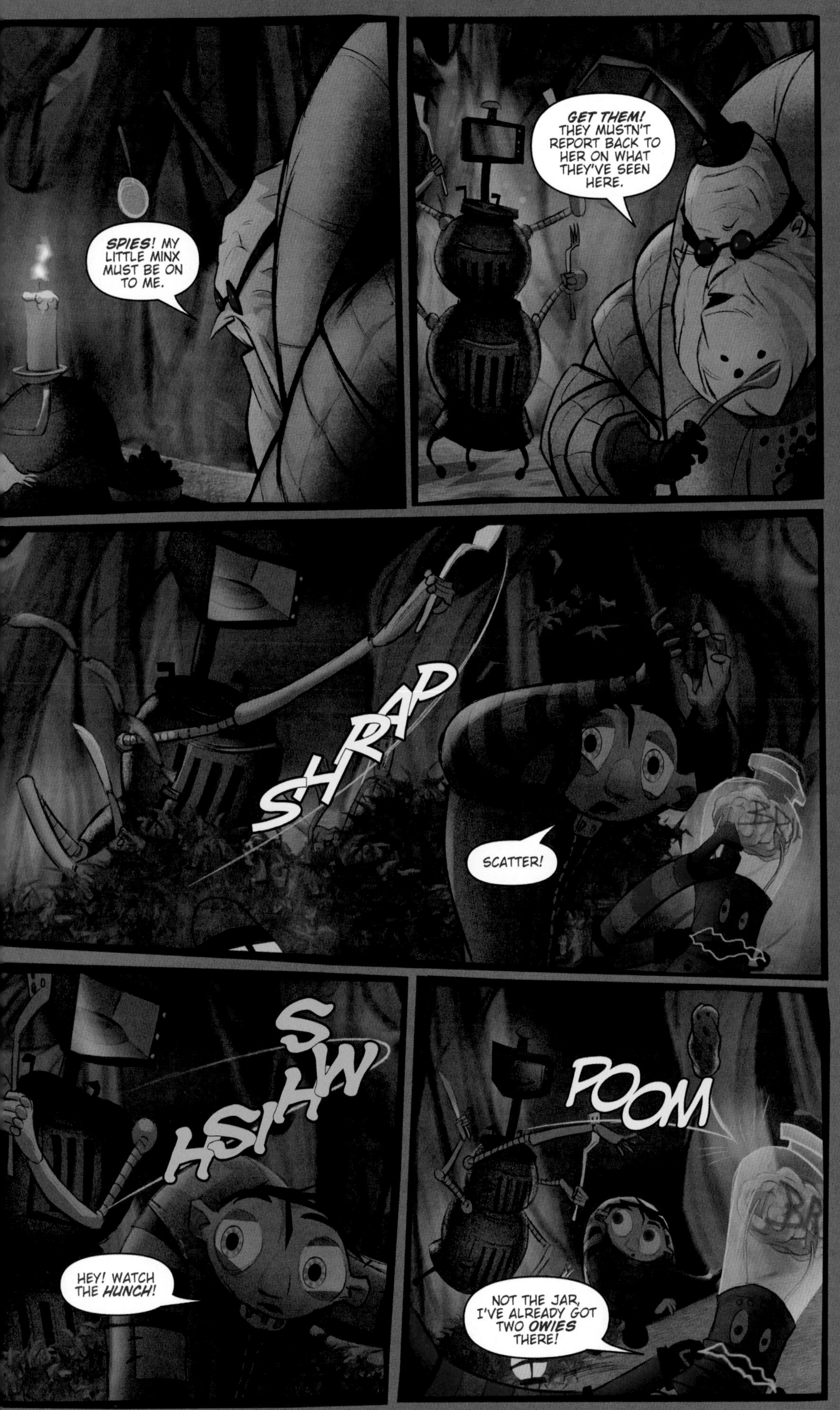
SPIES! MY LITTLE MINX MUST BE ON TO ME.
GET THEM! THEY MUSTN'T REPORT BACK TO HER ON WHAT THEY'VE SEEN HERE.
SHRAP
SCATTER!
SHHHWISH
HEY! WATCH THE HUNCH!
POOM
NOT THE JAR, I'VE ALREADY GOT TWO OWIES THERE!

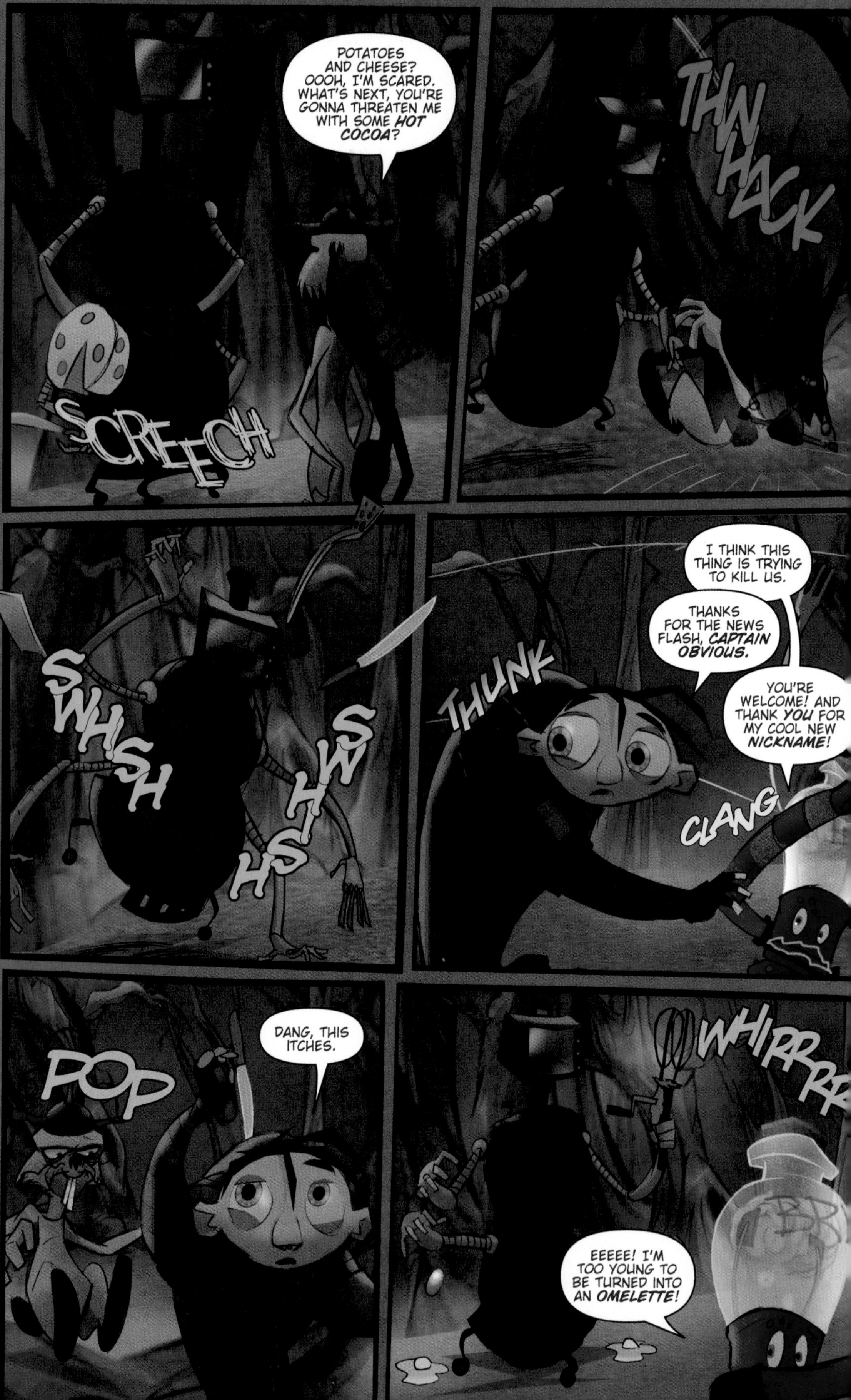

POTATOES AND CHEESE? OOOH, I'M SCARED. WHAT'S NEXT, YOU'RE GONNA THREATEN ME WITH SOME *HOT COCOA*?
SCREECH
THN
HACK
SWHISH
SWHISH
I THINK THIS THING IS TRYING TO KILL US.
THANKS FOR THE NEWS FLASH, *CAPTAIN OBVIOUS.*
THUNK
YOU'RE WELCOME! AND THANK *YOU* FOR MY COOL NEW *NICKNAME!*
CLANG
POP
DANG, THIS ITCHES.
WHIRRRR
EEEEE! I'M TOO YOUNG TO BE TURNED INTO AN *OMELETTE!*

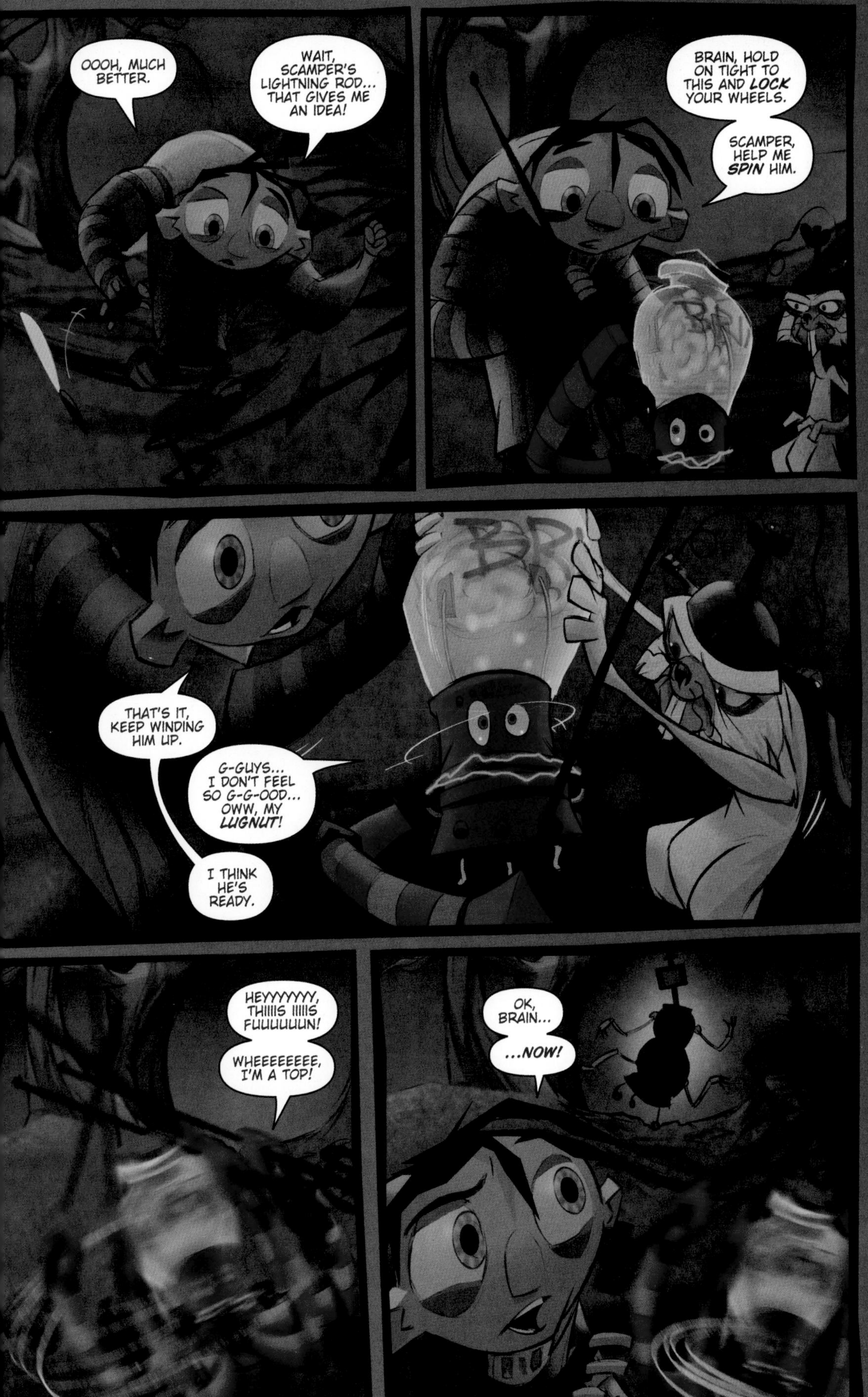
OOOH, MUCH BETTER.
WAIT, SCAMPER'S LIGHTNING ROD... THAT GIVES ME AN IDEA!
BRAIN, HOLD ON TIGHT TO THIS AND LOCK YOUR WHEELS.
SCAMPER, HELP ME SPIN HIM.
THAT'S IT, KEEP WINDING HIM UP.
G-GUYS... I DON'T FEEL SO G-G-OOD... OWW, MY LUGNUT!
I THINK HE'S READY.
HEYYYYYYY, THIIIIS IIIIIS FUUUUUUN!
WHEEEEEEEE, I'M A TOP!
OK, BRAIN...
...NOW!

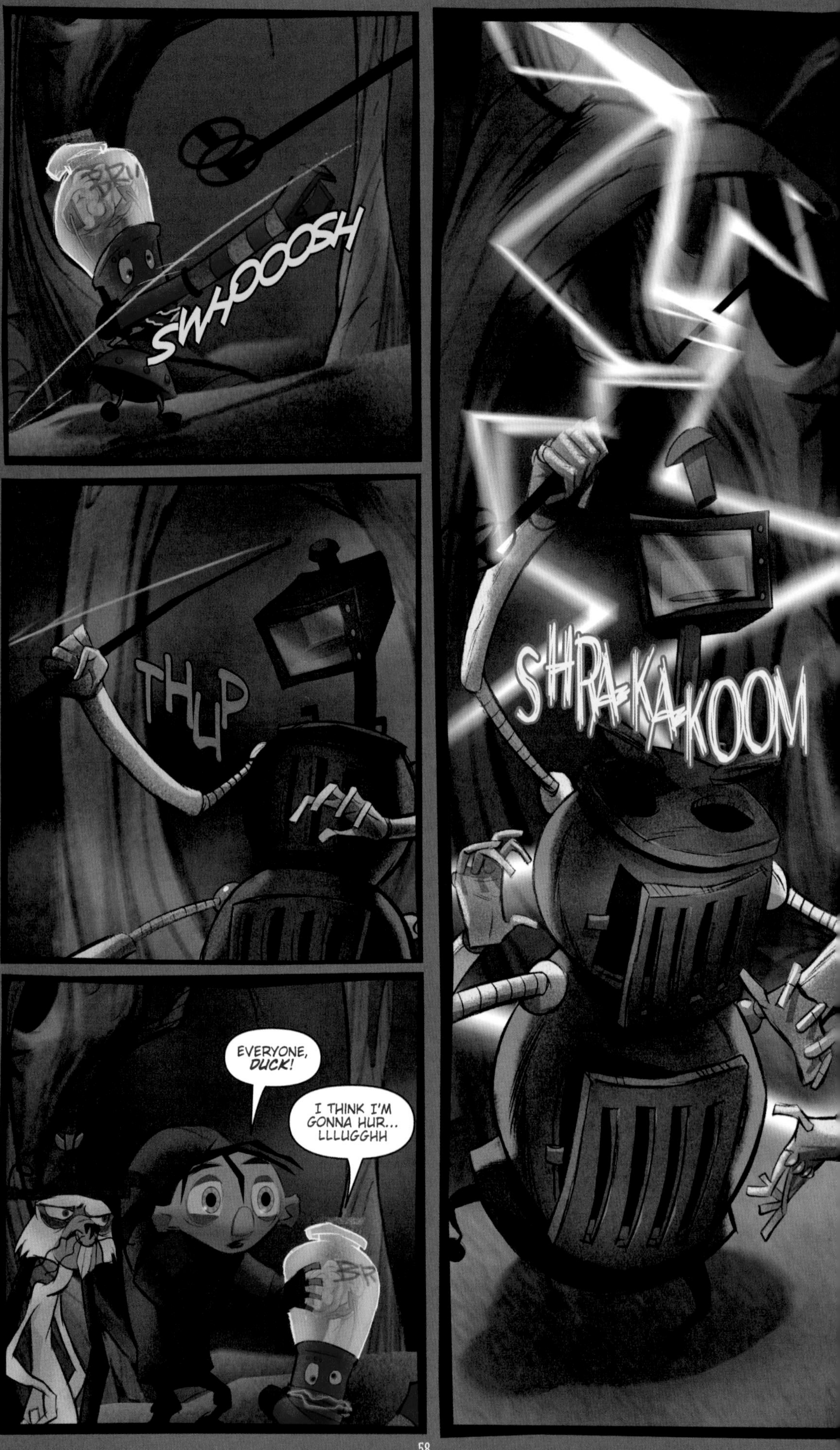
SWHOOOSH
THUP
SHRAKAKOOM
EVERYONE, DUCK!
I THINK I'M GONNA HUR... LLLUGGHH

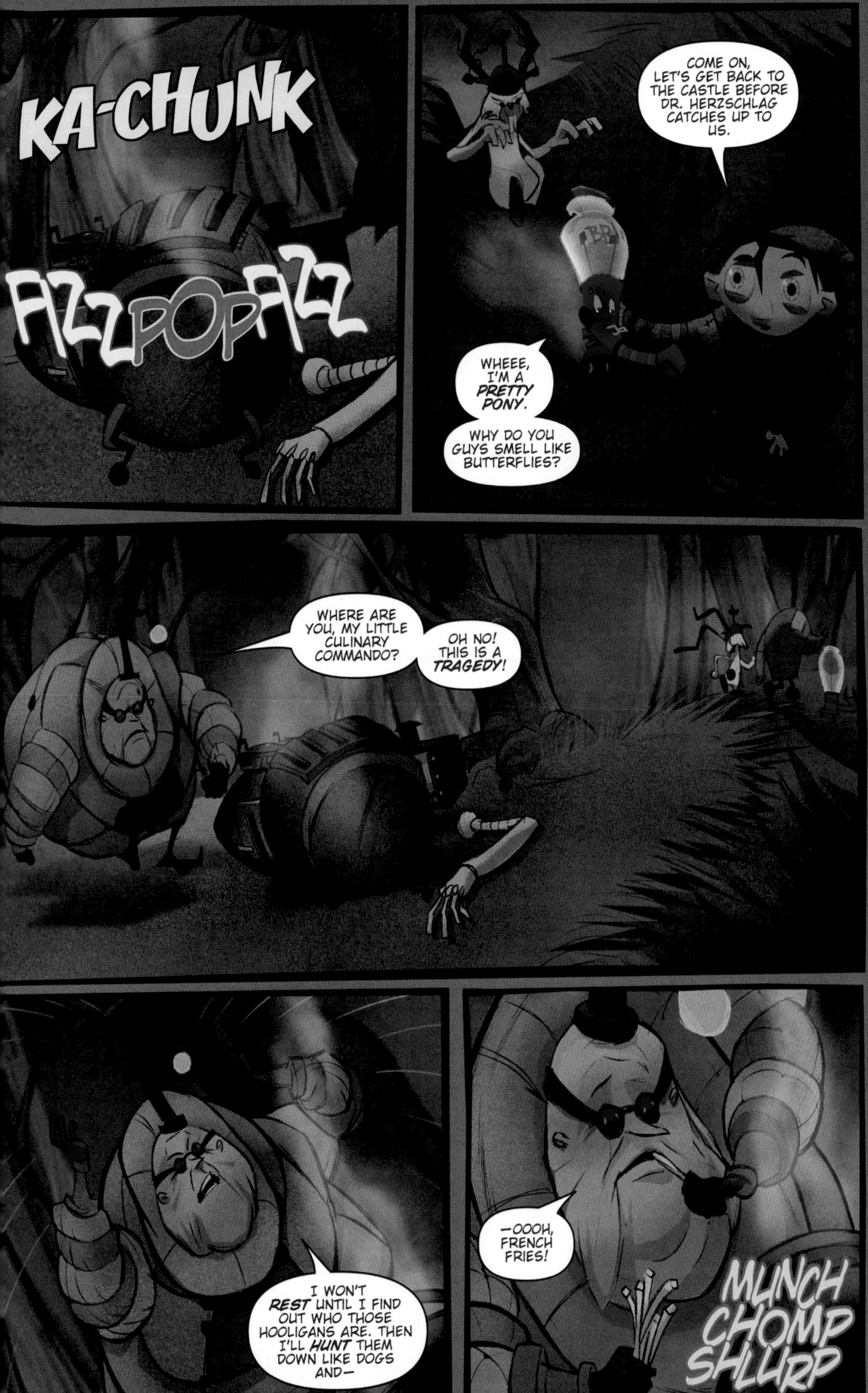
KA-CHUNK
FIZZPOPFIZZ
COME ON, LET'S GET BACK TO THE CASTLE BEFORE DR. HERZSCHLAG CATCHES UP TO US.
WHEEE, I'M A PRETTY PONY.
WHY DO YOU GUYS SMELL LIKE BUTTERFLIES?
WHERE ARE YOU, MY LITTLE CULINARY COMMANDO?
OH NO! THIS IS A TRAGEDY!
I WON'T REST UNTIL I FIND OUT WHO THOSE HOOLIGANS ARE. THEN I'LL HUNT THEM DOWN LIKE DOGS AND—
—OOOH, FRENCH FRIES!
MUNCH CHOMP SHLURP

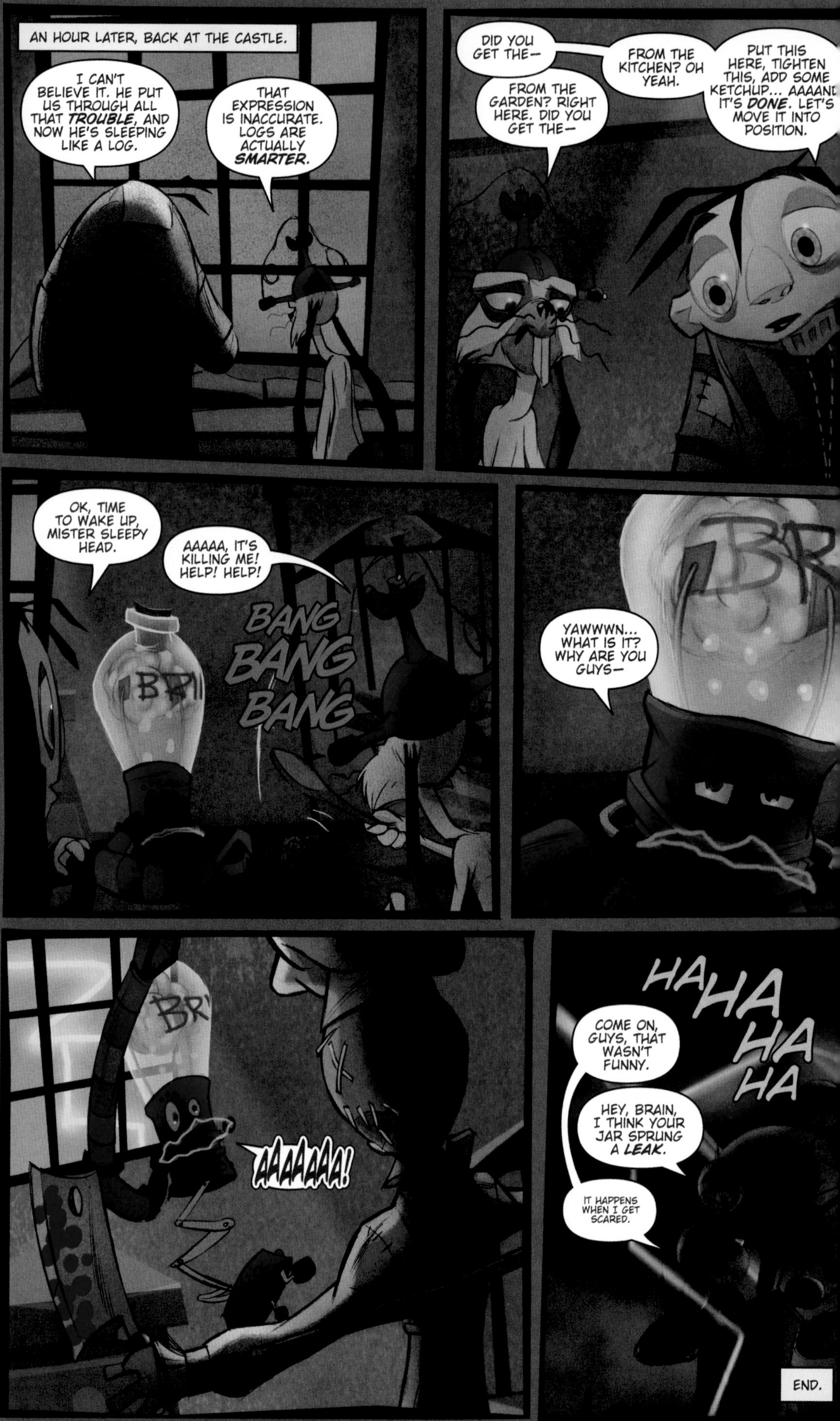

AN HOUR LATER, BACK AT THE CASTLE.
I CAN'T BELIEVE IT. HE PUT US THROUGH ALL THAT TROUBLE, AND NOW HE'S SLEEPING LIKE A LOG.
THAT EXPRESSION IS INACCURATE. LOGS ARE ACTUALLY SMARTER.
DID YOU GET THE—
FROM THE KITCHEN? OH YEAH.
FROM THE GARDEN? RIGHT HERE. DID YOU GET THE—
PUT THIS HERE, TIGHTEN THIS, ADD SOME KETCHUP... AAAAND IT'S DONE. LET'S MOVE IT INTO POSITION.
OK, TIME TO WAKE UP, MISTER SLEEPY HEAD.
AAAAA, IT'S KILLING ME! HELP! HELP!
BANG BANG BANG
YAWWWN... WHAT IS IT? WHY ARE YOU GUYS—
AAAAAAA!
HAHA HA HA HA
COME ON, GUYS, THAT WASN'T FUNNY.
HEY, BRAIN, I THINK YOUR JAR SPRUNG A LEAK.
IT HAPPENS WHEN I GET SCARED.
END.

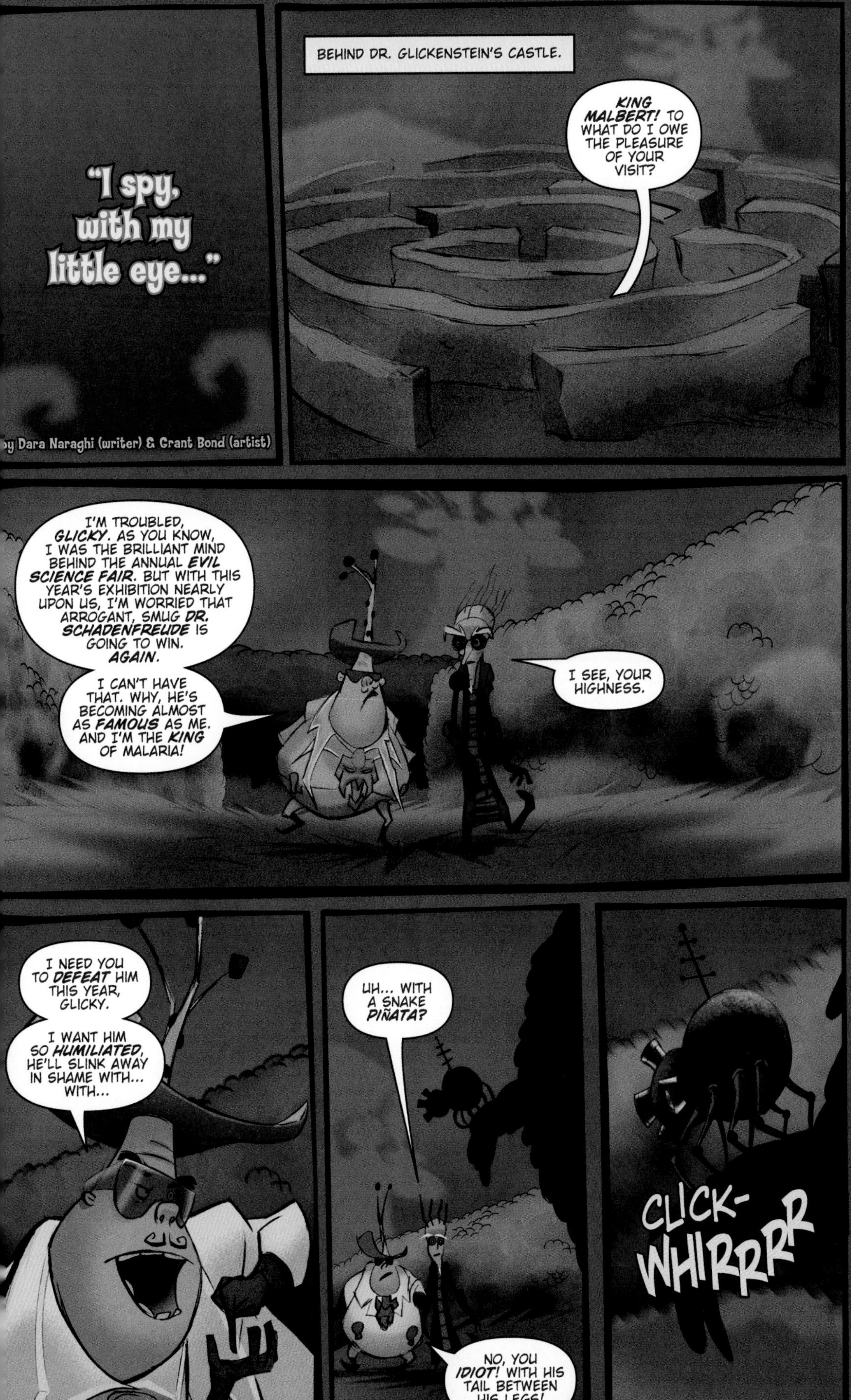
"I spy, with my little eye..."
by Dara Naraghi (writer) & Grant Bond (artist)
BEHIND DR. GLICKENSTEIN'S CASTLE.
KING MALBERT! TO WHAT DO I OWE THE PLEASURE OF YOUR VISIT?
I'M TROUBLED, GLICKY. AS YOU KNOW, I WAS THE BRILLIANT MIND BEHIND THE ANNUAL EVIL SCIENCE FAIR. BUT WITH THIS YEAR'S EXHIBITION NEARLY UPON US, I'M WORRIED THAT ARROGANT, SMUG DR. SCHADENFREUDE IS GOING TO WIN. AGAIN.
I CAN'T HAVE THAT. WHY, HE'S BECOMING ALMOST AS FAMOUS AS ME. AND I'M THE KING OF MALARIA!
I SEE, YOUR HIGHNESS.
I NEED YOU TO DEFEAT HIM THIS YEAR, GLICKY.
I WANT HIM SO HUMILIATED, HE'LL SLINK AWAY IN SHAME WITH... WITH...
UH... WITH A SNAKE PIÑATA?
NO, YOU IDIOT! WITH HIS TAIL BETWEEN HIS LEGS!
CLICK-WHIRRRR

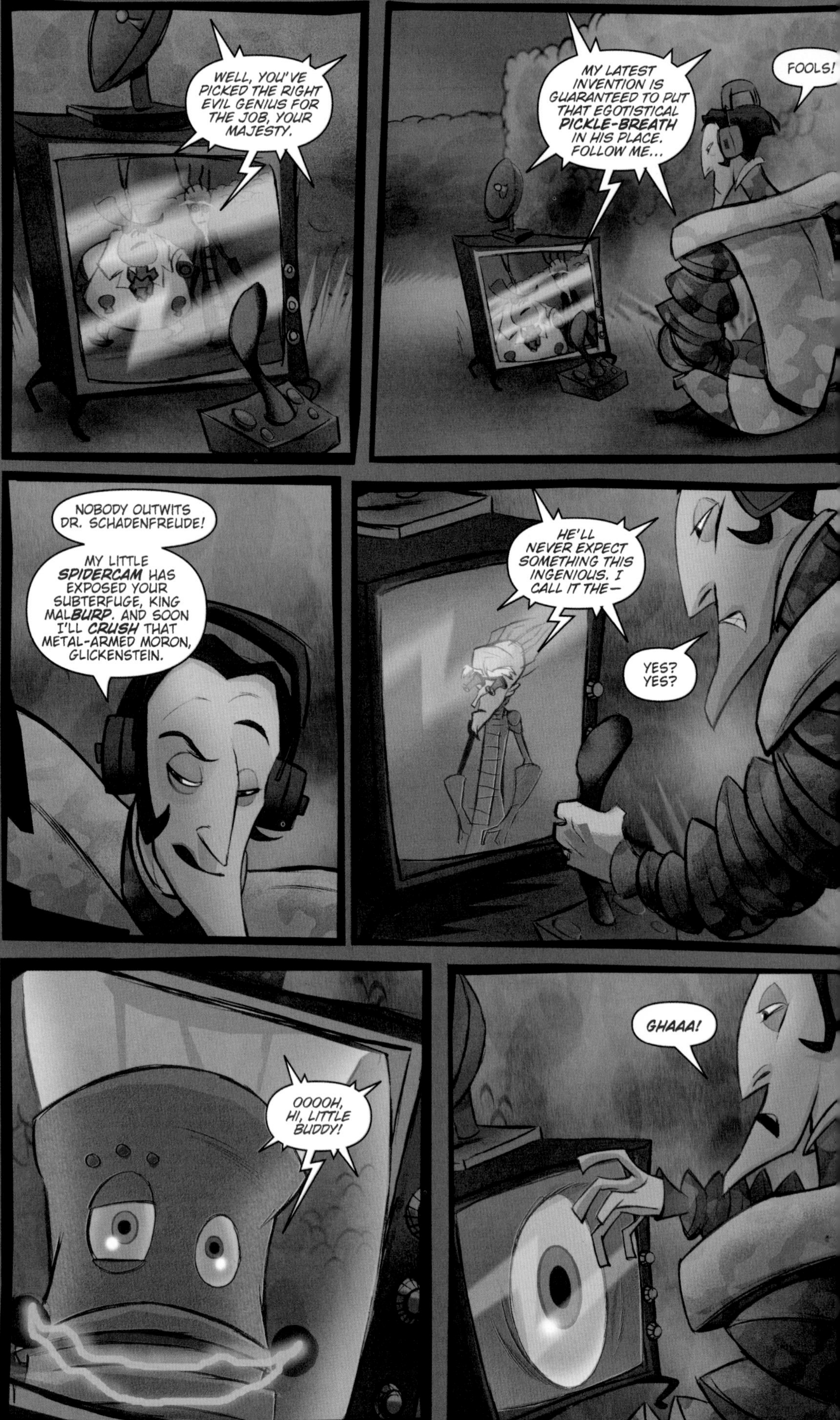
WELL, YOU'VE PICKED THE RIGHT EVIL GENIUS FOR THE JOB, YOUR MAJESTY.
MY LATEST INVENTION IS GUARANTEED TO PUT THAT EGOTISTICAL PICKLE-BREATH IN HIS PLACE. FOLLOW ME...
FOOLS!
NOBODY OUTWITS DR. SCHADENFREUDE!
MY LITTLE SPIDERCAM HAS EXPOSED YOUR SUBTERFUGE, KING MALBURP. AND SOON I'LL CRUSH THAT METAL-ARMED MORON, GLICKENSTEIN.
HE'LL NEVER EXPECT SOMETHING THIS INGENIOUS. I CALL IT THE—
YES? YES?
OOOOH, HI, LITTLE BUDDY!
GHAAA!

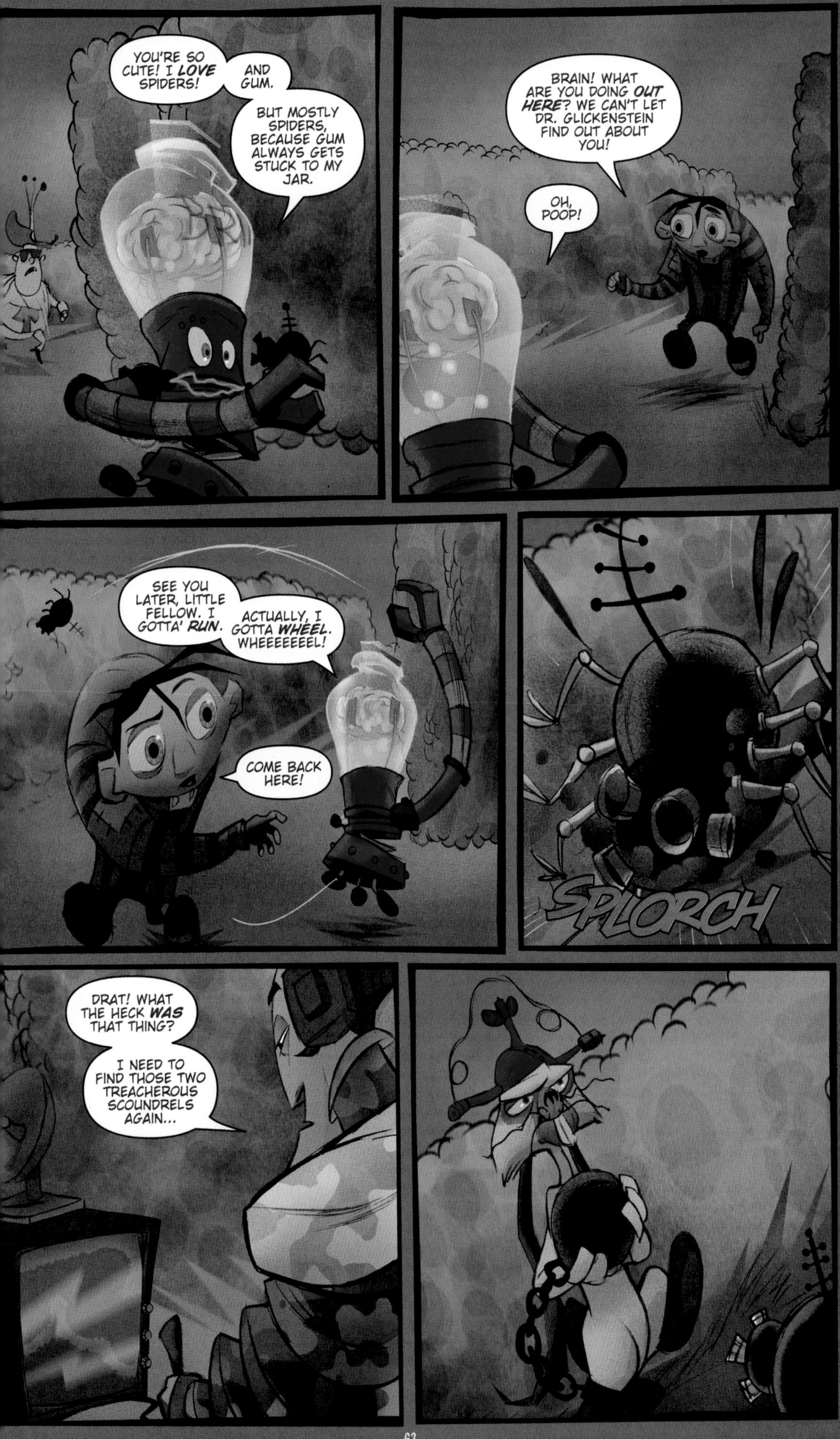
YOU'RE SO CUTE! I LOVE SPIDERS!
AND GUM.
BUT MOSTLY SPIDERS, BECAUSE GUM ALWAYS GETS STUCK TO MY JAR.
BRAIN! WHAT ARE YOU DOING OUT HERE? WE CAN'T LET DR. GLICKENSTEIN FIND OUT ABOUT YOU!
OH, POOP!
SEE YOU LATER, LITTLE FELLOW. I GOTTA' RUN.
ACTUALLY, I GOTTA WHEEL. WHEEEEEEEL!
COME BACK HERE!
SPLORCH
DRAT! WHAT THE HECK WAS THAT THING?
I NEED TO FIND THOSE TWO TREACHEROUS SCOUNDRELS AGAIN...

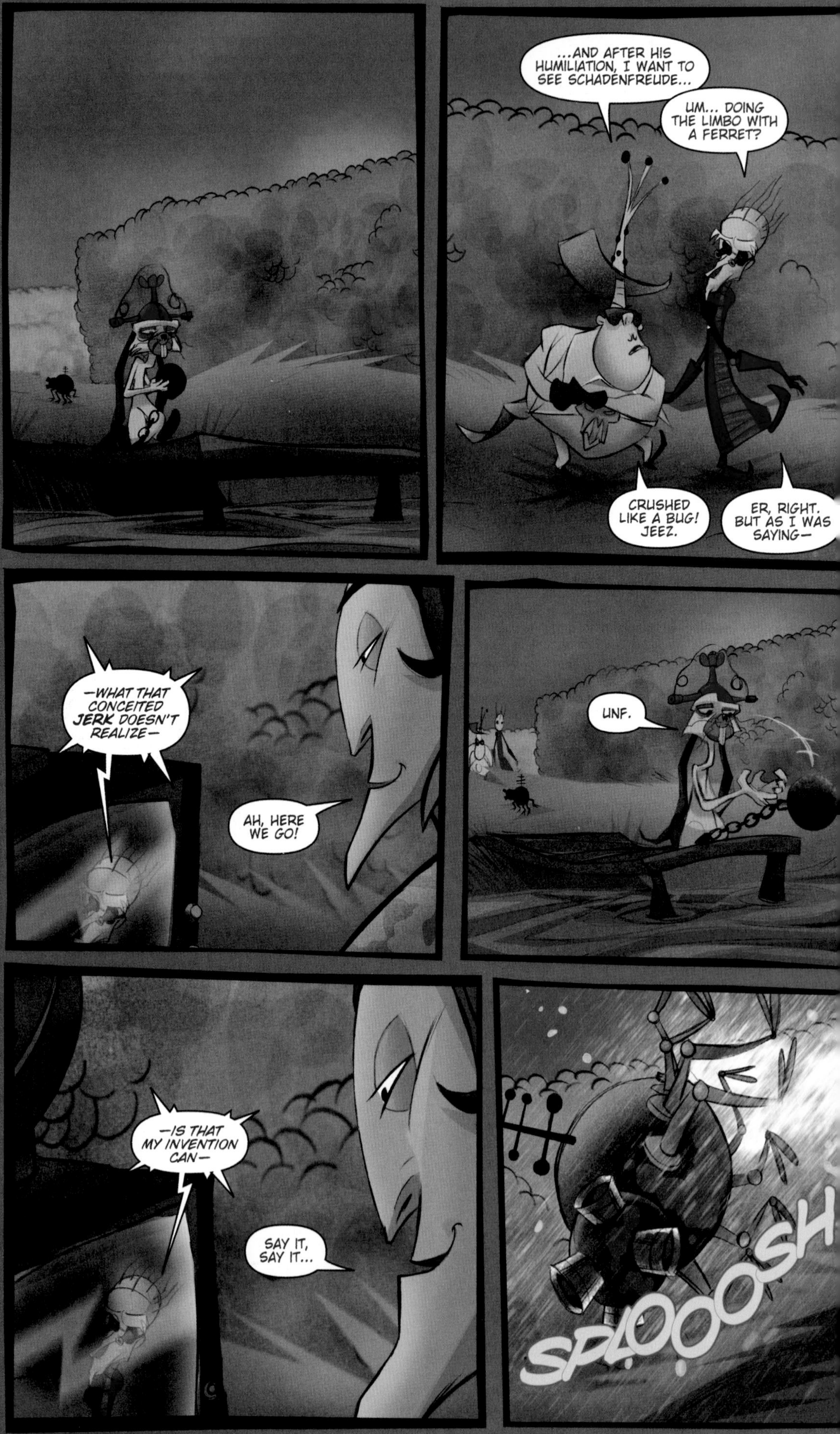
...AND AFTER HIS HUMILIATION, I WANT TO SEE SCHADENFREUDE...
UM... DOING THE LIMBO WITH A FERRET?
CRUSHED LIKE A BUG! JEEZ.
ER, RIGHT. BUT AS I WAS SAYING—
—WHAT THAT CONCEITED **JERK** DOESN'T REALIZE—
AH, HERE WE GO!
UNF.
—IS THAT MY INVENTION CAN—
SAY IT, SAY IT...
SPLOOOOSH

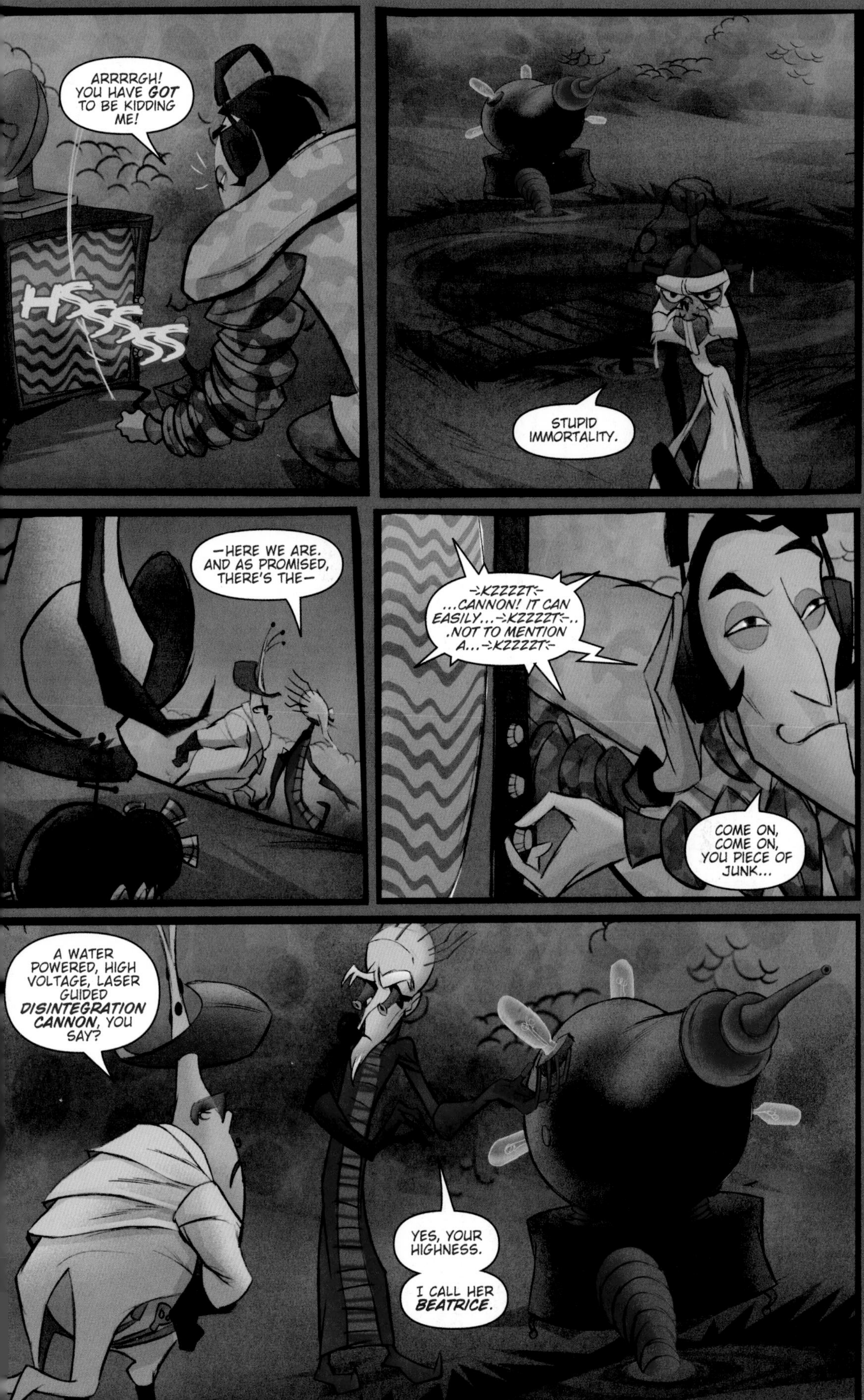

ARRRRGH! YOU HAVE GOT TO BE KIDDING ME!
HSSSSS
STUPID IMMORTALITY.
—HERE WE ARE. AND AS PROMISED, THERE'S THE—
-KZZZZT- ...CANNON! IT CAN EASILY... -KZZZZT-.. .NOT TO MENTION A... -KZZZZT-
COME ON, COME ON, YOU PIECE OF JUNK...
A WATER POWERED, HIGH VOLTAGE, LASER GUIDED DISINTEGRATION CANNON, YOU SAY?
YES, YOUR HIGHNESS.
I CALL HER BEATRICE.

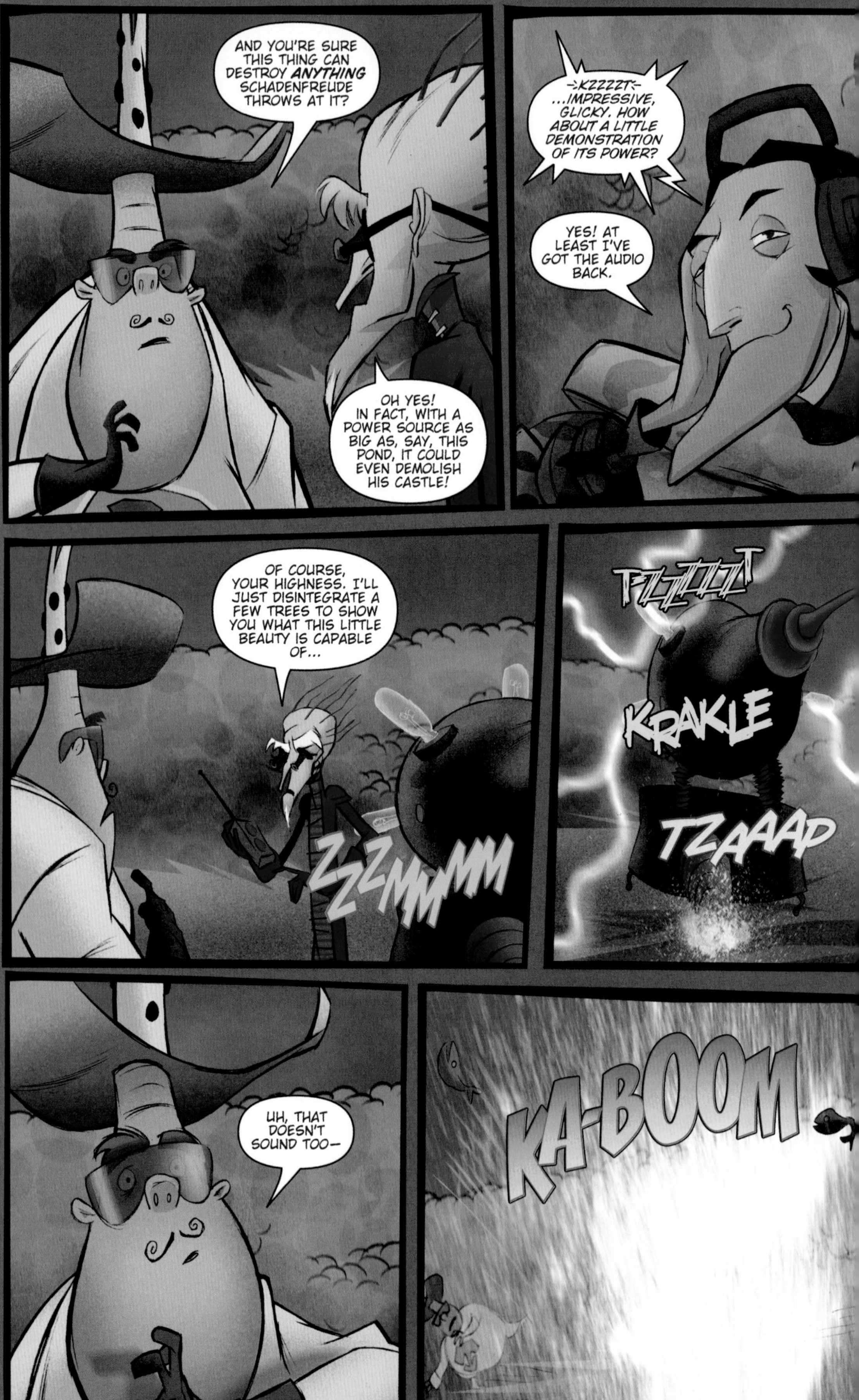
AND YOU'RE SURE THIS THING CAN DESTROY ***ANYTHING*** SCHADENFREUDE THROWS AT IT?
OH YES! IN FACT, WITH A POWER SOURCE AS BIG AS, SAY, THIS POND, IT COULD EVEN DEMOLISH HIS CASTLE!
-KZZZZT- ...IMPRESSIVE, GLICKY. HOW ABOUT A LITTLE DEMONSTRATION OF ITS POWER?
YES! AT LEAST I'VE GOT THE AUDIO BACK.
OF COURSE, YOUR HIGHNESS. I'LL JUST DISINTEGRATE A FEW TREES TO SHOW YOU WHAT THIS LITTLE BEAUTY IS CAPABLE OF...
ZZZMMMMM
TZZZZZT
KRAKLE
TZAAAP
UH, THAT DOESN'T SOUND TOO—
KA-BOOM

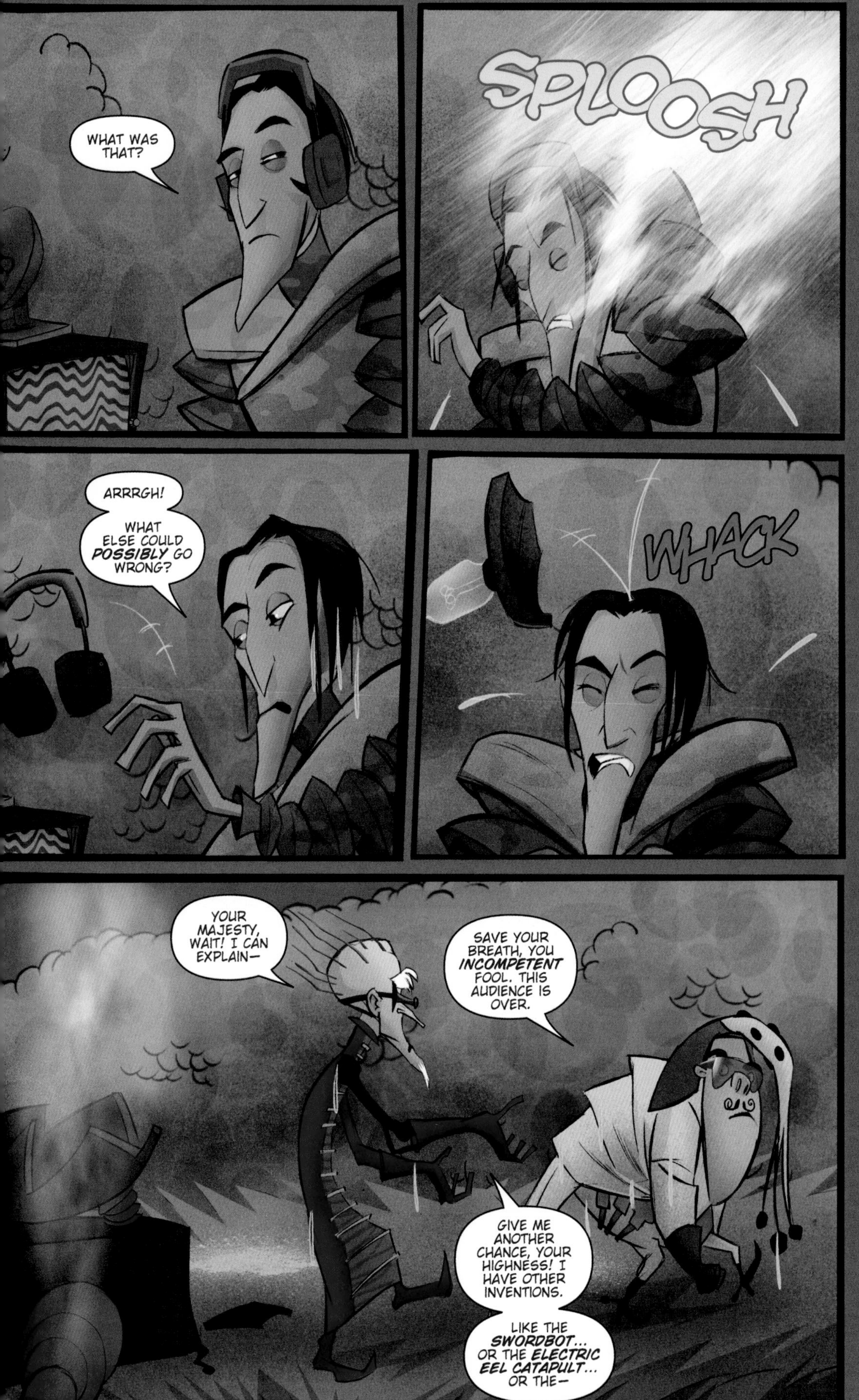
WHAT WAS THAT?
SPLOOSH
ARRRGH!
WHAT ELSE COULD **POSSIBLY** GO WRONG?
WHACK
YOUR MAJESTY, WAIT! I CAN EXPLAIN—
SAVE YOUR BREATH, YOU **INCOMPETENT** FOOL. THIS AUDIENCE IS OVER.
GIVE ME ANOTHER CHANCE, YOUR HIGHNESS! I HAVE OTHER INVENTIONS.
LIKE THE **SWORDBOT**... OR THE **ELECTRIC EEL CATAPULT**... OR THE—

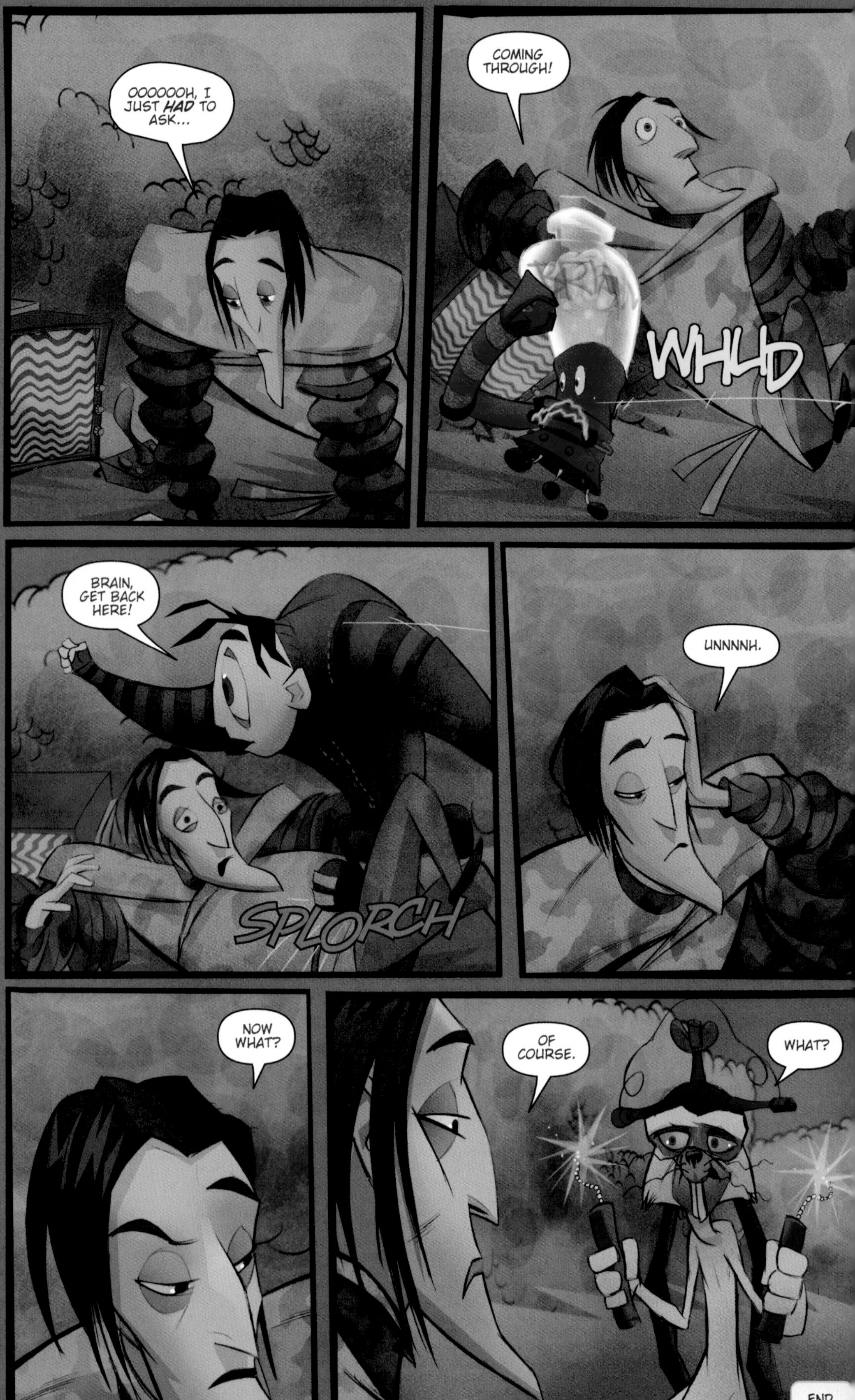
OOOOOOH, I JUST HAD TO ASK...
COMING THROUGH!
WHUD
BRAIN, GET BACK HERE!
SPLORCH
UNNNNH.
NOW WHAT?
OF COURSE.
WHAT?
END.

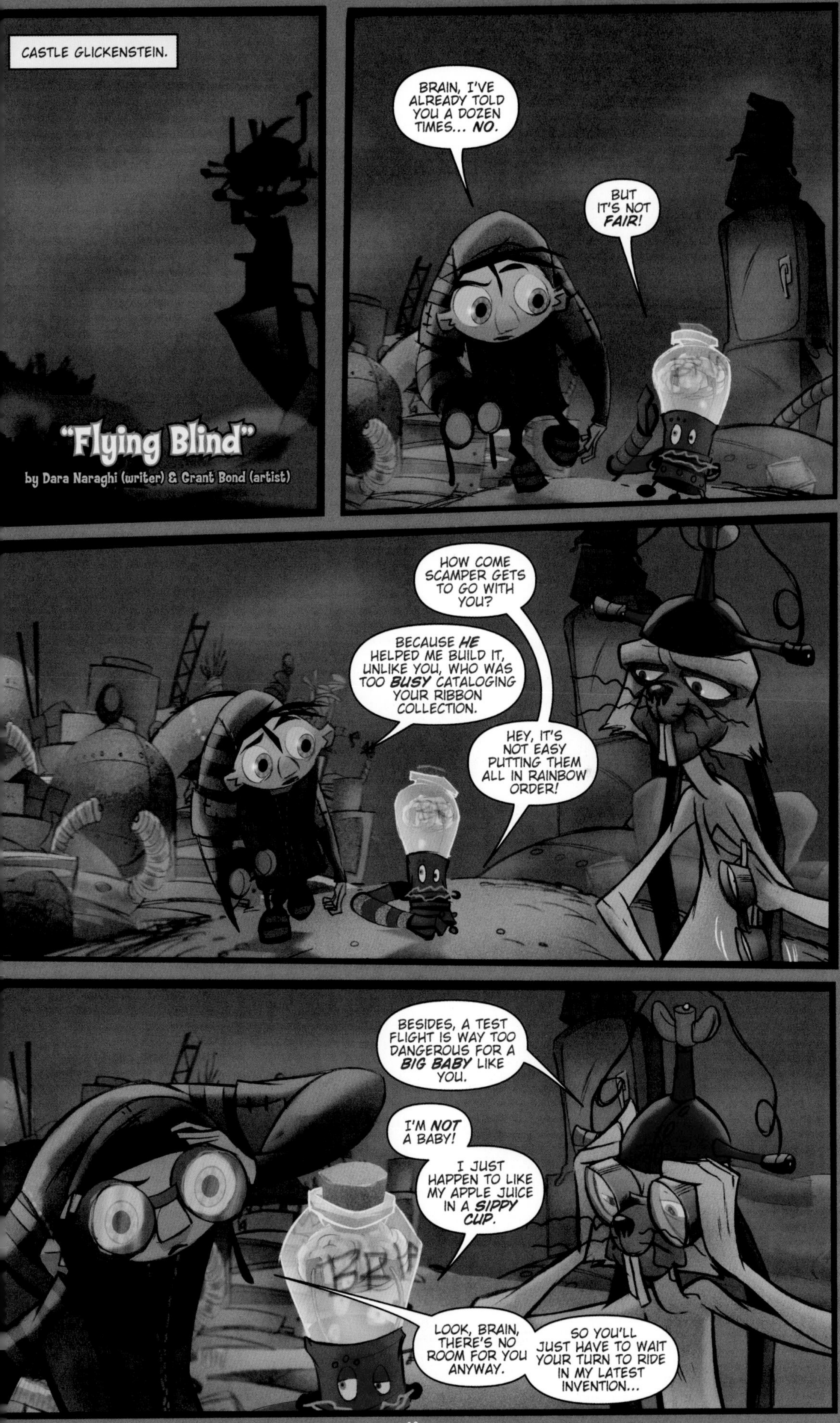

CASTLE GLICKENSTEIN.
"Flying Blind"
by Dara Naraghi (writer) & Grant Bond (artist)
BRAIN, I'VE ALREADY TOLD YOU A DOZEN TIMES... NO.
BUT IT'S NOT FAIR!
HOW COME SCAMPER GETS TO GO WITH YOU?
BECAUSE HE HELPED ME BUILD IT, UNLIKE YOU, WHO WAS TOO BUSY CATALOGING YOUR RIBBON COLLECTION.
HEY, IT'S NOT EASY PUTTING THEM ALL IN RAINBOW ORDER!
BESIDES, A TEST FLIGHT IS WAY TOO DANGEROUS FOR A BIG BABY LIKE YOU.
I'M NOT A BABY!
I JUST HAPPEN TO LIKE MY APPLE JUICE IN A SIPPY CUP.
LOOK, BRAIN, THERE'S NO ROOM FOR YOU ANYWAY.
SO YOU'LL JUST HAVE TO WAIT YOUR TURN TO RIDE IN MY LATEST INVENTION...

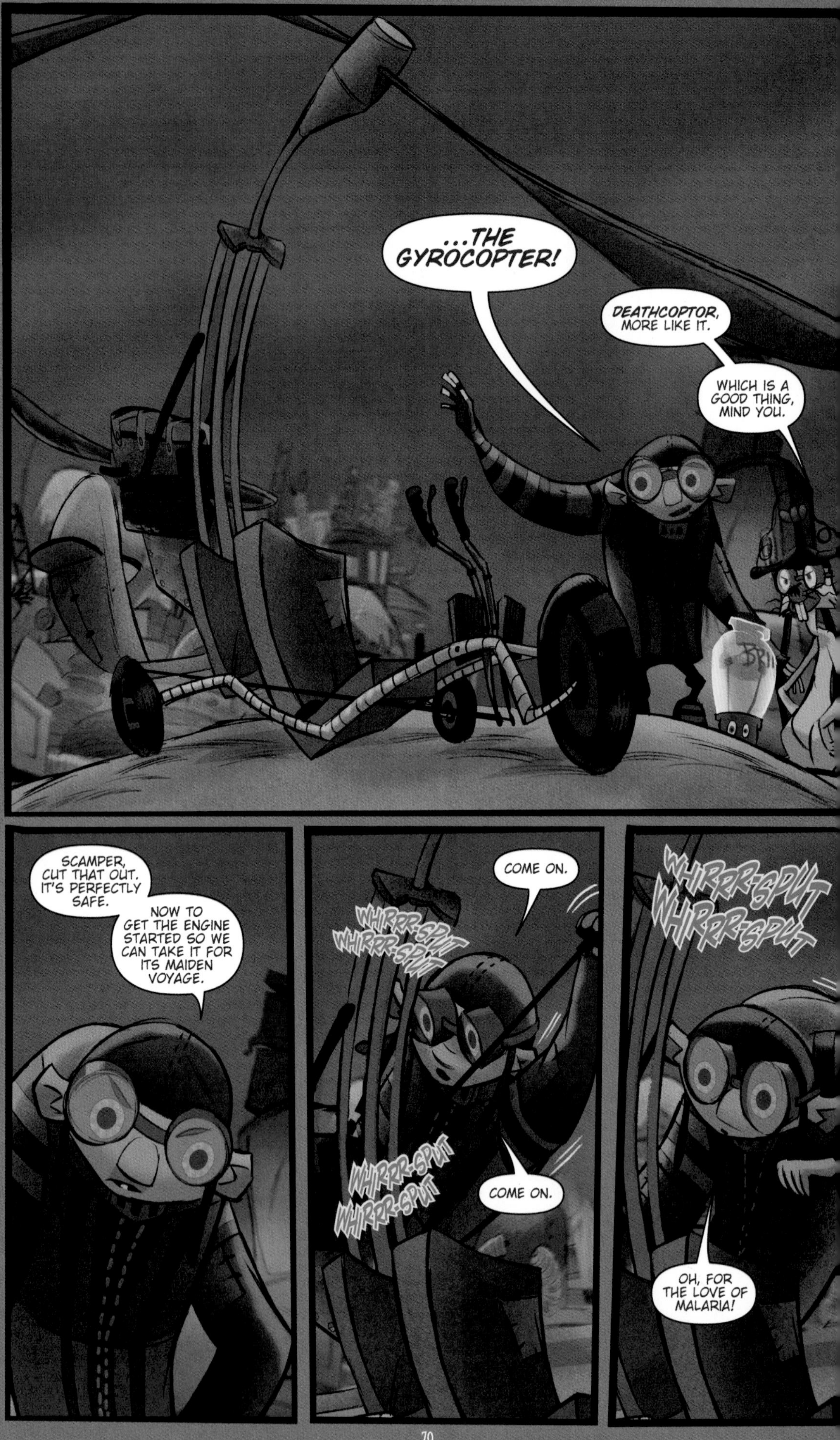
...THE GYROCOPTER!
DEATHCOPTOR, MORE LIKE IT.
WHICH IS A GOOD THING, MIND YOU.
SCAMPER, CUT THAT OUT. IT'S PERFECTLY SAFE.
NOW TO GET THE ENGINE STARTED SO WE CAN TAKE IT FOR ITS MAIDEN VOYAGE.
COME ON.
WHIRRR-SPUT WHIRRR-SPUT
WHIRRR-SPUT WHIRRR-SPUT
COME ON.
WHIRRR-SPUT WHIRRR-SPUT
OH, FOR THE LOVE OF MALARIA!

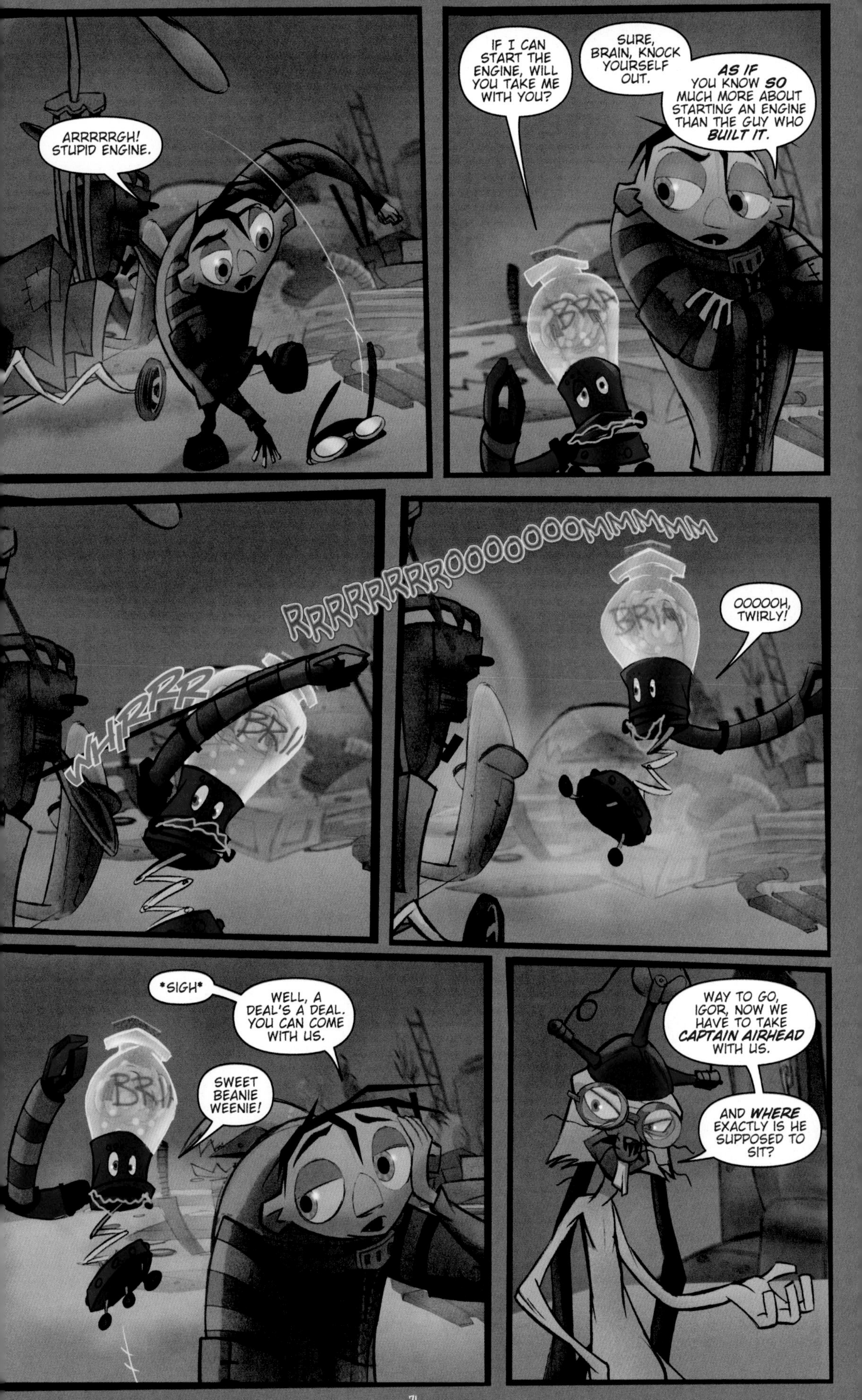
ARRRRRGH! STUPID ENGINE.
IF I CAN START THE ENGINE, WILL YOU TAKE ME WITH YOU?
SURE, BRAIN, KNOCK YOURSELF OUT.
AS IF YOU KNOW SO MUCH MORE ABOUT STARTING AN ENGINE THAN THE GUY WHO BUILT IT.
BRR
RRRRRRRROOOOOOOMMMMMM
WHIRRR
BRR
OOOOOH, TWIRLY!
SIGH
WELL, A DEAL'S A DEAL. YOU CAN COME WITH US.
SWEET BEANIE WEENIE!
WAY TO GO, IGOR, NOW WE HAVE TO TAKE CAPTAIN AIRHEAD WITH US.
AND WHERE EXACTLY IS HE SUPPOSED TO SIT?

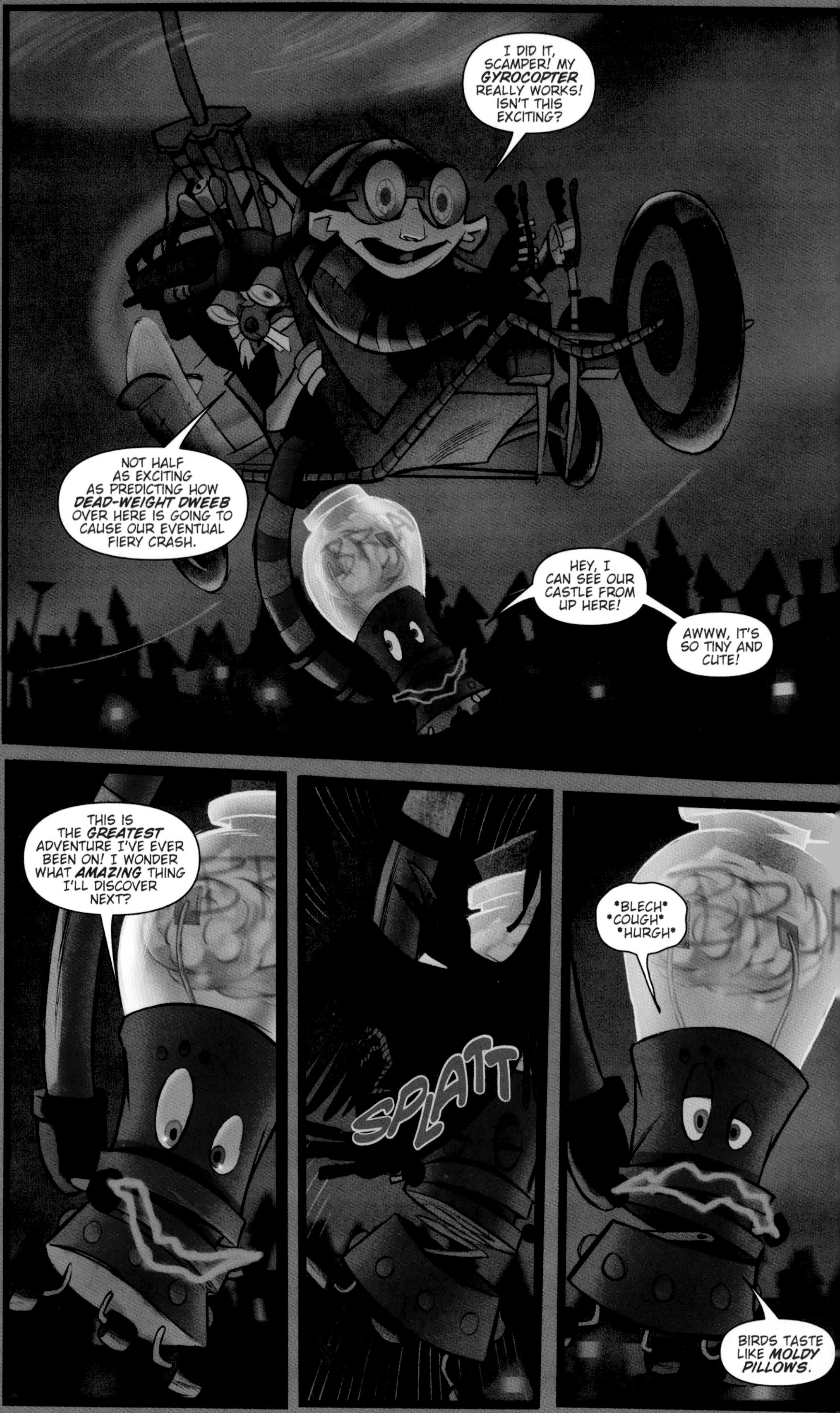

I DID IT, SCAMPER! MY **GYROCOPTER** REALLY WORKS! ISN'T THIS EXCITING?
NOT HALF AS EXCITING AS PREDICTING HOW **DEAD-WEIGHT DWEEB** OVER HERE IS GOING TO CAUSE OUR EVENTUAL FIERY CRASH.
HEY, I CAN SEE OUR CASTLE FROM UP HERE!
AWWW, IT'S SO TINY AND CUTE!
THIS IS THE **GREATEST** ADVENTURE I'VE EVER BEEN ON! I WONDER WHAT **AMAZING** THING I'LL DISCOVER NEXT?
SPLATT
BLECH *COUGH* *HURGH*
BIRDS TASTE LIKE **MOLDY PILLOWS**.

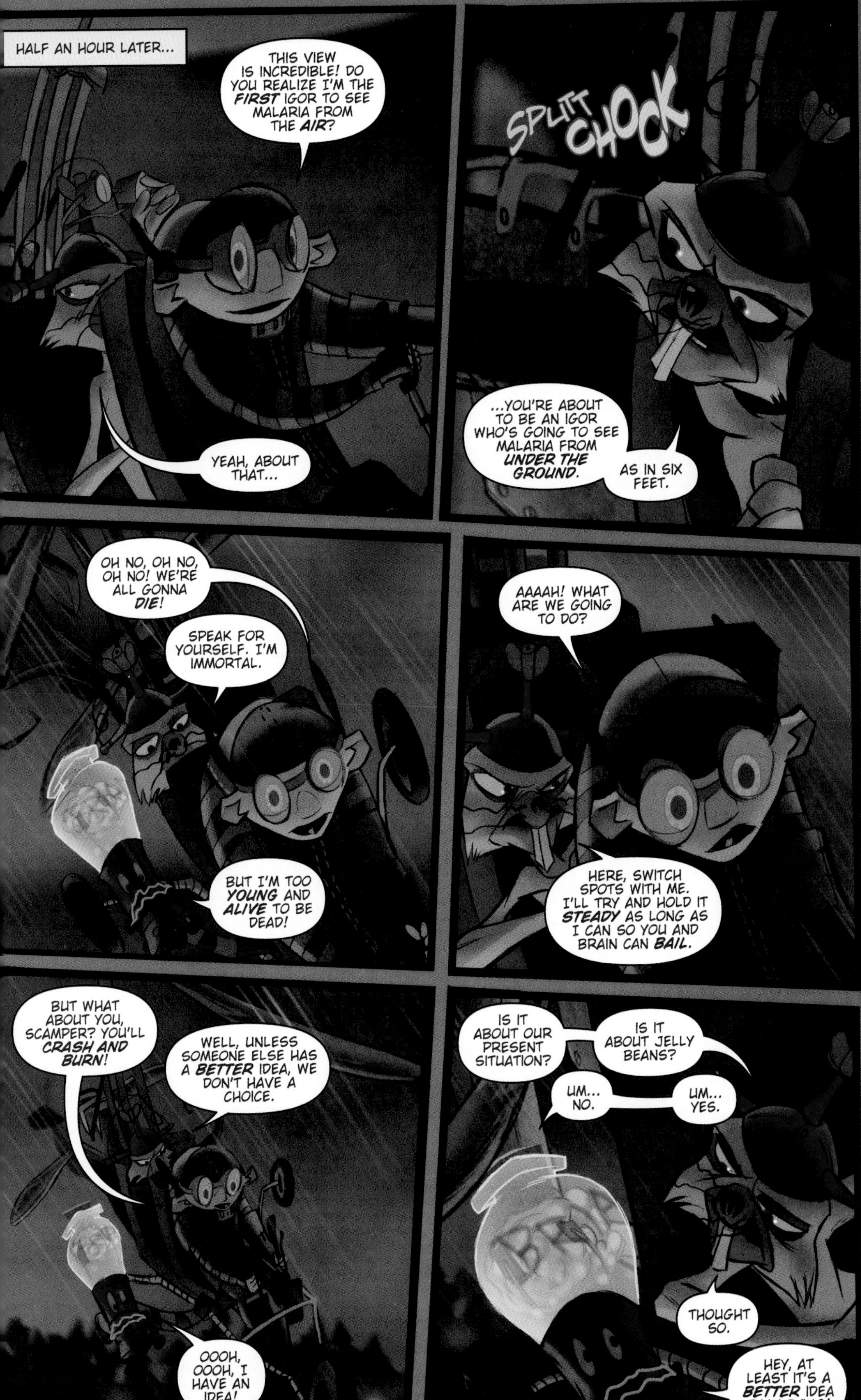

HALF AN HOUR LATER...
THIS VIEW IS INCREDIBLE! DO YOU REALIZE I'M THE FIRST IGOR TO SEE MALARIA FROM THE AIR?
YEAH, ABOUT THAT...
SPLUT
CHOCK
...YOU'RE ABOUT TO BE AN IGOR WHO'S GOING TO SEE MALARIA FROM UNDER THE GROUND.
AS IN SIX FEET.
OH NO, OH NO, OH NO! WE'RE ALL GONNA DIE!
SPEAK FOR YOURSELF. I'M IMMORTAL.
BUT I'M TOO YOUNG AND ALIVE TO BE DEAD!
AAAAH! WHAT ARE WE GOING TO DO?
HERE, SWITCH SPOTS WITH ME. I'LL TRY AND HOLD IT STEADY AS LONG AS I CAN SO YOU AND BRAIN CAN BAIL.
BUT WHAT ABOUT YOU, SCAMPER? YOU'LL CRASH AND BURN!
WELL, UNLESS SOMEONE ELSE HAS A BETTER IDEA, WE DON'T HAVE A CHOICE.
OOOH, OOOH, I HAVE AN IDEA!
IS IT ABOUT OUR PRESENT SITUATION?
IS IT ABOUT JELLY BEANS?
UM... NO.
UM... YES.
THOUGHT SO.
HEY, AT LEAST IT'S A BETTER IDEA THAN DYING!

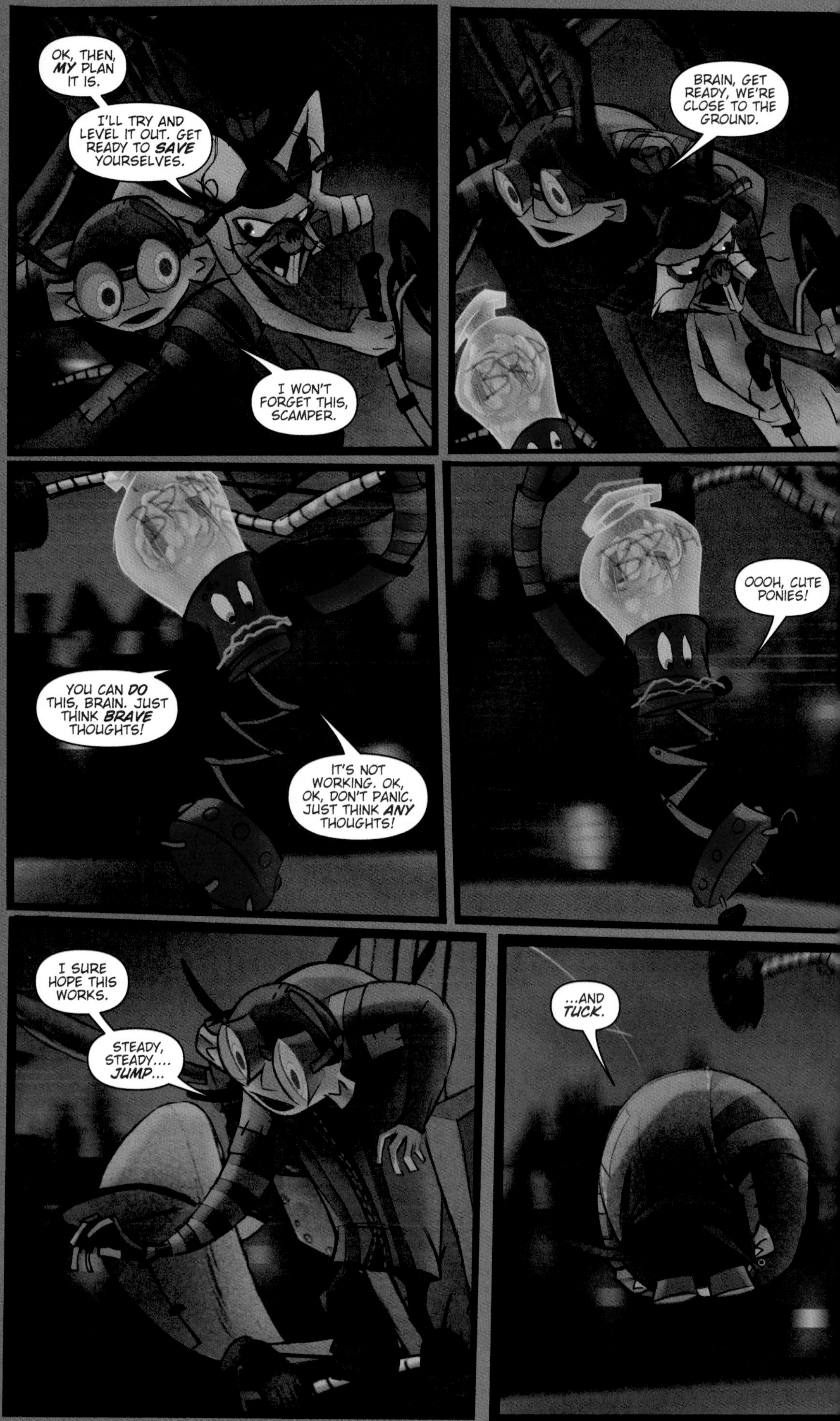
OK, THEN, MY PLAN IT IS.
I'LL TRY AND LEVEL IT OUT. GET READY TO SAVE YOURSELVES.
I WON'T FORGET THIS, SCAMPER.
BRAIN, GET READY, WE'RE CLOSE TO THE GROUND.
YOU CAN DO THIS, BRAIN. JUST THINK BRAVE THOUGHTS!
IT'S NOT WORKING. OK, OK, DON'T PANIC. JUST THINK ANY THOUGHTS!
OOOH, CUTE PONIES!
I SURE HOPE THIS WORKS.
STEADY, STEADY.... JUMP...
...AND TUCK.

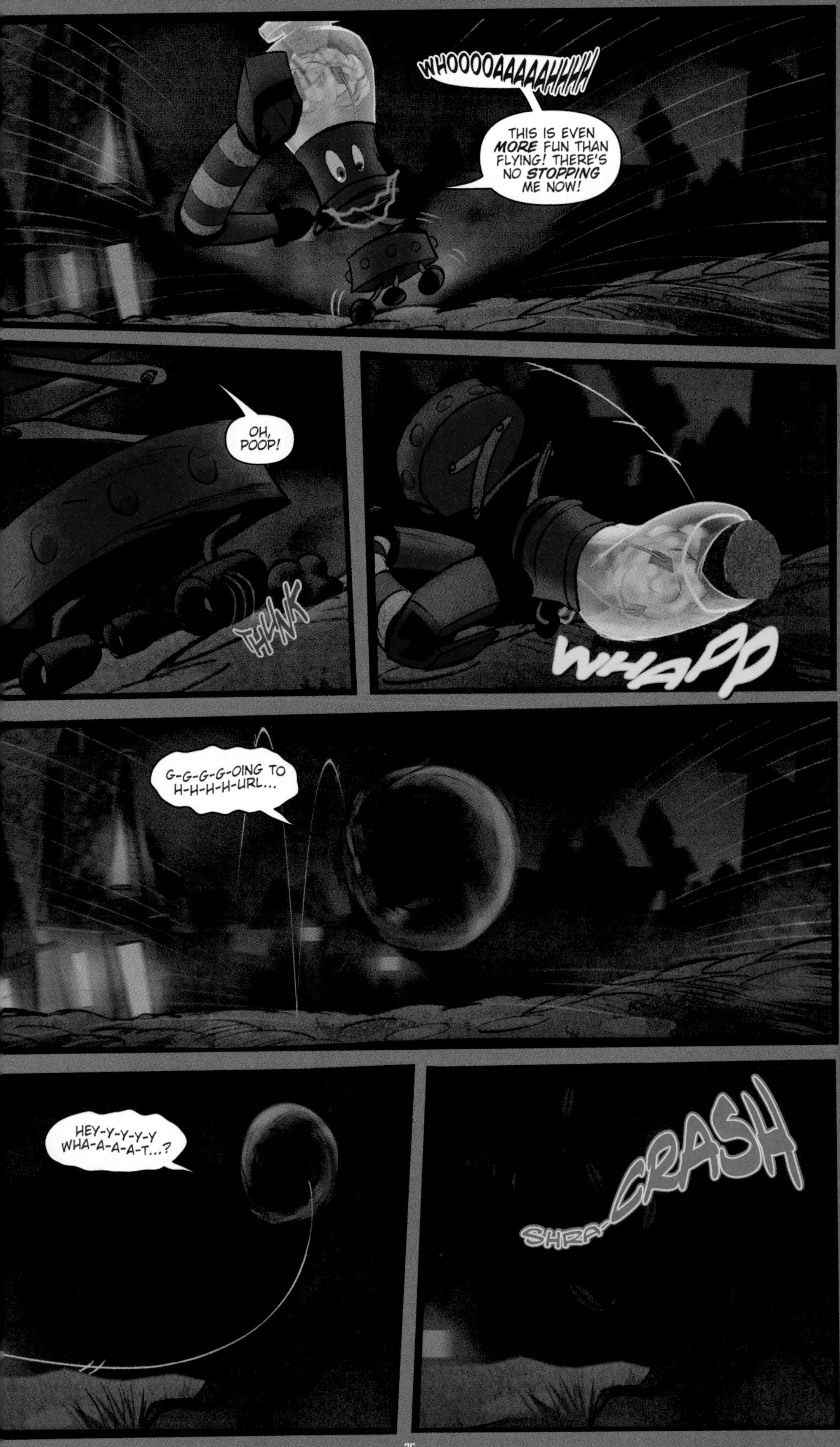
WHOOOOAAAAAHHHH
THIS IS EVEN MORE FUN THAN FLYING! THERE'S NO STOPPING ME NOW!
OH, POOP!
THUNK
WHAPP
G-G-G-G-OING TO H-H-H-H-URL...
HEY-Y-Y-Y-Y WHA-A-A-A-T...?
SHRA-CRASH

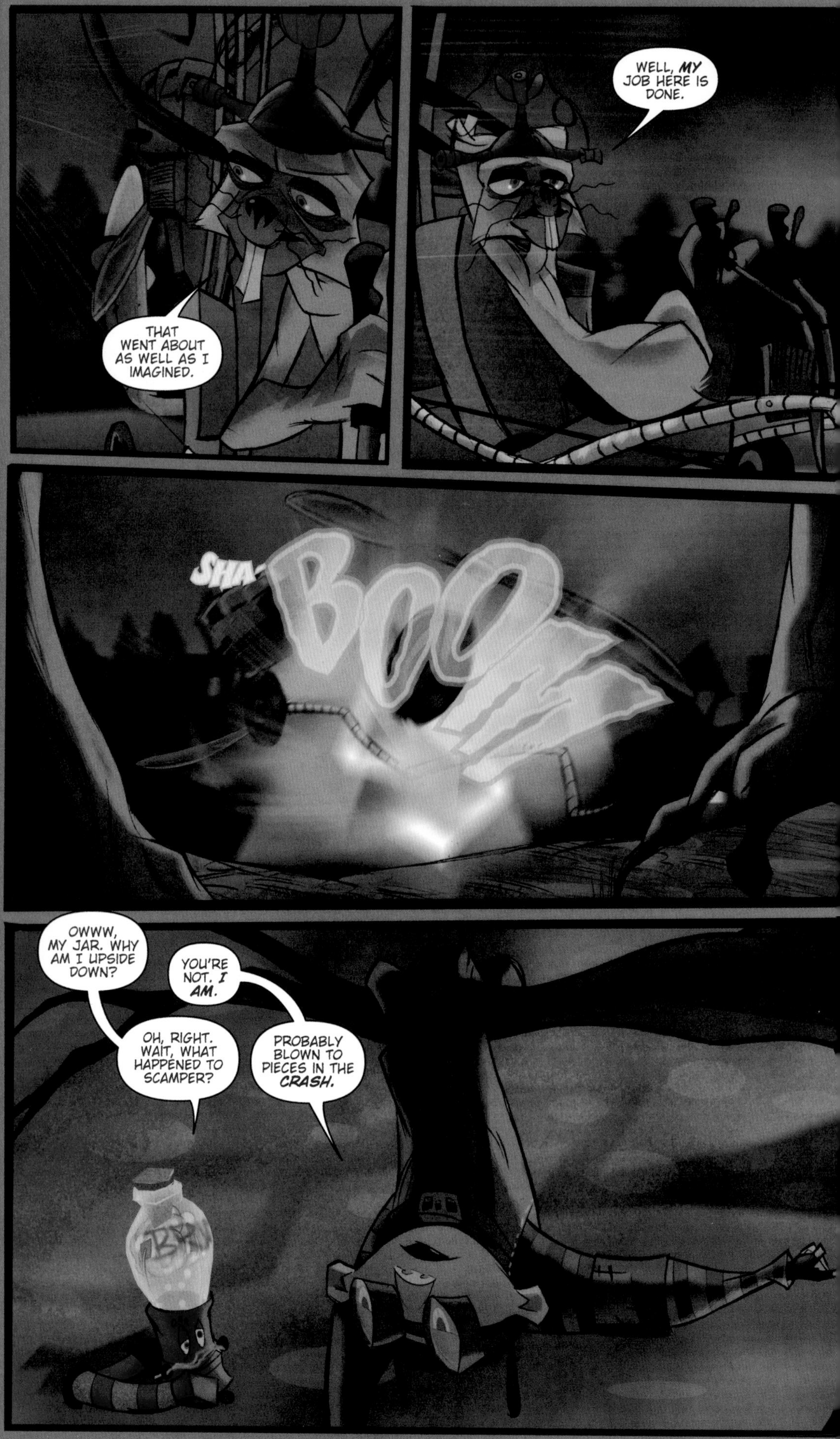

THAT WENT ABOUT AS WELL AS I IMAGINED.
WELL, MY JOB HERE IS DONE.
SHA-BOOM!
OWWW, MY JAR. WHY AM I UPSIDE DOWN?
YOU'RE NOT. I AM.
OH, RIGHT. WAIT, WHAT HAPPENED TO SCAMPER?
PROBABLY BLOWN TO PIECES IN THE CRASH.

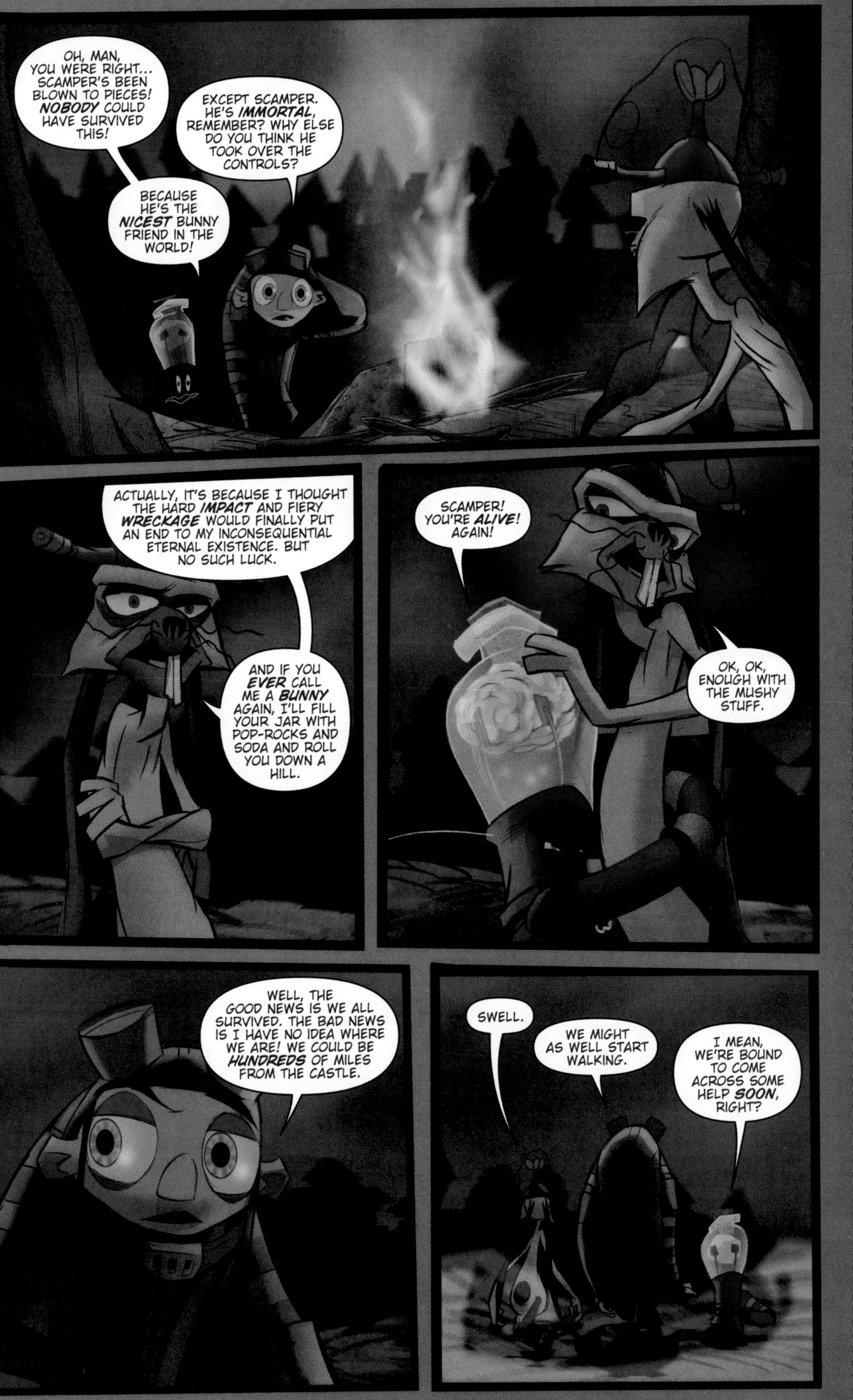
OH, MAN, YOU WERE RIGHT... SCAMPER'S BEEN BLOWN TO PIECES! NOBODY COULD HAVE SURVIVED THIS!
EXCEPT SCAMPER. HE'S IMMORTAL, REMEMBER? WHY ELSE DO YOU THINK HE TOOK OVER THE CONTROLS?
BECAUSE HE'S THE NICEST BUNNY FRIEND IN THE WORLD!
ACTUALLY, IT'S BECAUSE I THOUGHT THE HARD IMPACT AND FIERY WRECKAGE WOULD FINALLY PUT AN END TO MY INCONSEQUENTIAL ETERNAL EXISTENCE. BUT NO SUCH LUCK.
AND IF YOU EVER CALL ME A BUNNY AGAIN, I'LL FILL YOUR JAR WITH POP-ROCKS AND SODA AND ROLL YOU DOWN A HILL.
SCAMPER! YOU'RE ALIVE! AGAIN!
OK, OK, ENOUGH WITH THE MUSHY STUFF.
WELL, THE GOOD NEWS IS WE ALL SURVIVED. THE BAD NEWS IS I HAVE NO IDEA WHERE WE ARE! WE COULD BE HUNDREDS OF MILES FROM THE CASTLE.
SWELL.
WE MIGHT AS WELL START WALKING.
I MEAN, WE'RE BOUND TO COME ACROSS SOME HELP SOON, RIGHT?

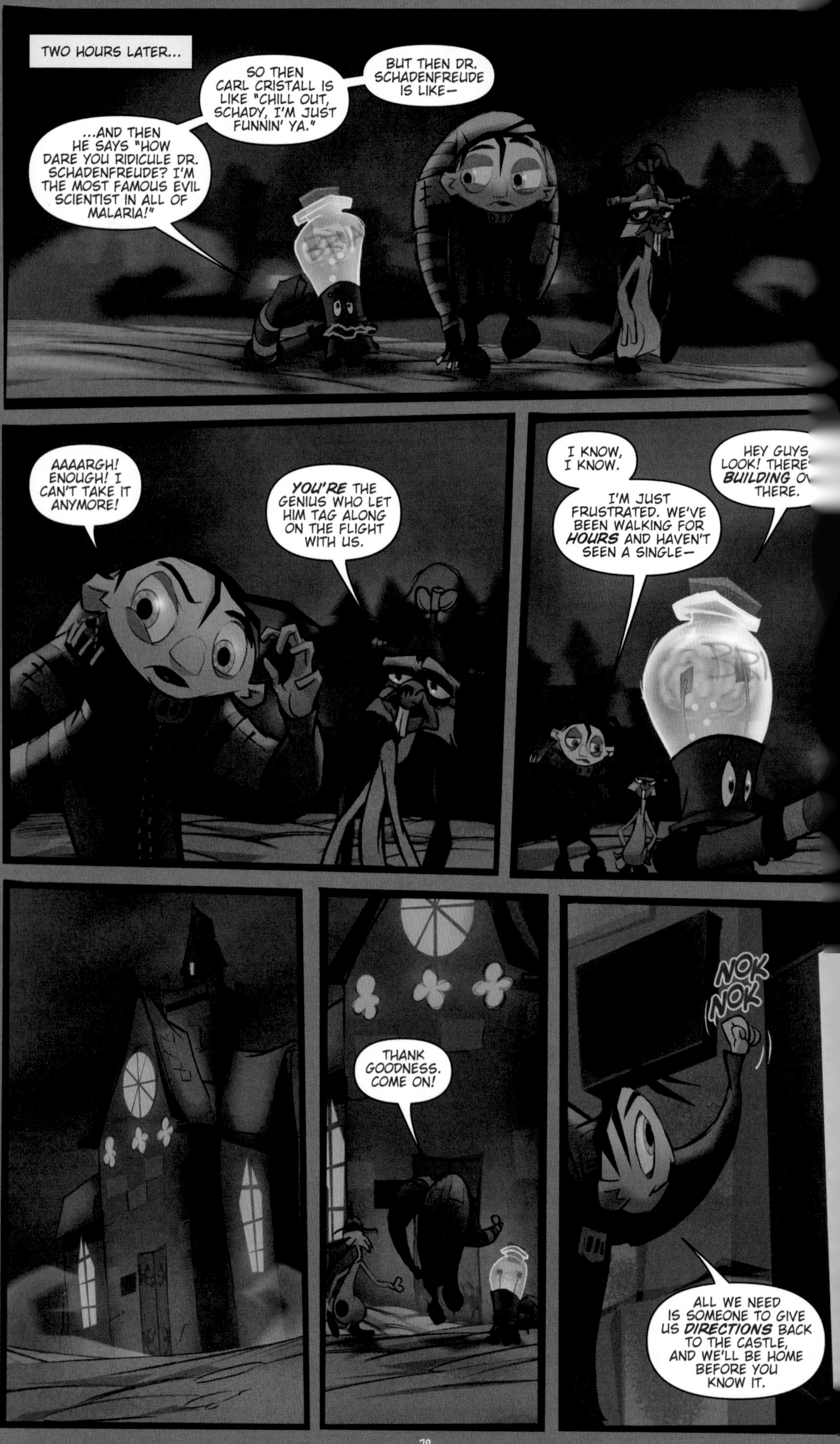
TWO HOURS LATER...
...AND THEN HE SAYS "HOW DARE YOU RIDICULE DR. SCHADENFREUDE? I'M THE MOST FAMOUS EVIL SCIENTIST IN ALL OF MALARIA!"
SO THEN CARL CRISTALL IS LIKE "CHILL OUT, SCHADY, I'M JUST FUNNIN' YA."
BUT THEN DR. SCHADENFREUDE IS LIKE—
AAAARGH! ENOUGH! I CAN'T TAKE IT ANYMORE!
YOU'RE THE GENIUS WHO LET HIM TAG ALONG ON THE FLIGHT WITH US.
I KNOW, I KNOW.
I'M JUST FRUSTRATED. WE'VE BEEN WALKING FOR HOURS AND HAVEN'T SEEN A SINGLE—
HEY GUYS, LOOK! THERE'S BUILDING OV THERE.
THANK GOODNESS. COME ON!
NOK NOK
ALL WE NEED IS SOMEONE TO GIVE US DIRECTIONS BACK TO THE CASTLE, AND WE'LL BE HOME BEFORE YOU KNOW IT.

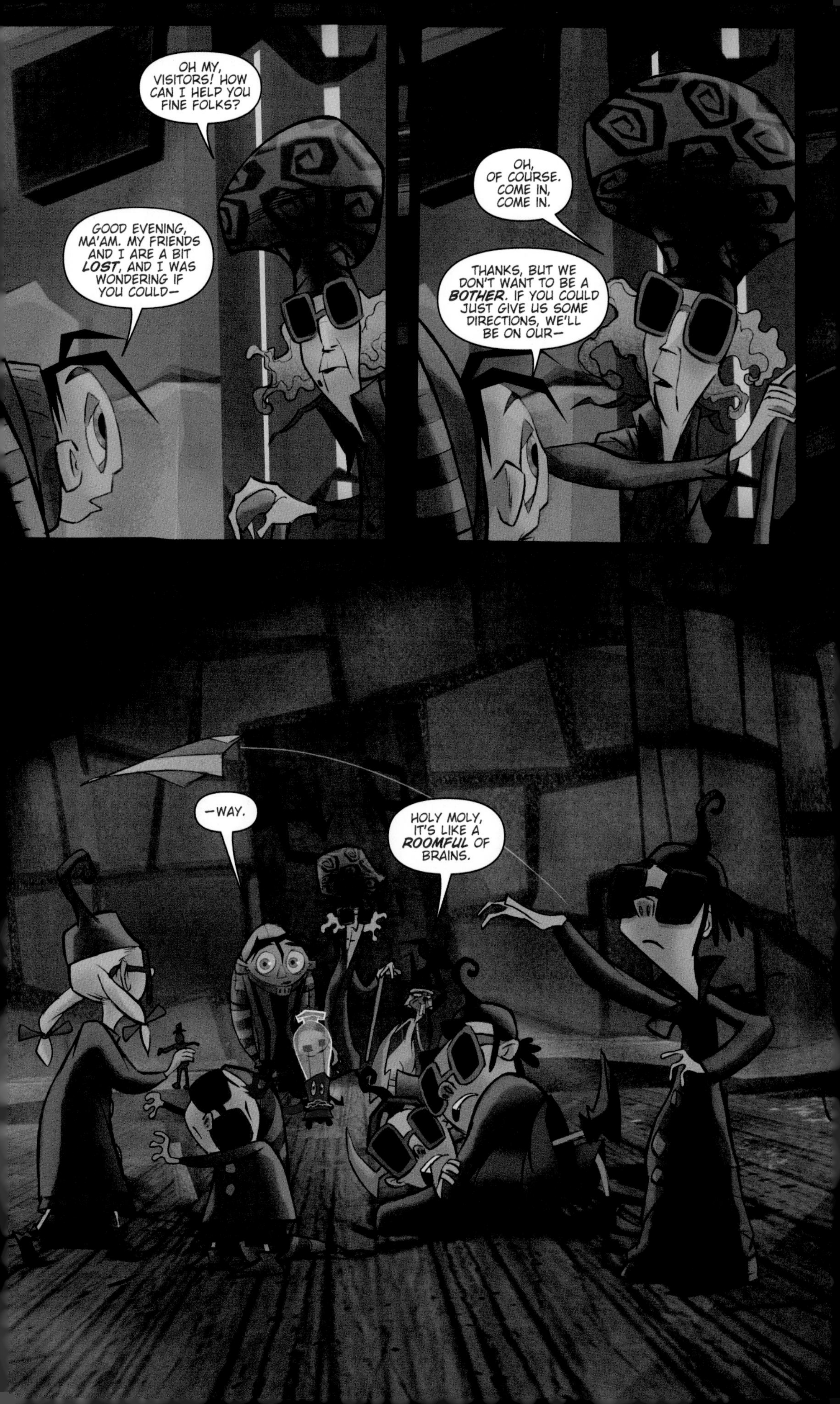

OH MY, VISITORS! HOW CAN I HELP YOU FINE FOLKS?
GOOD EVENING, MA'AM. MY FRIENDS AND I ARE A BIT LOST, AND I WAS WONDERING IF YOU COULD—
OH, OF COURSE. COME IN, COME IN.
THANKS, BUT WE DON'T WANT TO BE A BOTHER. IF YOU COULD JUST GIVE US SOME DIRECTIONS, WE'LL BE ON OUR—
—WAY.
HOLY MOLY, IT'S LIKE A ROOMFUL OF BRAINS.

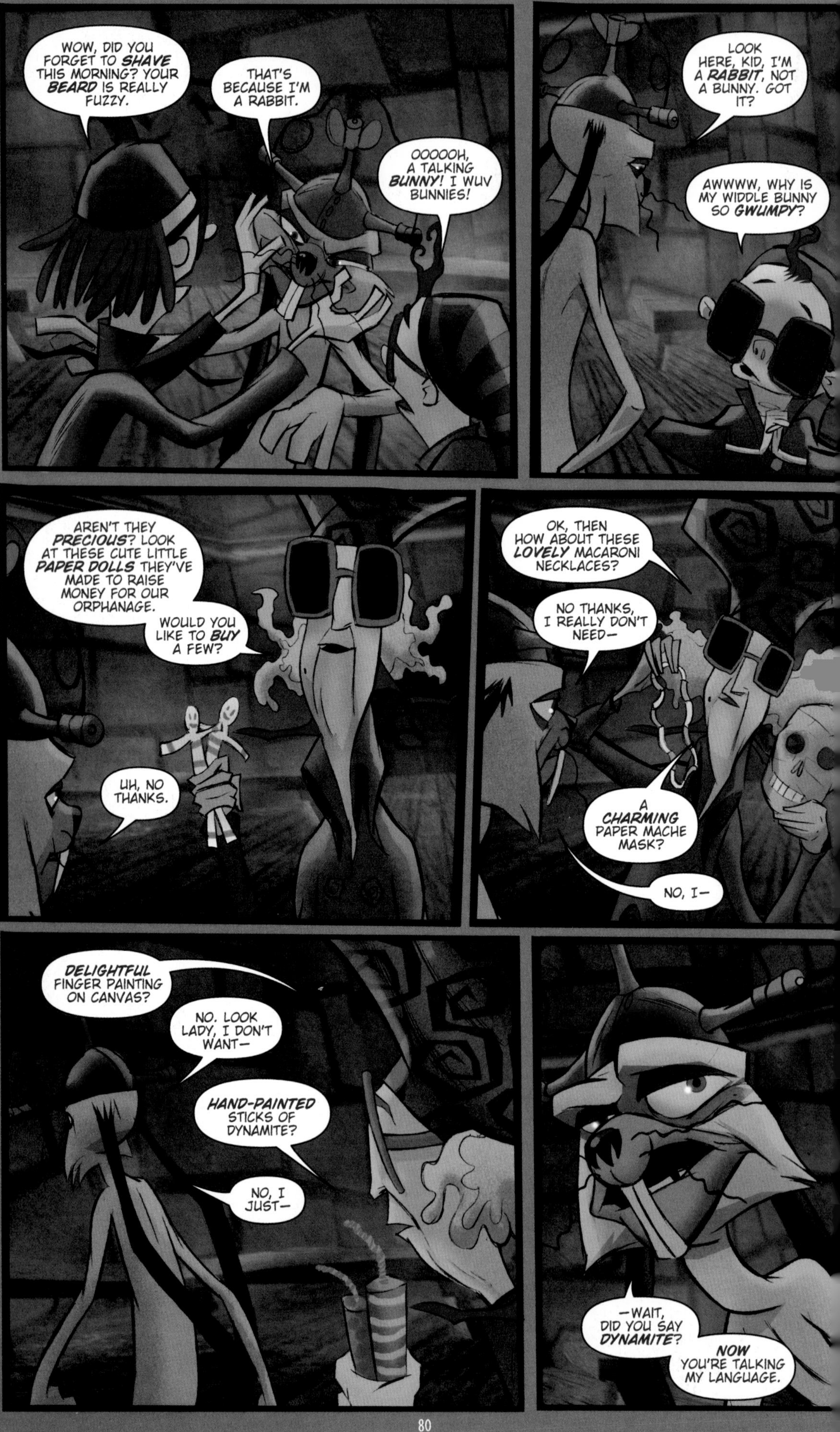

WOW, DID YOU FORGET TO SHAVE THIS MORNING? YOUR BEARD IS REALLY FUZZY.
THAT'S BECAUSE I'M A RABBIT.
OOOOOH, A TALKING BUNNY! I WUV BUNNIES!
LOOK HERE, KID, I'M A RABBIT, NOT A BUNNY. GOT IT?
AWWWW, WHY IS MY WIDDLE BUNNY SO GWUMPY?
AREN'T THEY PRECIOUS? LOOK AT THESE CUTE LITTLE PAPER DOLLS THEY'VE MADE TO RAISE MONEY FOR OUR ORPHANAGE.
WOULD YOU LIKE TO BUY A FEW?
UH, NO THANKS.
OK, THEN HOW ABOUT THESE LOVELY MACARONI NECKLACES?
NO THANKS, I REALLY DON'T NEED—
A CHARMING PAPER MACHE MASK?
NO, I—
DELIGHTFUL FINGER PAINTING ON CANVAS?
NO. LOOK LADY, I DON'T WANT—
HAND-PAINTED STICKS OF DYNAMITE?
NO, I JUST—
—WAIT, DID YOU SAY DYNAMITE?
NOW YOU'RE TALKING MY LANGUAGE.

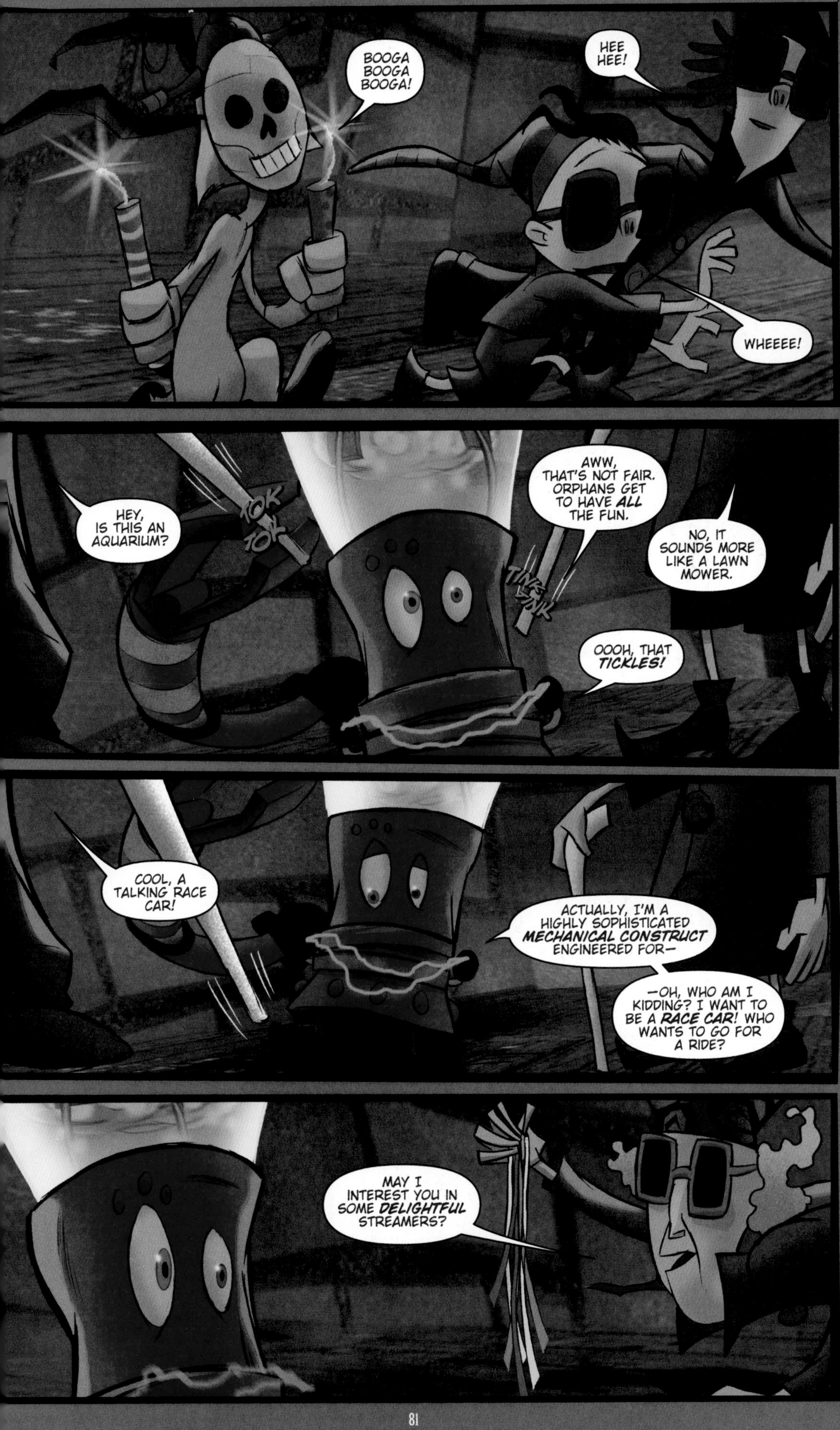
BOOGA BOOGA BOOGA!
HEE HEE!
WHEEEE!
HEY, IS THIS AN AQUARIUM?
TOK TOK
AWW, THAT'S NOT FAIR. ORPHANS GET TO HAVE ALL THE FUN.
TINK
NO, IT SOUNDS MORE LIKE A LAWN MOWER.
OOOH, THAT TICKLES!
COOL, A TALKING RACE CAR!
ACTUALLY, I'M A HIGHLY SOPHISTICATED MECHANICAL CONSTRUCT ENGINEERED FOR—
—OH, WHO AM I KIDDING? I WANT TO BE A RACE CAR! WHO WANTS TO GO FOR A RIDE?
MAY I INTEREST YOU IN SOME DELIGHTFUL STREAMERS?

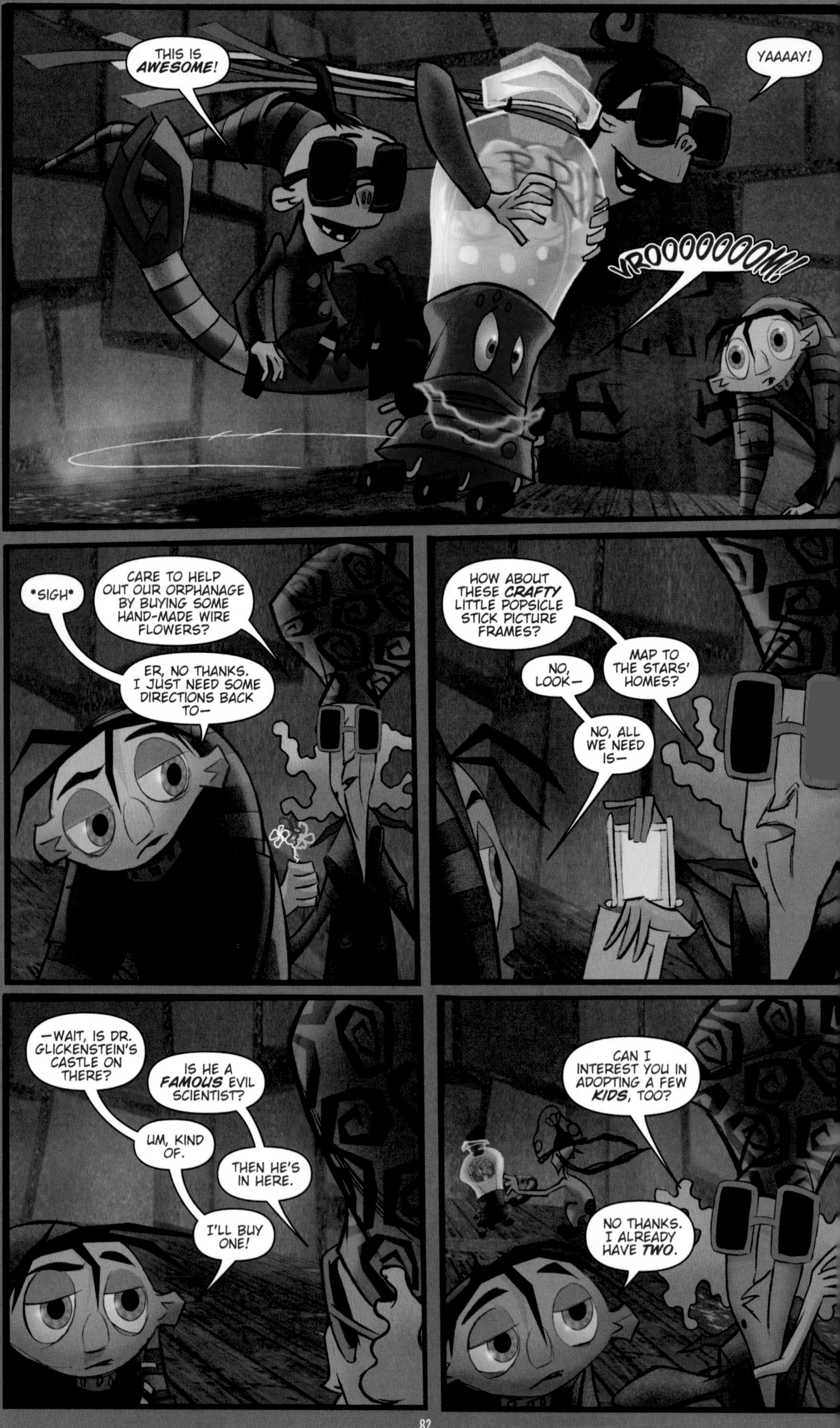
THIS IS AWESOME!
YAAAAY!
VROOOOOOOM!
SIGH
CARE TO HELP OUT OUR ORPHANAGE BY BUYING SOME HAND-MADE WIRE FLOWERS?
ER, NO THANKS. I JUST NEED SOME DIRECTIONS BACK TO—
HOW ABOUT THESE CRAFTY LITTLE POPSICLE STICK PICTURE FRAMES?
MAP TO THE STARS' HOMES?
NO, LOOK—
NO, ALL WE NEED IS—
—WAIT, IS DR. GLICKENSTEIN'S CASTLE ON THERE?
IS HE A FAMOUS EVIL SCIENTIST?
UM, KIND OF.
THEN HE'S IN HERE.
I'LL BUY ONE!
CAN I INTEREST YOU IN ADOPTING A FEW KIDS, TOO?
NO THANKS. I ALREADY HAVE TWO.

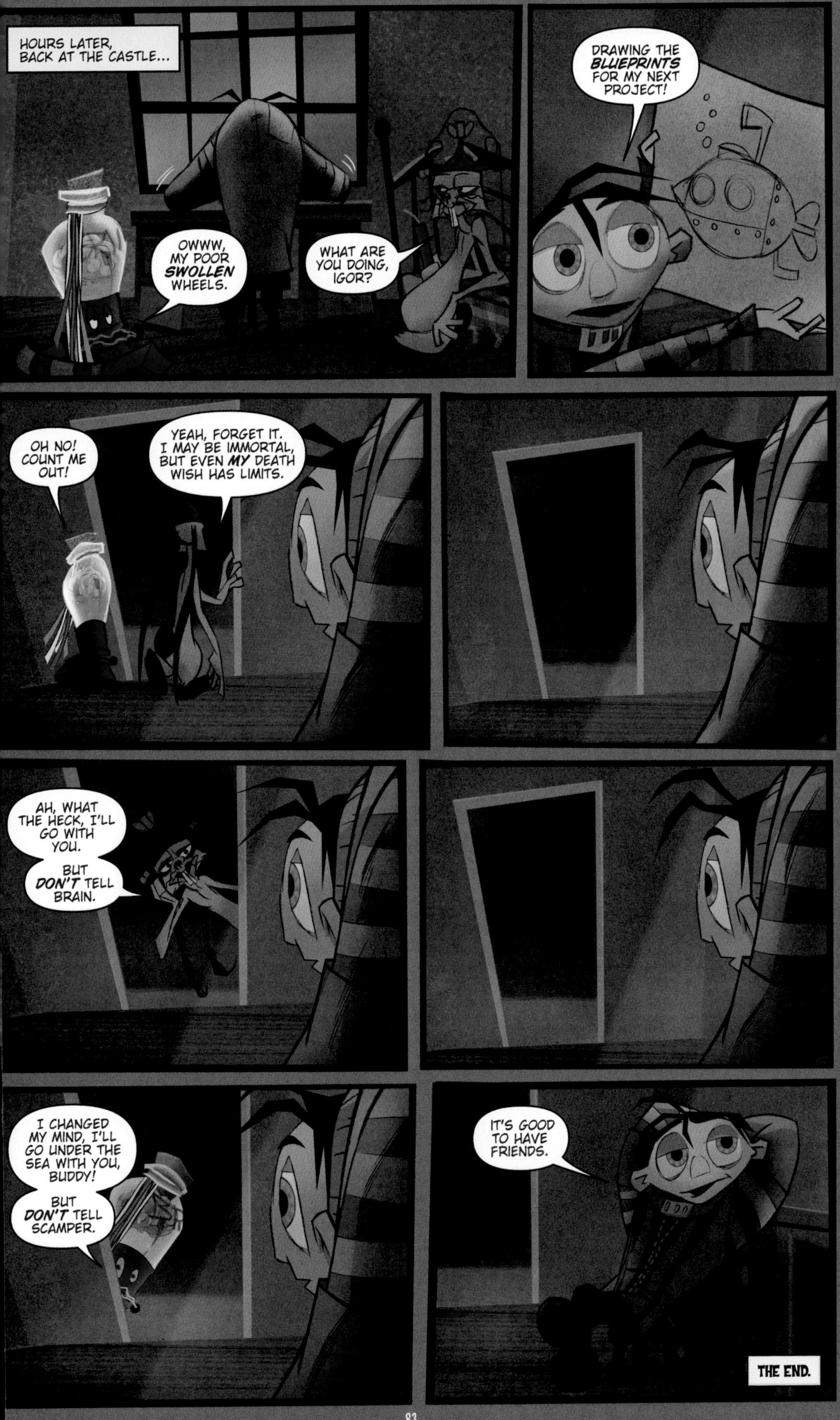
HOURS LATER, BACK AT THE CASTLE...
OWWW, MY POOR SWOLLEN WHEELS.
WHAT ARE YOU DOING, IGOR?
DRAWING THE BLUEPRINTS FOR MY NEXT PROJECT!
OH NO! COUNT ME OUT!
YEAH, FORGET IT. I MAY BE IMMORTAL, BUT EVEN MY DEATH WISH HAS LIMITS.
AH, WHAT THE HECK, I'LL GO WITH YOU.
BUT DON'T TELL BRAIN.
I CHANGED MY MIND, I'LL GO UNDER THE SEA WITH YOU, BUDDY!
BUT DON'T TELL SCAMPER.
IT'S GOOD TO HAVE FRIENDS.
THE END.

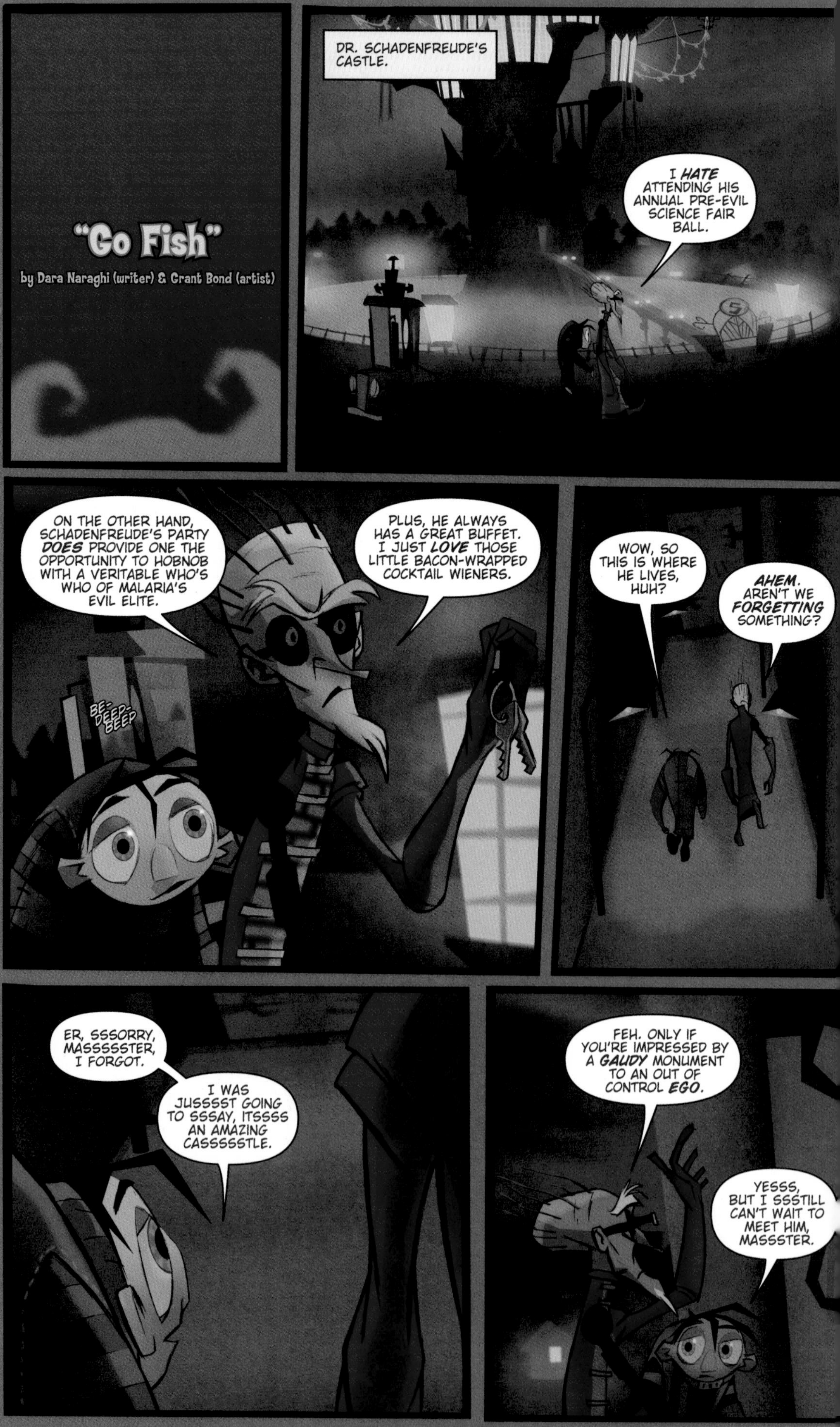
"Go Fish"
by Dara Naraghi (writer) & Grant Bond (artist)
DR. SCHADENFREUDE'S CASTLE.
I HATE ATTENDING HIS ANNUAL PRE-EVIL SCIENCE FAIR BALL.
ON THE OTHER HAND, SCHADENFREUDE'S PARTY DOES PROVIDE ONE THE OPPORTUNITY TO HOBNOB WITH A VERITABLE WHO'S WHO OF MALARIA'S EVIL ELITE.
PLUS, HE ALWAYS HAS A GREAT BUFFET. I JUST LOVE THOSE LITTLE BACON-WRAPPED COCKTAIL WIENERS.
BE-DEEP-BEEP
WOW, SO THIS IS WHERE HE LIVES, HUH?
AHEM. AREN'T WE FORGETTING SOMETHING?
ER, SSSORRY, MASSSSSTER, I FORGOT.
I WAS JUSSSST GOING TO SSSAY, ITSSSS AN AMAZING CASSSSSTLE.
FEH. ONLY IF YOU'RE IMPRESSED BY A GAUDY MONUMENT TO AN OUT OF CONTROL EGO.
YESSS, BUT I SSSTILL CAN'T WAIT TO MEET HIM, MASSSTER.

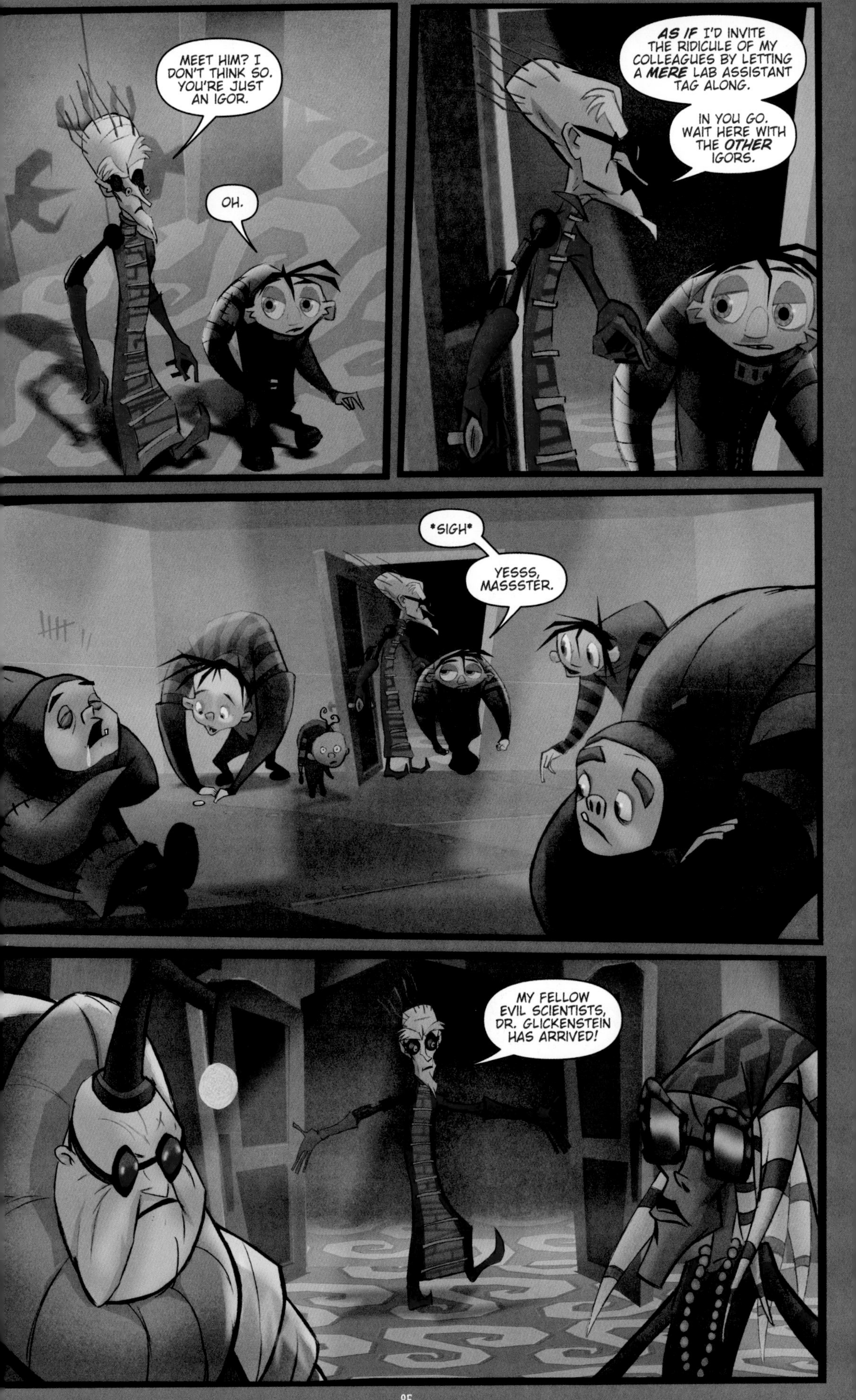
MEET HIM? I DON'T THINK SO. YOU'RE JUST AN IGOR.
OH.
AS IF I'D INVITE THE RIDICULE OF MY COLLEAGUES BY LETTING A MERE LAB ASSISTANT TAG ALONG.
IN YOU GO. WAIT HERE WITH THE OTHER IGORS.
SIGH
YESSS, MASSSTER.
MY FELLOW EVIL SCIENTISTS, DR. GLICKENSTEIN HAS ARRIVED!

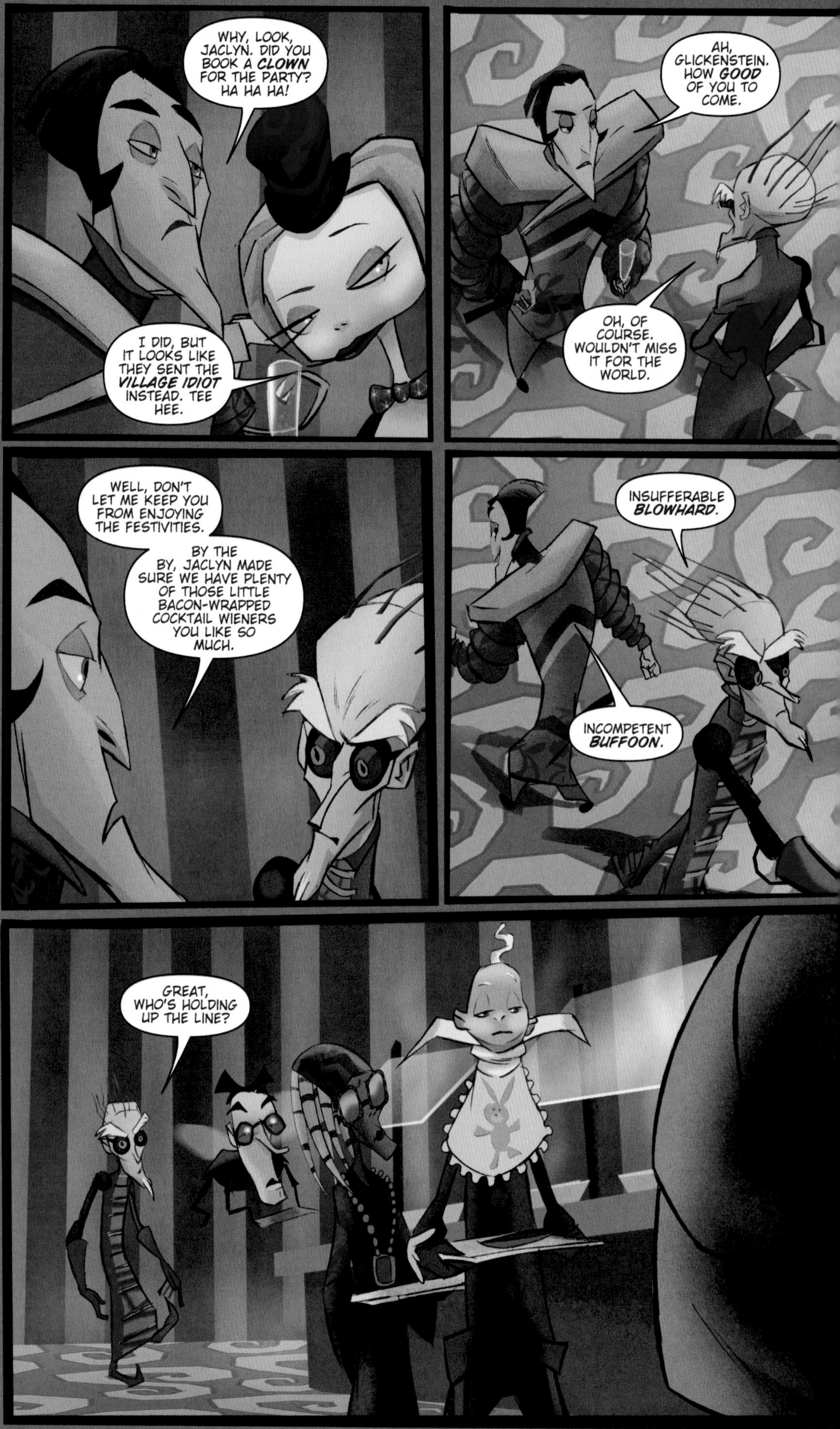
WHY, LOOK, JACLYN. DID YOU BOOK A CLOWN FOR THE PARTY? HA HA HA!
I DID, BUT IT LOOKS LIKE THEY SENT THE VILLAGE IDIOT INSTEAD. TEE HEE.
AH, GLICKENSTEIN. HOW GOOD OF YOU TO COME.
OH, OF COURSE. WOULDN'T MISS IT FOR THE WORLD.
WELL, DON'T LET ME KEEP YOU FROM ENJOYING THE FESTIVITIES.
BY THE BY, JACLYN MADE SURE WE HAVE PLENTY OF THOSE LITTLE BACON-WRAPPED COCKTAIL WIENERS YOU LIKE SO MUCH.
INSUFFERABLE BLOWHARD.
INCOMPETENT BUFFOON.
GREAT, WHO'S HOLDING UP THE LINE?

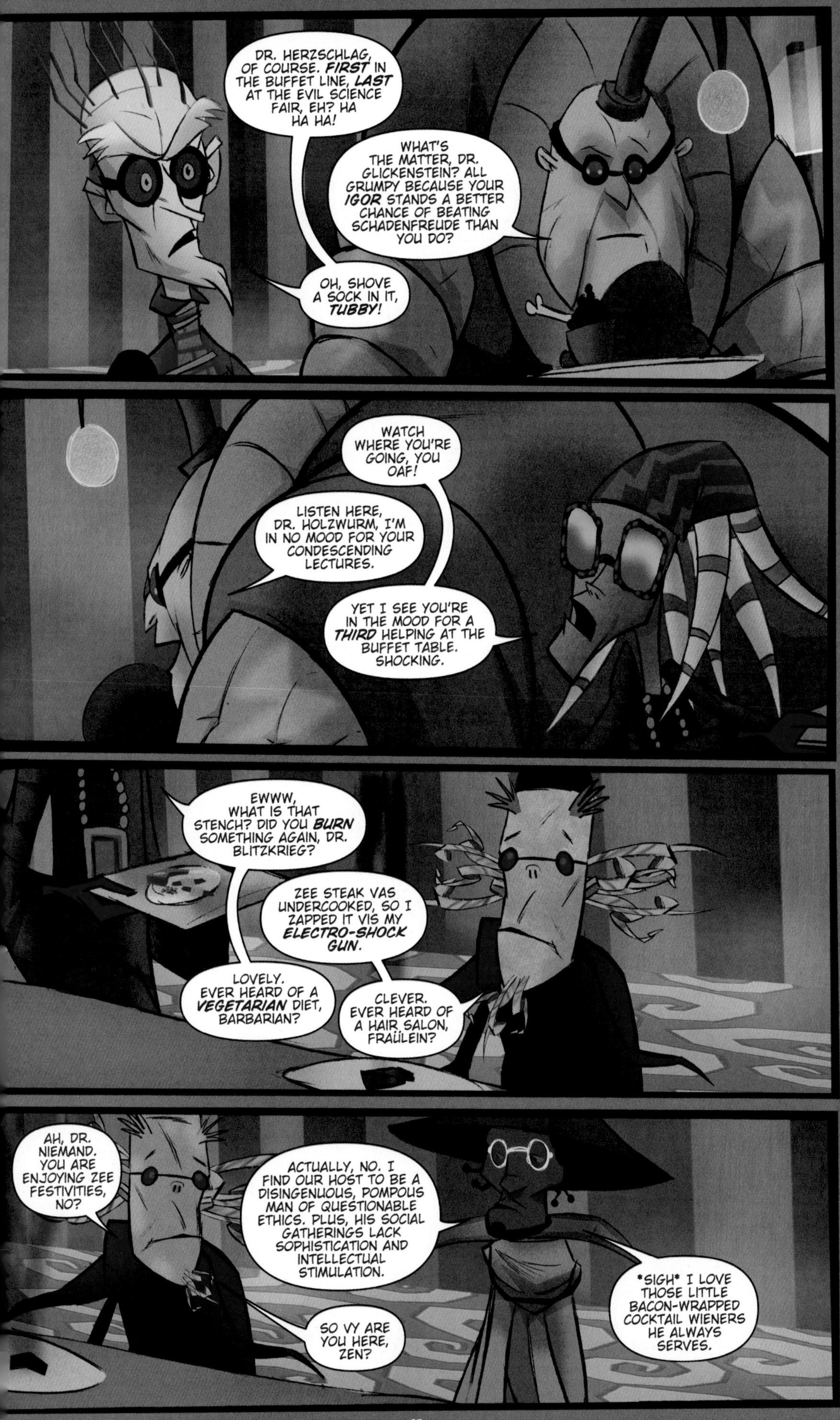
DR. HERZSCHLAG, OF COURSE. FIRST IN THE BUFFET LINE, LAST AT THE EVIL SCIENCE FAIR, EH? HA HA HA!
WHAT'S THE MATTER, DR. GLICKENSTEIN? ALL GRUMPY BECAUSE YOUR IGOR STANDS A BETTER CHANCE OF BEATING SCHADENFREUDE THAN YOU DO?
OH, SHOVE A SOCK IN IT, TUBBY!
WATCH WHERE YOU'RE GOING, YOU OAF!
LISTEN HERE, DR. HOLZWURM, I'M IN NO MOOD FOR YOUR CONDESCENDING LECTURES.
YET I SEE YOU'RE IN THE MOOD FOR A THIRD HELPING AT THE BUFFET TABLE. SHOCKING.
EWWW, WHAT IS THAT STENCH? DID YOU BURN SOMETHING AGAIN, DR. BLITZKRIEG?
ZEE STEAK VAS UNDERCOOKED, SO I ZAPPED IT VIS MY ELECTRO-SHOCK GUN.
LOVELY. EVER HEARD OF A VEGETARIAN DIET, BARBARIAN?
CLEVER. EVER HEARD OF A HAIR SALON, FRAÜLEIN?
AH, DR. NIEMAND. YOU ARE ENJOYING ZEE FESTIVITIES, NO?
ACTUALLY, NO. I FIND OUR HOST TO BE A DISINGENUOUS, POMPOUS MAN OF QUESTIONABLE ETHICS. PLUS, HIS SOCIAL GATHERINGS LACK SOPHISTICATION AND INTELLECTUAL STIMULATION.
SO VY ARE YOU HERE, ZEN?
SIGH I LOVE THOSE LITTLE BACON-WRAPPED COCKTAIL WIENERS HE ALWAYS SERVES.

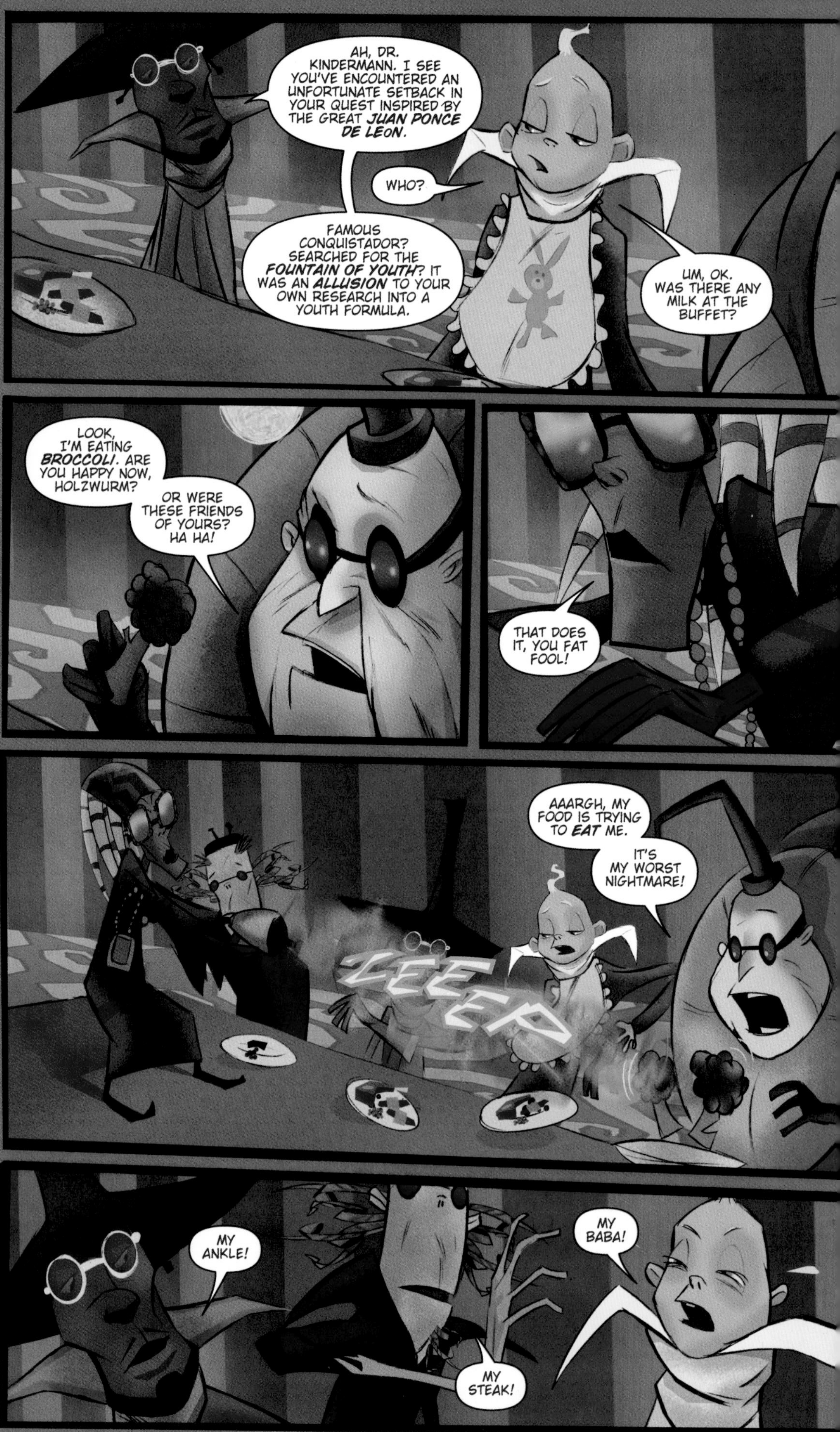
AH, DR. KINDERMANN. I SEE YOU'VE ENCOUNTERED AN UNFORTUNATE SETBACK IN YOUR QUEST INSPIRED BY THE GREAT JUAN PONCE DE LEON.
WHO?
FAMOUS CONQUISTADOR? SEARCHED FOR THE FOUNTAIN OF YOUTH? IT WAS AN ALLUSION TO YOUR OWN RESEARCH INTO A YOUTH FORMULA.
UM, OK. WAS THERE ANY MILK AT THE BUFFET?
LOOK, I'M EATING BROCCOLI. ARE YOU HAPPY NOW, HOLZWURM?
OR WERE THESE FRIENDS OF YOURS? HA HA!
THAT DOES IT, YOU FAT FOOL!
ZEEEP
AAARGH, MY FOOD IS TRYING TO EAT ME.
IT'S MY WORST NIGHTMARE!
MY ANKLE!
MY STEAK!
MY BABA!

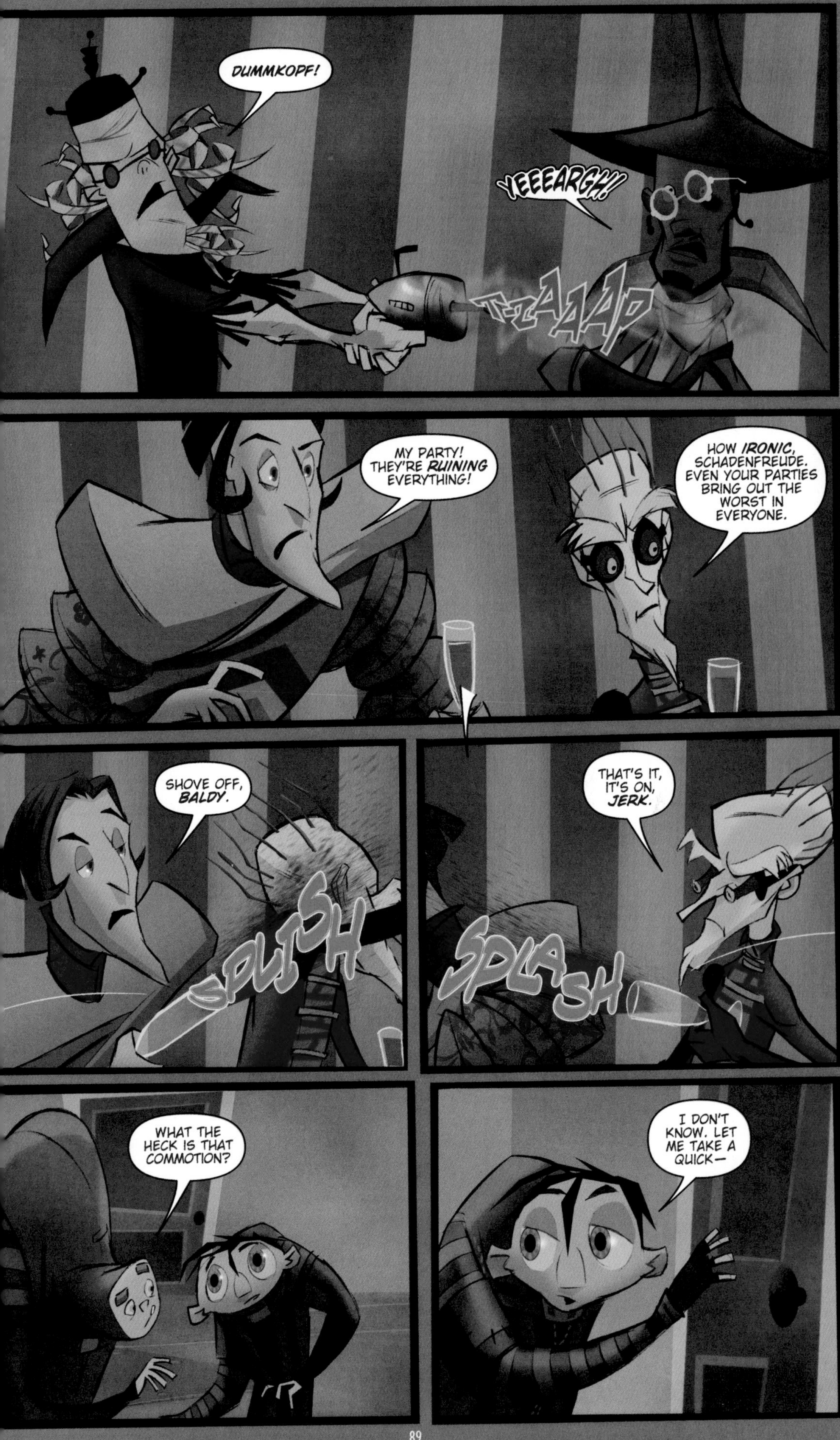
DUMMKOPF!
YEEEARGH!
T-ZAAAP
MY PARTY! THEY'RE RUINING EVERYTHING!
HOW IRONIC, SCHADENFREUDE. EVEN YOUR PARTIES BRING OUT THE WORST IN EVERYONE.
SHOVE OFF, BALDY.
SPLISH
THAT'S IT, IT'S ON, JERK.
SPLASH
WHAT THE HECK IS THAT COMMOTION?
I DON'T KNOW. LET ME TAKE A QUICK—

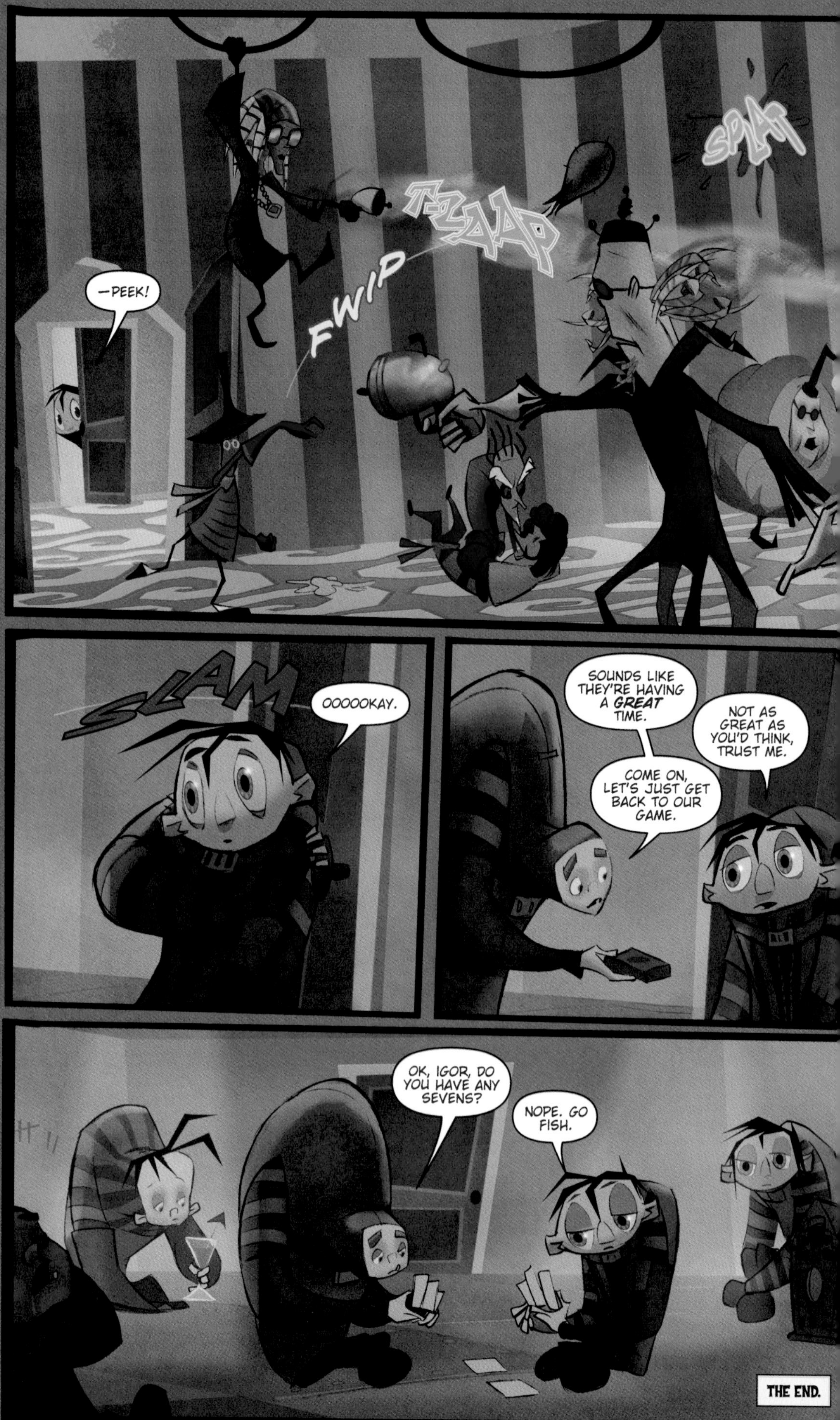

SPLAT
T-ZAAP
FWIP
—PEEK!
SLAM
OOOOOKAY.
SOUNDS LIKE THEY'RE HAVING A **GREAT** TIME.
COME ON, LET'S JUST GET BACK TO OUR GAME.
NOT AS GREAT AS YOU'D THINK, TRUST ME.
OK, IGOR, DO YOU HAVE ANY SEVENS?
NOPE. GO FISH.
THE END.

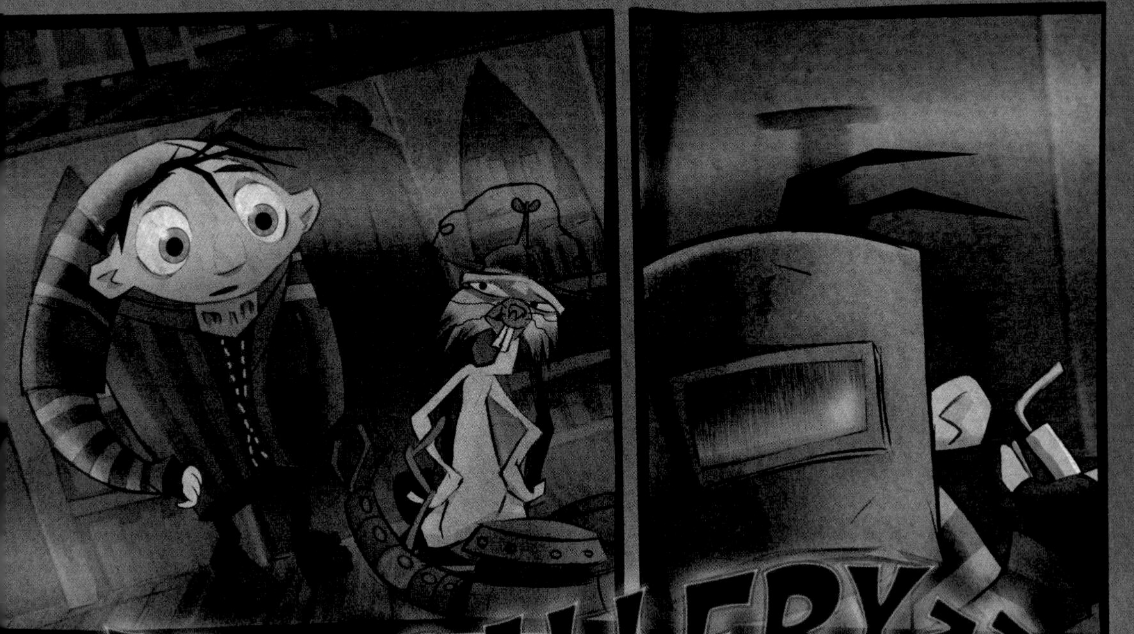

ART GALLERY >>

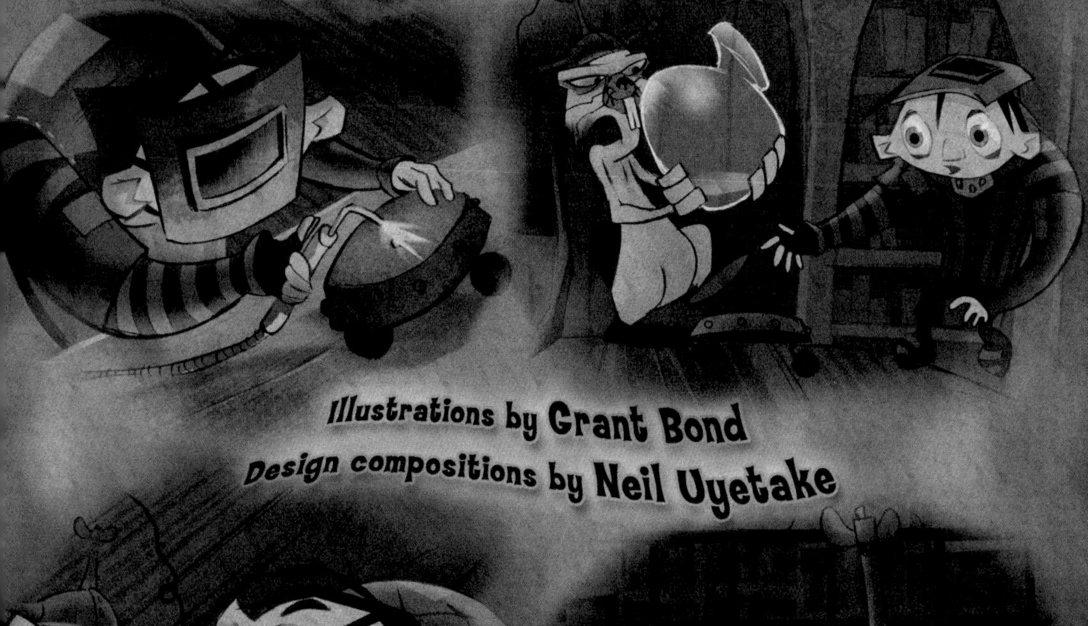

Illustrations by Grant Bond
Design compositions by Neil Uyetake

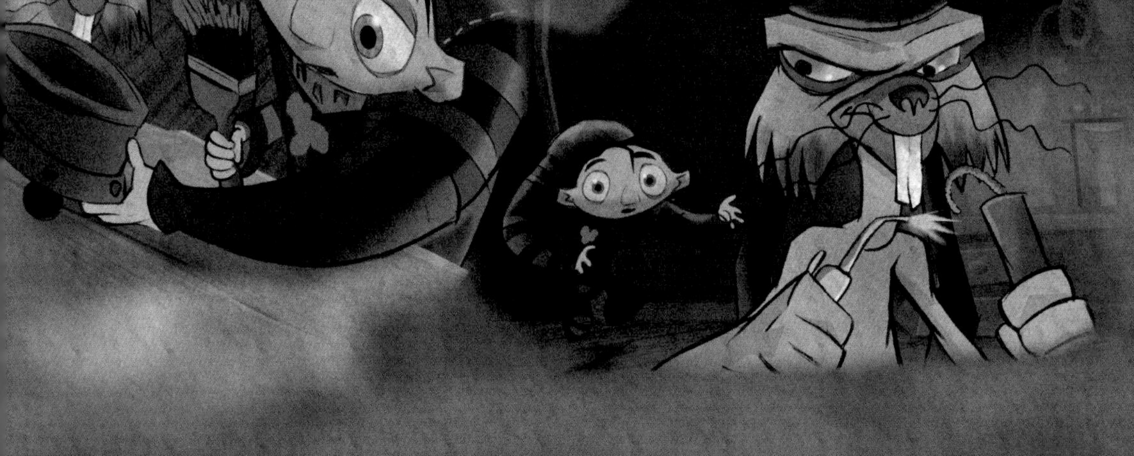

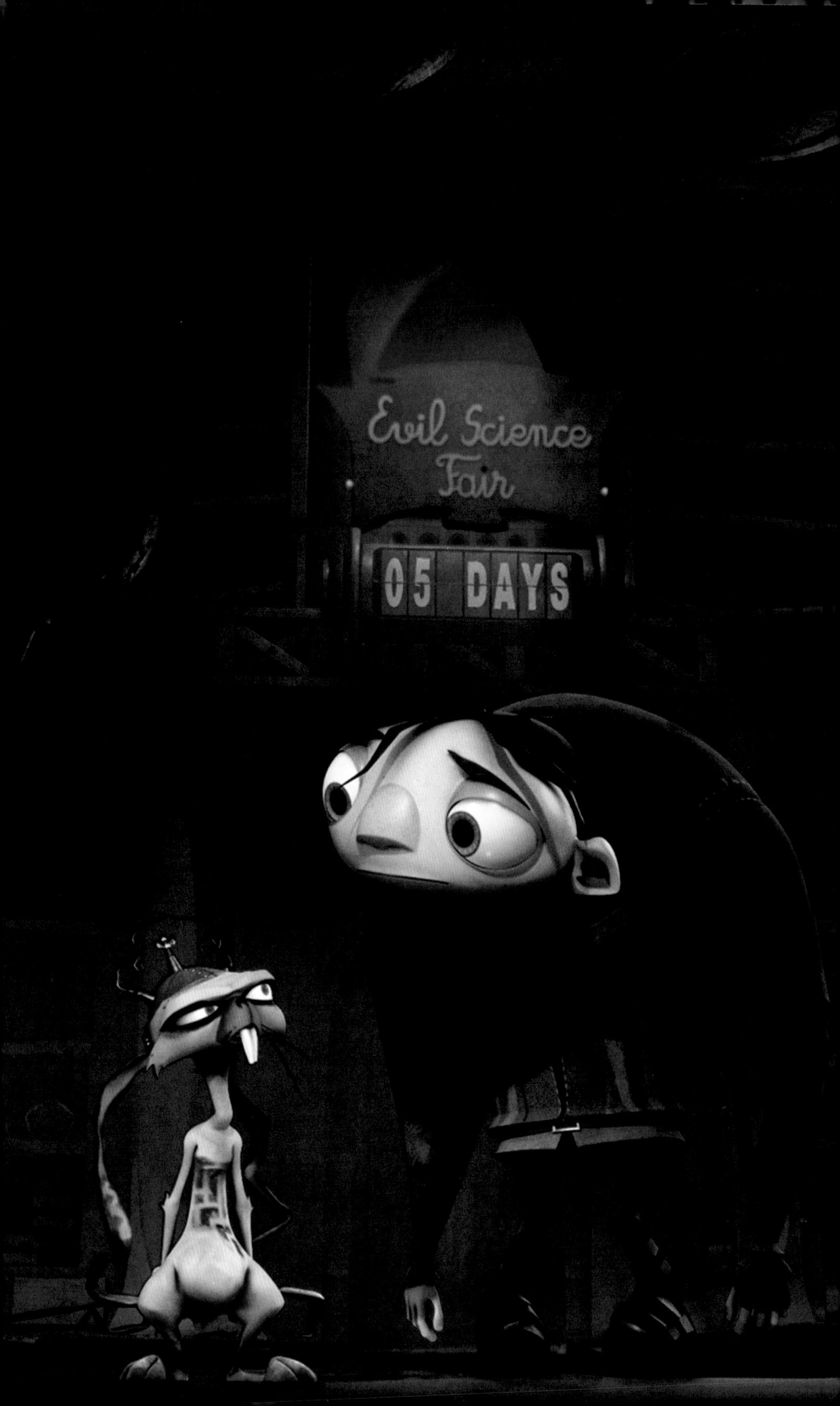
Evil Science
Fair
05 DAYS

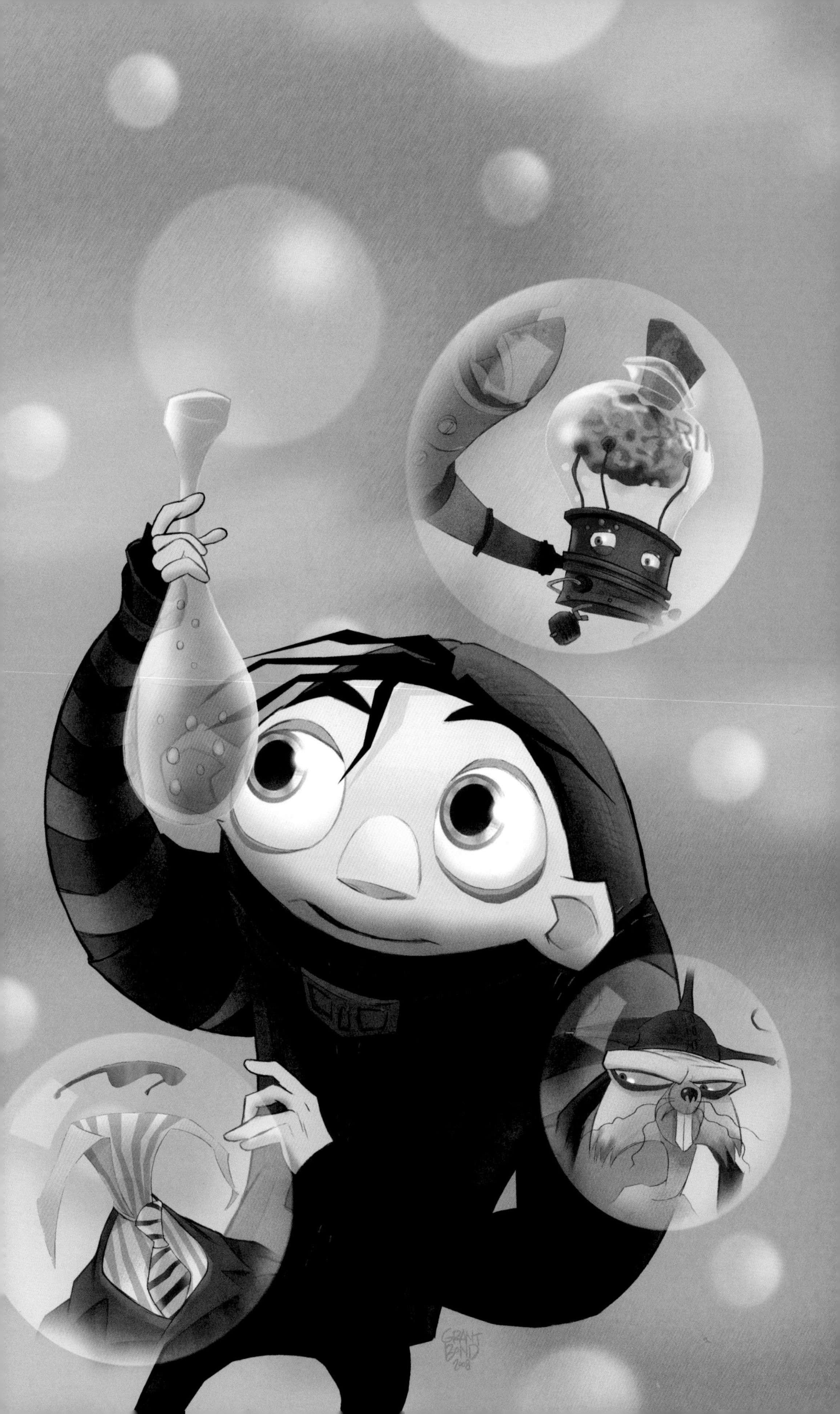
GRANT BOND 2008

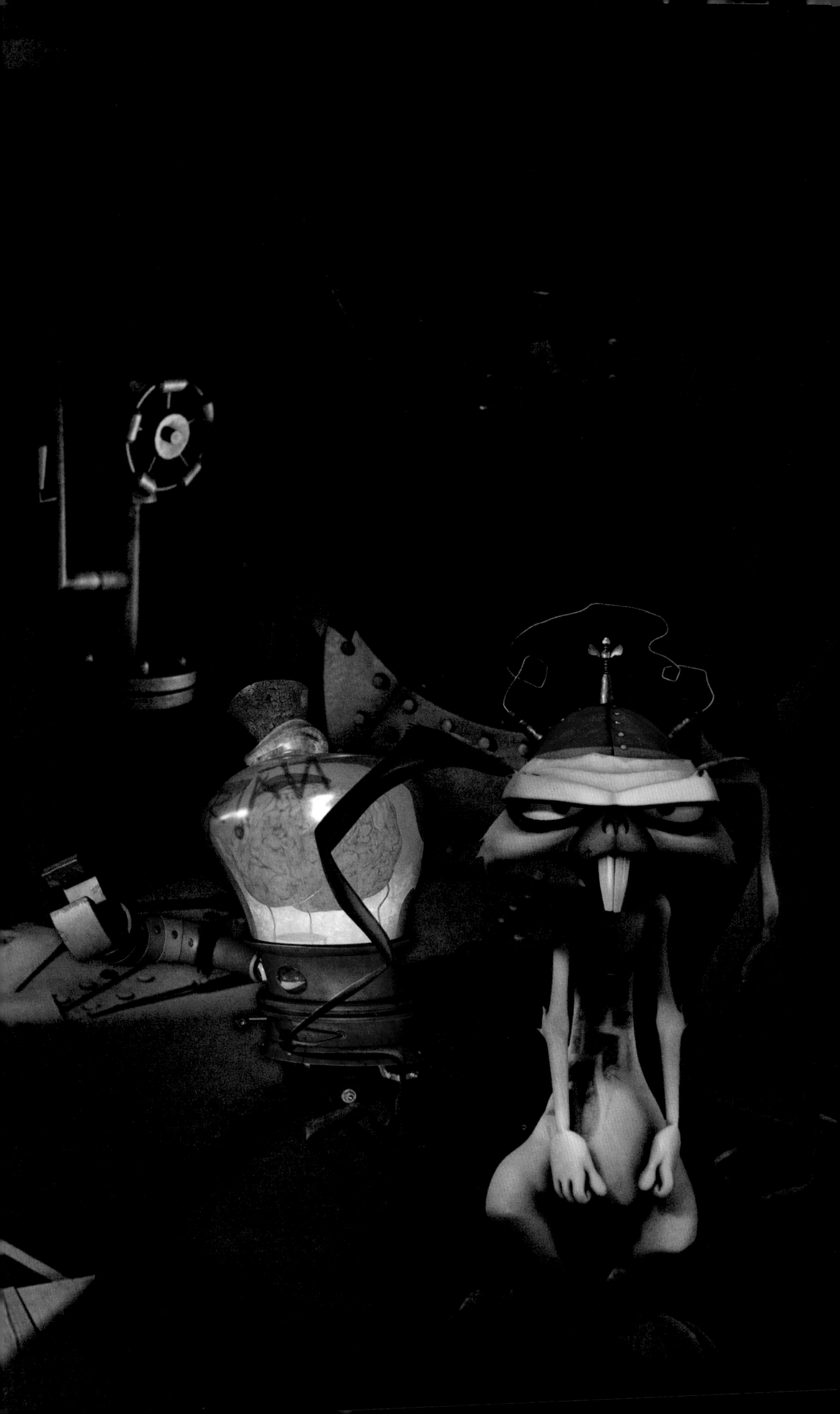

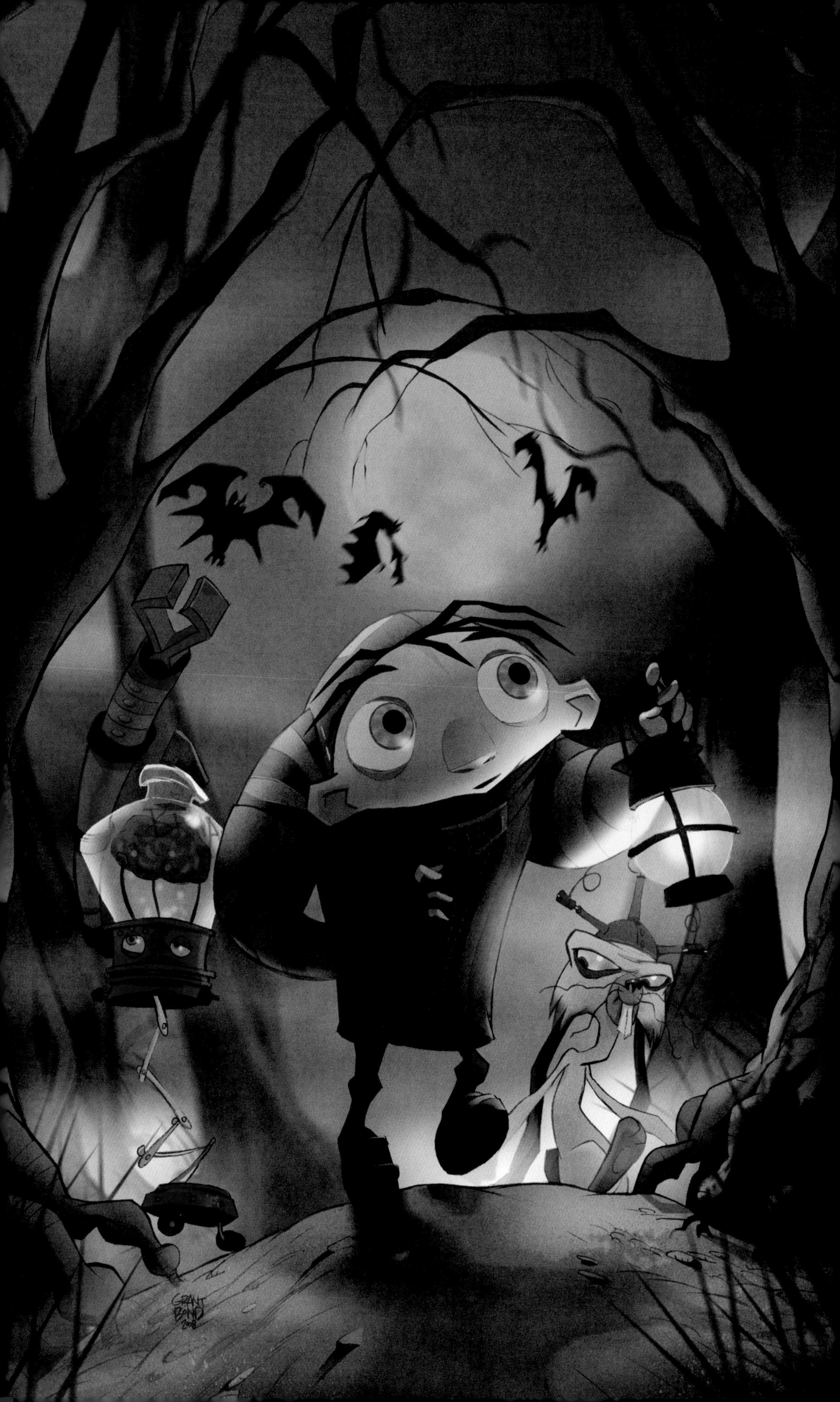

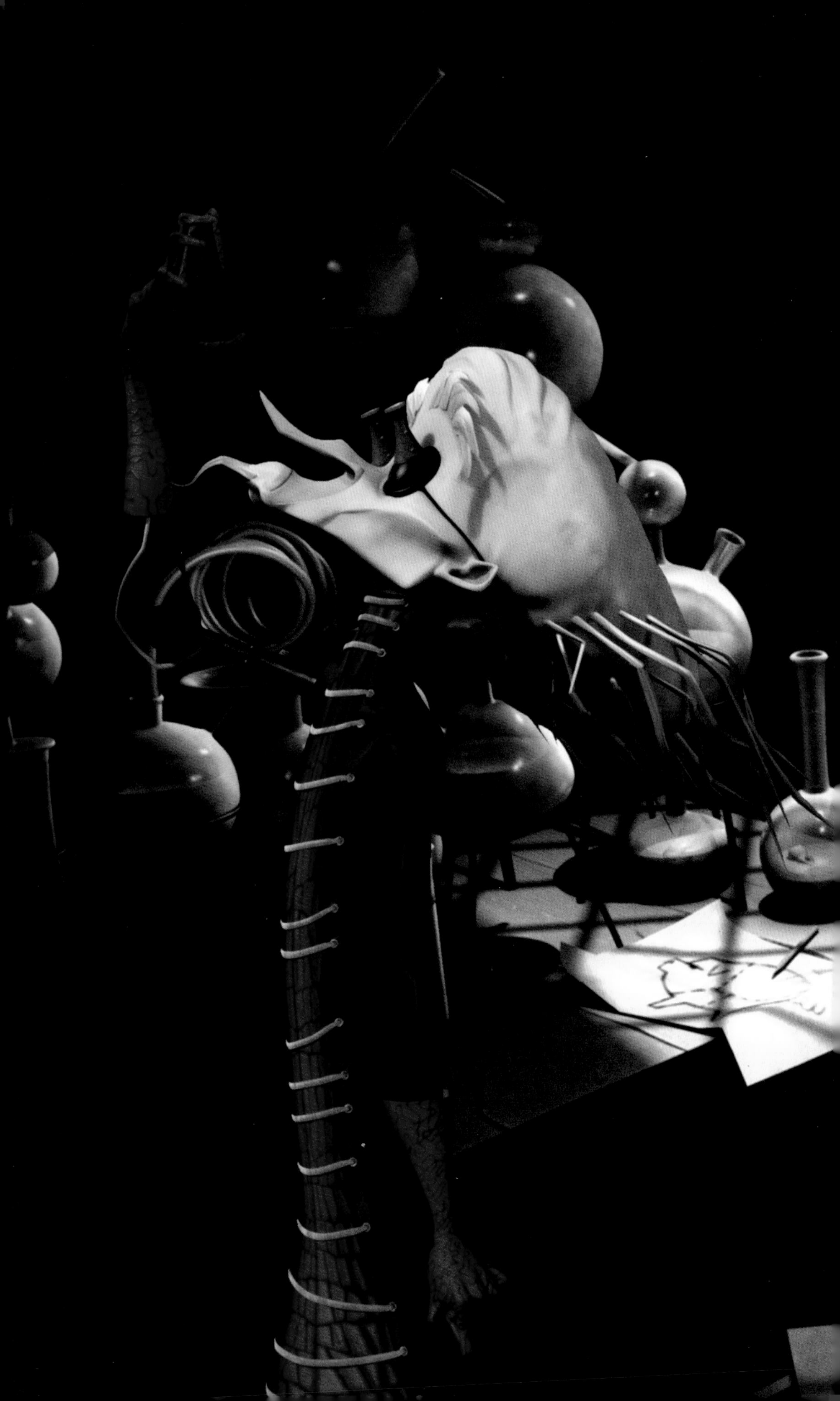

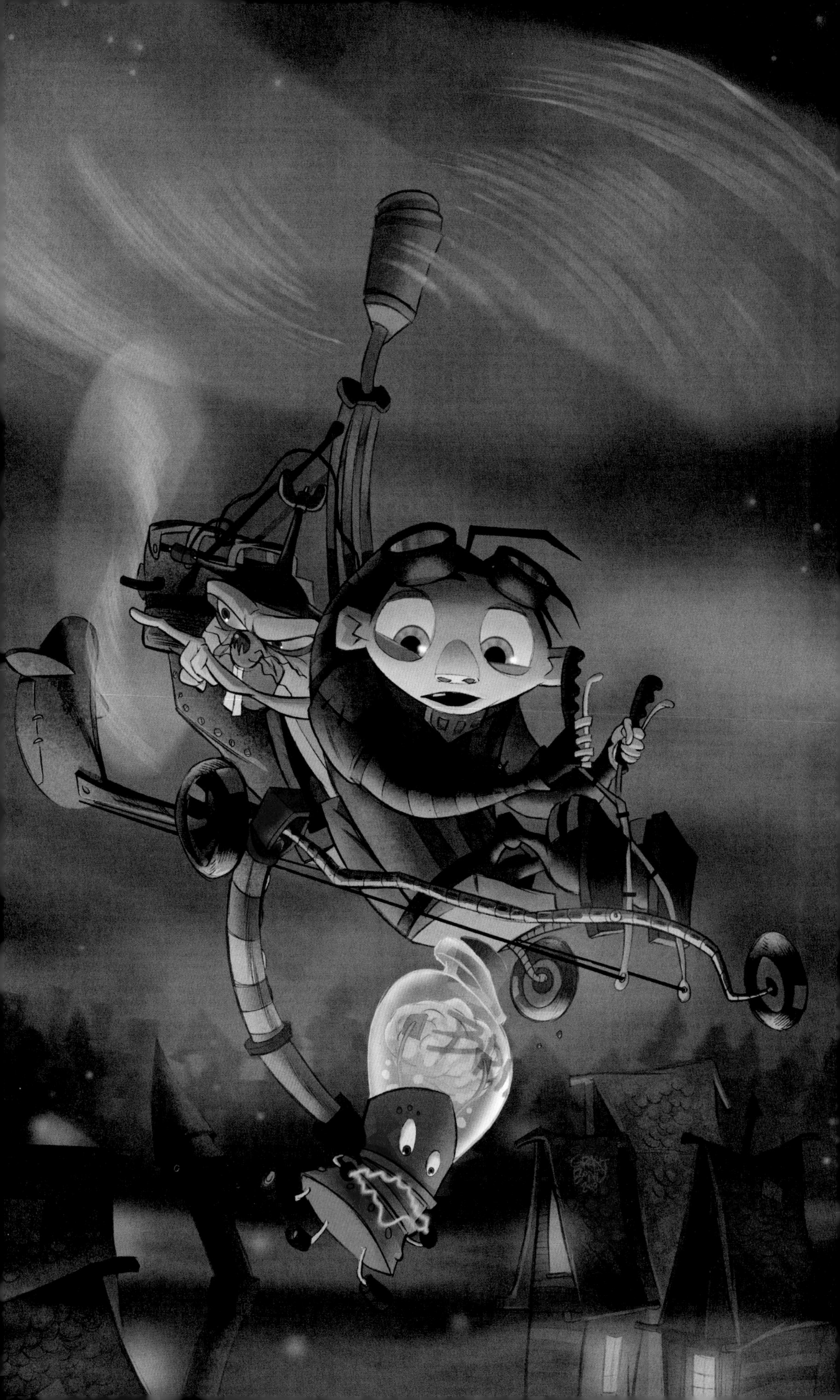

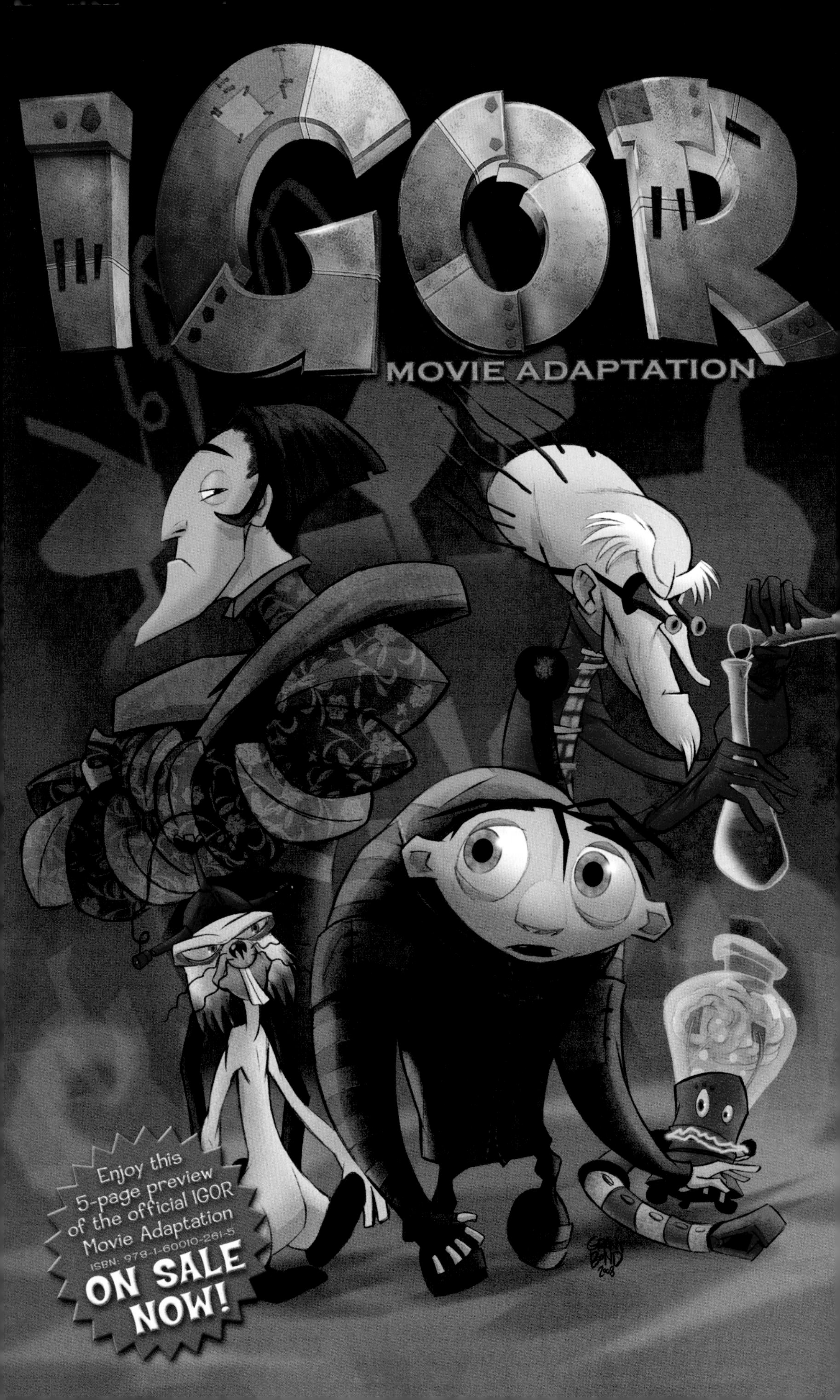
IGOR
MOVIE ADAPTATION
Enjoy this
5-page preview
of the official IGOR
Movie Adaptation
ISBN: 978-1-60010-261-5
ON SALE
NOW!

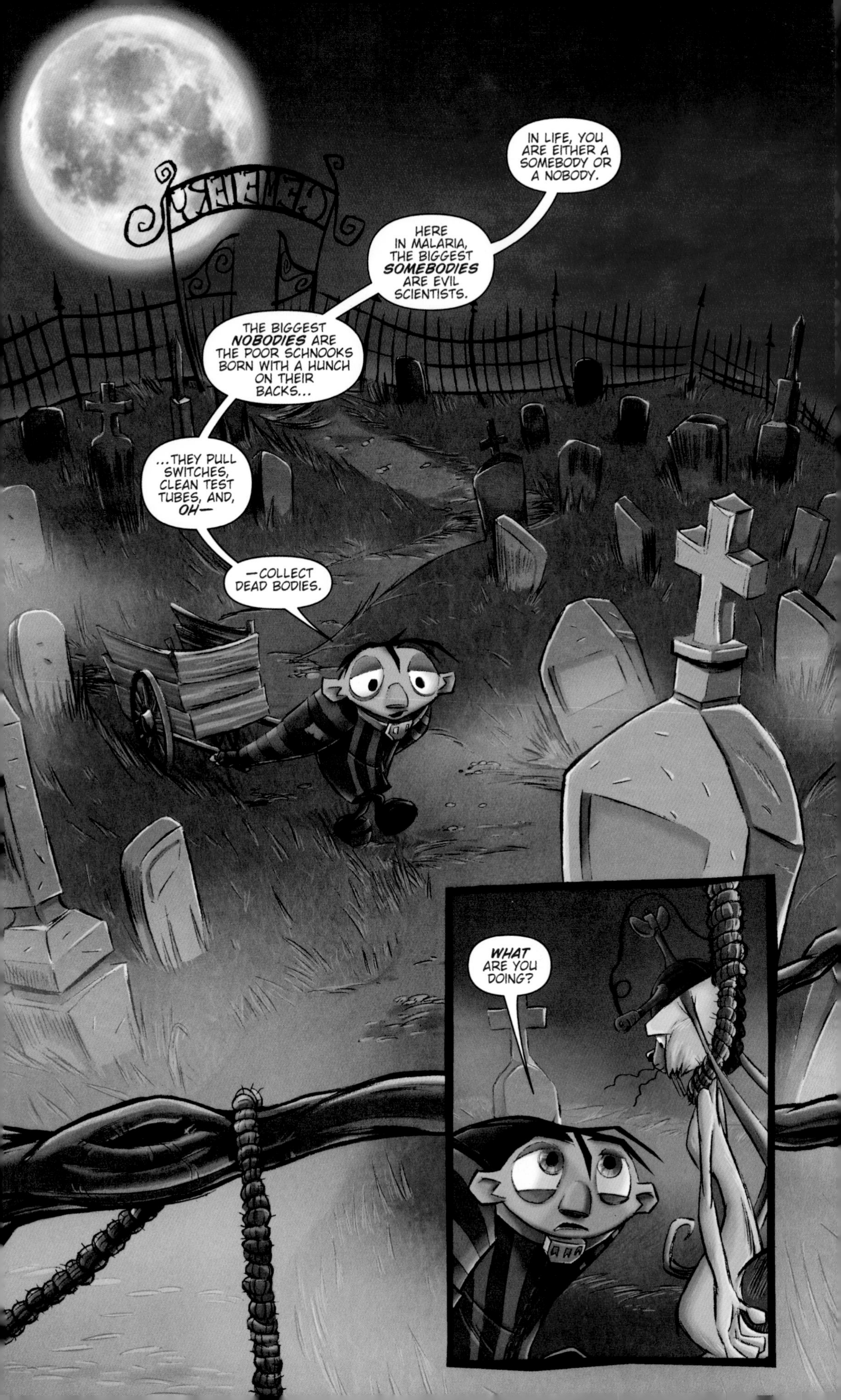
CEMETERY
IN LIFE, YOU ARE EITHER A SOMEBODY OR A NOBODY.
HERE IN MALARIA, THE BIGGEST SOMEBODIES ARE EVIL SCIENTISTS.
THE BIGGEST NOBODIES ARE THE POOR SCHNOOKS BORN WITH A HUNCH ON THEIR BACKS...
...THEY PULL SWITCHES, CLEAN TEST TUBES, AND, OH—
—COLLECT DEAD BODIES.
WHAT ARE YOU DOING?

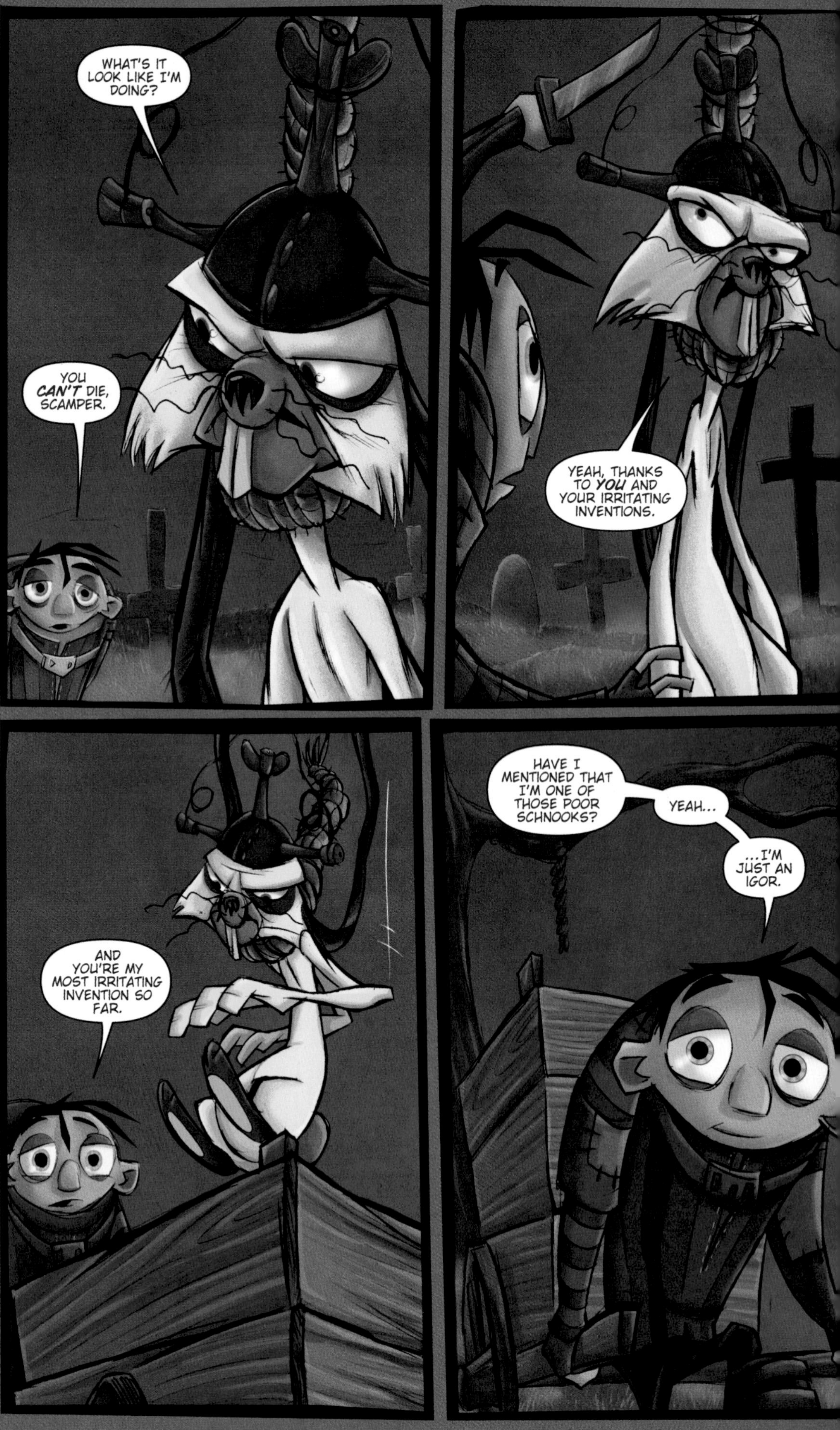
WHAT'S IT LOOK LIKE I'M DOING?
YOU CAN'T DIE, SCAMPER.
YEAH, THANKS TO YOU AND YOUR IRRITATING INVENTIONS.
AND YOU'RE MY MOST IRRITATING INVENTION SO FAR.
HAVE I MENTIONED THAT I'M ONE OF THOSE POOR SCHNOOKS?
YEAH...
...I'M JUST AN IGOR.

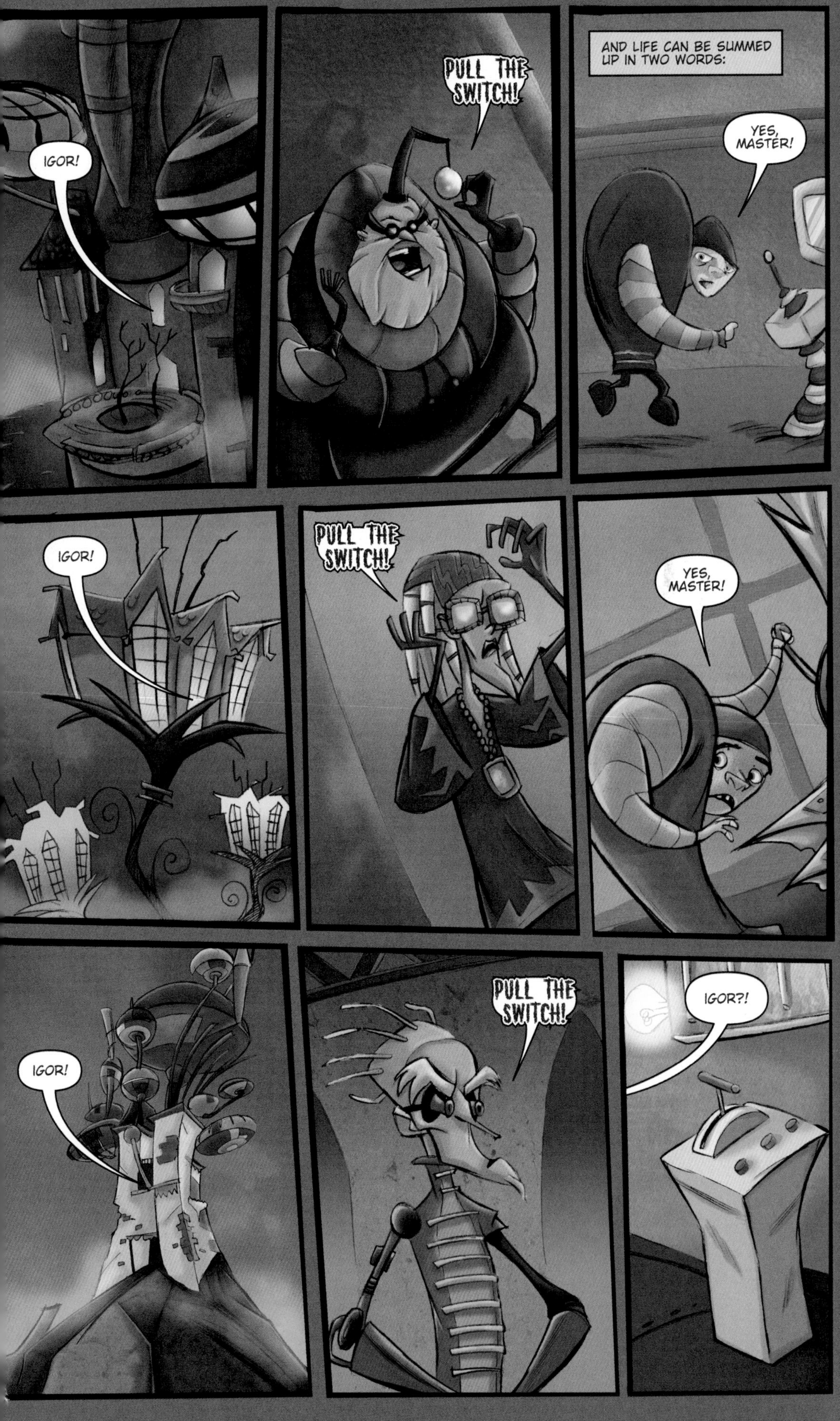
IGOR!
PULL THE SWITCH!
AND LIFE CAN BE SUMMED UP IN TWO WORDS:
YES, MASTER!
IGOR!
PULL THE SWITCH!
YES, MASTER!
IGOR!
PULL THE SWITCH!
IGOR?!

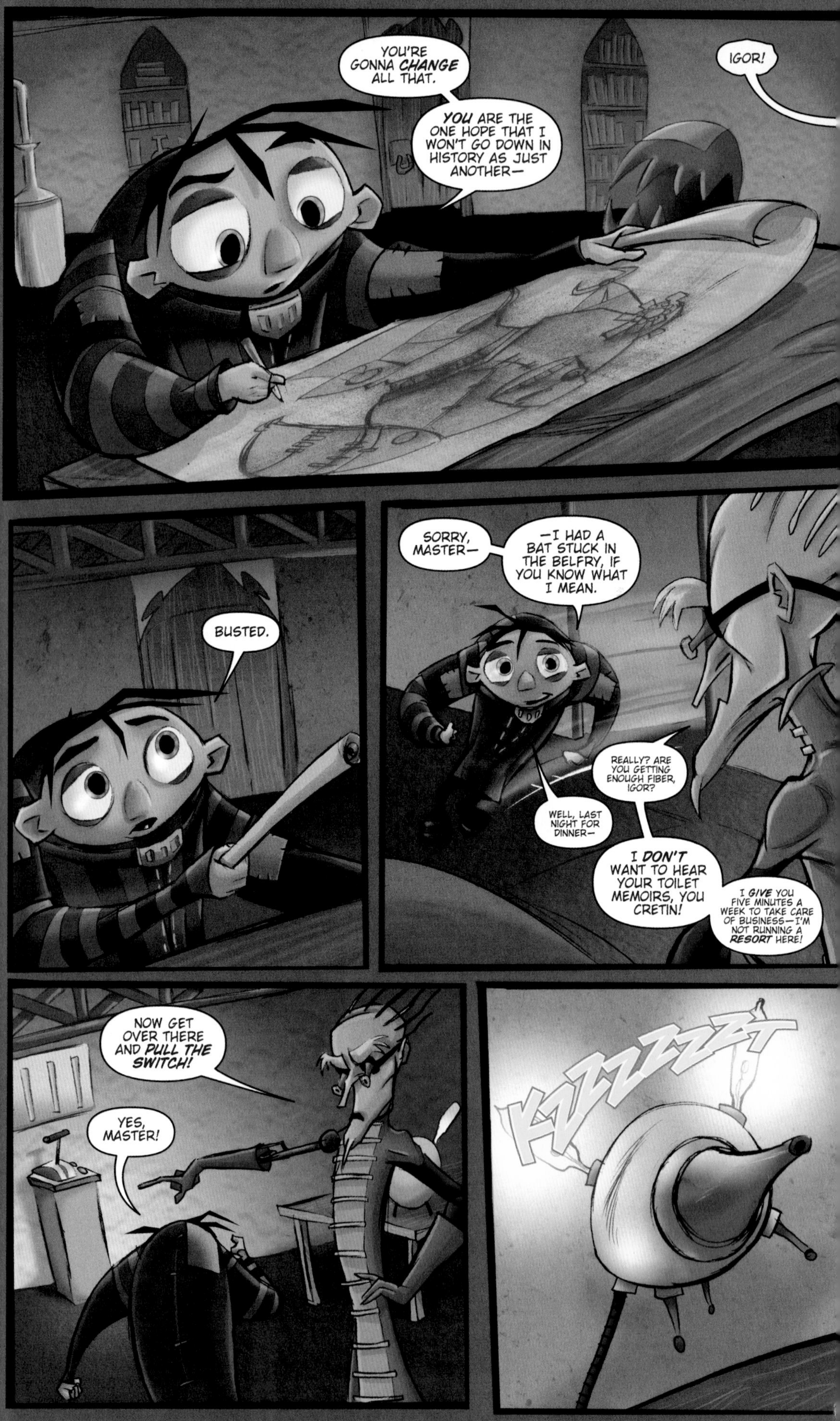
YOU'RE GONNA CHANGE ALL THAT.
YOU ARE THE ONE HOPE THAT I WON'T GO DOWN IN HISTORY AS JUST ANOTHER—
IGOR!
BUSTED.
SORRY, MASTER—
—I HAD A BAT STUCK IN THE BELFRY, IF YOU KNOW WHAT I MEAN.
REALLY? ARE YOU GETTING ENOUGH FIBER, IGOR?
WELL, LAST NIGHT FOR DINNER—
I DON'T WANT TO HEAR YOUR TOILET MEMOIRS, YOU CRETIN!
I GIVE YOU FIVE MINUTES A WEEK TO TAKE CARE OF BUSINESS—I'M NOT RUNNING A RESORT HERE!
NOW GET OVER THERE AND PULL THE SWITCH!
YES, MASTER!
KZZZZZZZT

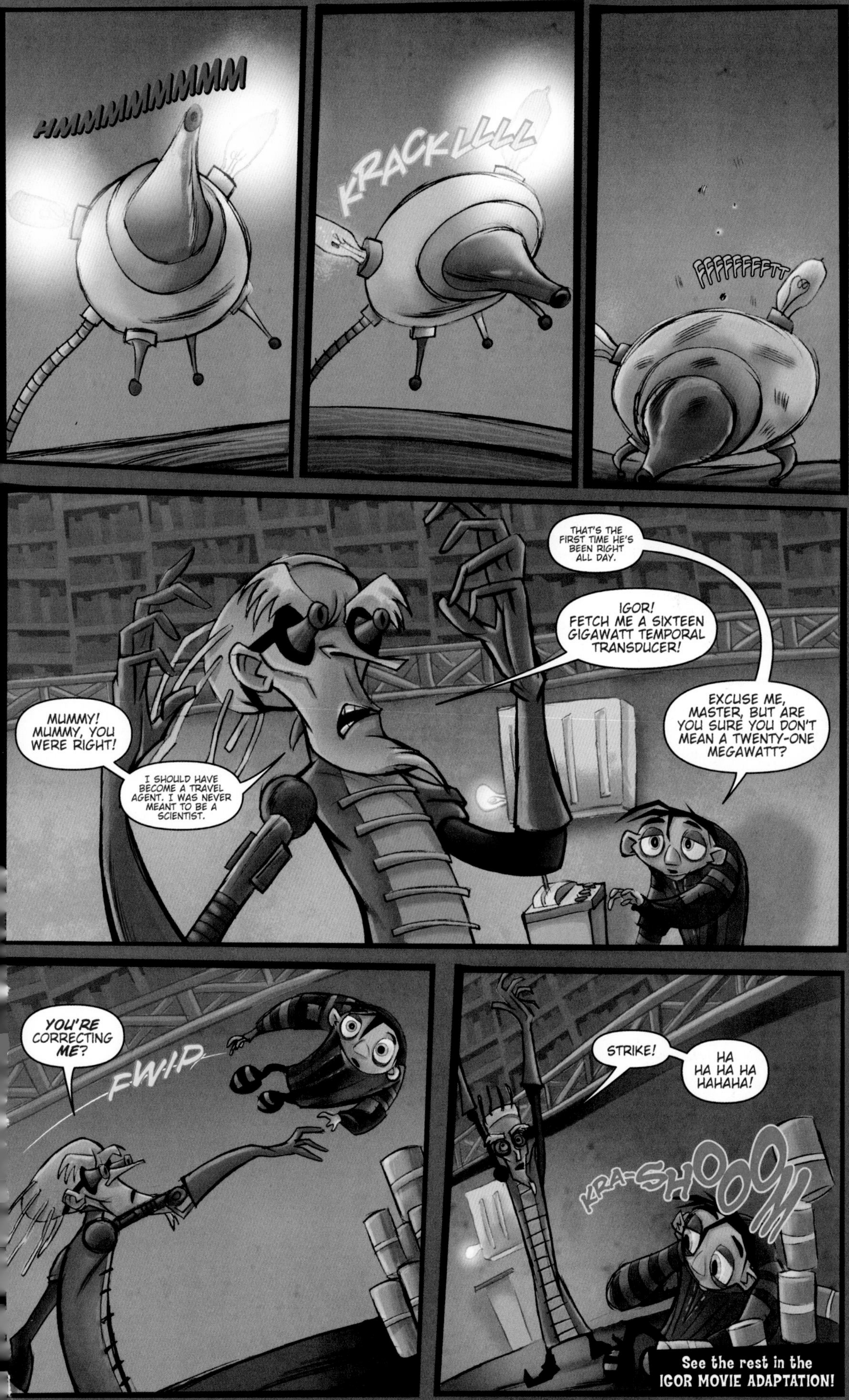
HMMMMMMMMMM
KRACKLLLL
FFFFFFFFFTT
THAT'S THE FIRST TIME HE'S BEEN RIGHT ALL DAY.
IGOR! FETCH ME A SIXTEEN GIGAWATT TEMPORAL TRANSDUCER!
EXCUSE ME, MASTER, BUT ARE YOU SURE YOU DON'T MEAN A TWENTY-ONE MEGAWATT?
MUMMY! MUMMY, YOU WERE RIGHT!
I SHOULD HAVE BECOME A TRAVEL AGENT. I WAS NEVER MEANT TO BE A SCIENTIST.
YOU'RE CORRECTING ME?
F-W-I-P
STRIKE!
HA HA HA HA HAHAHA!
KRA-SHOOOM
See the rest in the IGOR MOVIE ADAPTATION!

www.IDWpublishing.com